The Education of the Black Child in Britain

Maureen Stone was born and brought up in Barbados. She went to Calcutta University where she studied history, before coming to Britain where she has lived for the past fifteen years. She has been a social worker (specializing for a time in school liaison) and a Community and Adult Education officer. She is currently a lecturer in Applied Social Sciences at Surrey University. *The Education of the Black Child in Britain* is her first book.

Maureen Stone

The Education of the Black Child in Britain

The Myth of Multiracial Education

Fontana Paperbacks

First published by Fontana Paperbacks 1981
Copyright © Maureen Stone 1981

Set in Lasercomp Garamond

Made and printed in Great Britain
by William Collins Sons & Co. Ltd, Glasgow

Contents

Preface and Acknowledgements

The area covered by this piece of work lies broadly in the overlap between social-psychology and sociology. Aspects of identity, self-concept and self-esteem which are essentially psychological are examined in relation to sociological processes of adaptation by (a) social institutions (schools) and (b) the West Indian community in London, to the situation which has arisen in inner-city urban schools.

The emphasis on self-concept and self-esteem reflects the belief of educationalists and practitioners that schooling should concern itself with the affective as well as the cognitive domain of learning. This relates in turn to the belief that the school failure of certain groups of children in British society is related to poor self-concept and that the school has a duty to provide the type of curricula and teaching methods which will enable these children to develop more positive self-feelings.

The children of West Indian people living in Britain are seen as being particularly in need of treatment to enhance self-concept. West Indians as a group are concentrated in deprived inner-city areas of poor housing and low employment. They suffer the effects of discrimination, prejudice and racism and their children under-achieve in school. It is assumed that these children more than any others must suffer from negative self-concept and poor self-image. There is a belief that teachers must address themselves to these problems and offer children the opportunity to 'enhance' their self-concept. It is further assumed that one of the effects of this 'enhanced' self-concept will be more positive attitudes to school, leading in turn to improved attainment.

Whilst some schools are trying to 'compensate' black children for the deprivations of inner-city urban life and to enhance their self-concept, West Indian community groups and parents are trying to 'supplement' what they regard as the inadequate schooling given to their children. The schools blame parents, poor self-concept and the general 'deprivation' suffered by the children for their inability to make use of what the school has to offer. The community blames the schools, poor teaching, low standards, racism and prejudice for the poor performance of West Indian children in British schools. In this book these two responses are examined: the school-based multiracial education response emphasizing the affective component in learning and the community-based 'supplementary education' response, emphasizing the cognitive, skills-mastering approach to achieving improved attainment in West Indian school children.

Official policy supports the schools definition of the situation – and it may be argued, if it becomes generally accepted in the teaching profession and amongst educationalists, that a major part of the reason for poor achievement of West Indian children lies in personality factors. The situation may arise or may possibly have arisen (see Box 1977) where sections of urban schools with large numbers of West Indian pupils come to resemble psychiatric or social work units. The objectives of schooling become those of therapy with the teachers as therapists and children as patients.

This book sets out to examine critically the implications of these developments and to outline some of the consequences of the muddled, if well-intentioned thinking in this area.

My thanks to the schools and community groups and to the teachers and workers in the various projects. Special thanks to the children and young people who took part in the study, and to the DES whose financial assistance enabled the research to be completed. I must also record my thanks to Annette Bryce who gave unstintingly of her time and who remained keen and enthusiastic even when assisting in the most routine tasks. Thanks also to Professor Robert Ziller for permission to use his self-esteem measure and to Dr Margaret Norris for permission to use her diagrammatic presentation of styles of community work.

1. Defining the Problem

An article in the *Guardian* in 1977, 'Teaching the EEC Jet Set', reported that Britain was to have its first European school for the children of European scientists and bureaucrats:

> The school, which will take children between the ages of 5 and 18, has 200 purpose-built study-bedrooms and the DES is also hoping to offer a boarding-school education to the children of British diplomats working for the EEC and other people working overseas.
>
> The facilities and education offered at the school will be equal to a public school education . . . tuition in five languages with the possibility of Danish being taught if there is enough demand. Class size is unlikely to exceed 30 in any subject and will be reduced to single figures in some subjects . . . Facilities include a superb chapel, a well-equipped library, playing fields, music rooms, science laboratories and a large hall and stage.

The article was sub-titled 'Elite School for EEC Children', and made clear that those of elite status know what sort of education they want for their own children. The 'education debate' is really about the education provided for the mass of other people's children, and the potential elites amongst them. The elites do not agonize about the aims of education – they know them – five or six languages, science, music, sports and a 'superb chapel'. If their children are 'unhappy' or their self-concepts are poor or damaged or their self-esteem suffers, then they can always take a course in co-counselling or sign up with one of the many therapists or psychoanalysts who minister to the damaged self-concepts of the rich and well-off. Of course they will be able to afford the price of therapy (about £25 per hour) having 'achieved' their rightful status in the job market, with annual salaries in the five-figure range.

The same edition of the *Guardian* which carried the article on 'Elite Schools' also published an account of the Department of Education and Science and Welsh Office report, *A Study of School Buildings*. The *Guardian* reported the study as saying that:

> the main problem in schools is lack of space. Some statistics included: 37 per cent of primary schools overcrowded. 8,000 out of 23,000 were built before 1903. Of the 12,500 primary schools built before 1946, 49 per cent had outdoor lavatories, 80 per cent inadequate staff accommodation, 26 per cent 'grossly inadequate sites' and 18 per cent were in poor environments. Just under half the 5,000 secondary schools were overcrowded. Over half did not have enough practical facilities such as laboratories and workshops and 36 per cent insufficient large spaces, such as halls. One-fifth were built before 1946 and of these 83 per cent had inadequate staff accommodation, 28 per cent had outdoor lavatories and 22 per cent temporary prefab kitchens.

The tale of woe continued, ending with a statement that £1500 million were needed to put things right by 1986.

In recent years it has become increasingly fashionable to argue that the educational failure of working-class and black children is due to poor self-concept and self-esteem, and that if this is treated they will achieve better in school. This is a false and dangerous argument based on incomplete and unsound theoretical assumptions and biased research findings. By focusing on self-esteem, it manages to ignore the vast body of evidence showing that working-class and black families have much less access to power, to resources of every kind, than middle-class children. 'Self-concept' becomes a way of evading the real, and uncomfortable, issue of class and privilege in our society. Furthermore no body of research has ever demonstrated unequivocally that the children of the working-class as a whole, poor children or black children in particular, suffer from poor self-image or self-esteem. Rather the reverse is true – self-esteem, unlike school and life success, is *not* related to socio-economic status (Rosenberg); if anything, children of parents of low socio-economic status have higher self-concept scores than those of higher socio-economic status. In analysing the perception of education and aspiration in middle-class and working-class children, Swift (1967) observed: 'There is an enormous amount of research evidence to show that middle-class children aspire to higher occupational and economic levels than working-class children.' He also suggested that it is probable that they try harder at all tasks, presumably because of the view of 'themselves in relation to tasks' which they are taught. He linked this discussion to the child-rearing methods of middle-class parents (Davis) which tend to produce high levels of anxiety about all forms of achievement. Recent work by John and Elizabeth Newson does in fact support the suggestion that middle-class parents tend to produce high levels of anxiety in children and to offer 'conditional love' – conditional upon achieving success in schools and acquiring appropriate skills. Two major effects of this type of child-rearing will be:

a. high achievement;
b. high anxiety/low self-concept.

This is essentially the argument which Musgrove advanced to explain the low self-concept and the self-hatred which he found in his sample of grammar school boys. In his chapter entitled 'The Good Home', he described the effective home as the 'demanding' home: the parents set high standards from an early age; they are ambitious for their children; they reward infrequently and without generosity; approval and affection are conditional upon achievement. But within the framework of high demands and expectations the child is free to learn and good opportunities are afforded for him to do so. He concludes:

> The driving, demanding home, with exacting standards and expectations and remorseless pressure on the children appears to be the 'good home' in terms of achievement at school and economic success in later life. Schools reflect middle-class values and middle-class children experience a continuation of these 'child care' methods at school – if they continue to achieve they are valued; acceptance and affection are conditional upon performance.

Thus Musgrove argued that the grammar school may be failing to promote 'self-confidence' amongst youngsters in the sixth form and he called for further investigation of the role of grammar schools in creating anxiety and low self-concept in children. His concluding remarks included this observation: 'negative self-concept may be a necessary price of high academic attainment under highly competitive conditions.'

If we accept Ford's analysis of comprehensive schools as largely mirroring the tripartite system of grammar, technical and secondary modern education, we may assume that Musgrove's comments hold good for middle-class children in comprehensive schools today. In contrast to this is Bagley's view that lower streamed children develop negative self-concepts because of their lower stream status. Historically, middle-class parents welcomed formal education much more than working-class parents and they have always regarded the school as an extension of the home, extolling the same virtues, upholding the same values and having the same objectives. Middle-class children fit nicely into the school system and have little alternative. Working-class children and minority group children do have alternatives and do not need to accept the low status value which society places on their groups or to internalize it by developing low self-concepts or poor self-esteem. Their 'reference groups', unlike those of the middle-class child, have different values from those which obtain in the school system. To many working- and lower-class children, school is of marginal importance, especially in the later years of the secondary school. To many black children, using the language of the Rastafarian religion, school is 'Babylon' – it is unlikely that these children will regard teachers as 'significant others' and internalize the negative way in which they are viewed by them.

One interpretation of the influence of Carl Rogers, Maslow, Kelly and the self-theorists may be that this internalization and resulting poor self-concept are the reactions of sensitive middle-class people to the faults of their own system of child-rearing and they would like to humanize that system of child-care and the kind of schooling which it has given rise to. This is clearly a desirable objective – but it is difficult to equate the reasons for working-class and minority group failure in school with the poor self-concept of the successful middle-class child.

Whatever the real aims of education are – whether to service the capitalist system, to supply the meritocracy with brains and manpower, to exercise control and custody over children – the fact is that formal education is here to stay. The deschooled Utopia will never come, not least because it too depends on the results of formal education – computers, link-ups, 'freeway learning'; all these ideas emerged from those who had gone through the formal education system, indeed who had spent much longer than most people within it, either as learners or as teachers. So, because formal education is here to stay, sociologists must study it in all its manifestations, particularly when it seems to be 'innovative'. Herein lies the rationale for research on self-concept and education. The move towards looking at children's self-concept and self-esteem is innovative, seems worthy and potentially rewarding and, linked to the 'new' sociology of education and to the stress on individual meaning and subjective experience as a means of defining social reality, appears a desirable advance on current sociological and psychological theories and research. On closer examination, however, it may not be an advance at all, not least because it mainly serves to obscure the real issues, which are ones of power, class and racial oppression. For a number of reasons, many teachers are firmly committed to the idea of improving working-class and black self-concept. Their commitment may be as much a function of their own personality or need for job satisfaction as of the needs they perceive the children to have. Many teachers perceive themselves as doing the best for the children in their care, and would be surprised, even shocked, by the extent of disenchantment that some parents and community groups feel with what the educational system has to offer their children. Black parents in particular feel short-changed by the school system (Report of Select Committee on Race Relations, 1974). While schools try to compensate children by offering Black Studies and steel bands, black parents and community groups are organizing Saturday schools – to supplement the second-rate education which the school system offers their children. There is a mismatch between the system and the community, and with the best of intentions the system is offering the community the worst possible options. It is this mismatch, and how it could be corrected, which this book will be largely concerned with. Although the book will focus on the education of the black child, the argument can be extended to the whole of working-class education.

The Crisis in Urban Schools and the Shift towards Social-psychological Solutions – Self-concept in the Classroom

> Nurture groups, withdrawal and adjustment units, special counselling schemes, behaviour modification techniques and school-based social workers are all currently being used to reduce violence and disruption [in schools].
>
> National Children's Bureau, *Highlight* (October 1977)

The Size of the Problem

The existing statistics on the extent of violent and disruptive behaviour are limited by inexact record-keeping and problems of definition. Recent studies indicate, however, that it is more common in secondary than in primary schools, among boys than among girls (Power), in urban rather than rural areas, and among low-ability disadvantaged pupils (Pack; West and Farrington). A recent DES study (Lassett) found that 40 per cent of schools reported a significant rise in violence and estimated an average of one violent act per hundred pupils.

Background

Mass formal education and urbanization developed as products of industrialization, and the crises that beset industry and cities are reflected in schools to a greater or lesser degree (Field). In recent years, urban schools have suffered a variety of problems which have been manifested by:

1. Increasing rates of truancy (Pack; Turner, 1974).
2. Increasing rates of vandalism, violence, disruption and general 'misbehaviour' (Home Office, *Protection Against Vandalism*; National Association of School Masters, *Discipline in Schools* and *The Retreat from Authority* document the concern of

teachers, administrators and others with aspects of the crisis in schools).

3. Increasing rates of 'stress' illnesses amongst teachers and pupils (Clegg and Mogson; NAS/NUWT, *Effects of Stress on Teachers*).

Although urban schools are not alone in having problems of the type outlined above, it is true to say that the difficulties are accentuated in cities. Thus, for example, the schools which feature in the press and on television as sensational illustrations of decay and degeneracy have all been urban schools: 'They Turn our Schools into a Jungle of Violence' – *Sunday Express* (9 June 1974); 'Control Experiment' – the *Guardian* (18 March 1975); 'Discipline or Terror' – *Sunday People* (16 June 1974); *The Best Years* – BBC television (23 March 1977).

The problems associated with increases in maladjustment, truancy, delinquency and vandalism in schools have been well documented. What have received far less attention are the responses of the Local Education Authorities, the DES and the teaching, medical and social work professions to the problem of urban schooling. Very little research has been carried out, for example, on the use of drugs and psychotherapy in treating the problems of urban school children in the normal school population as distinct from those in residential or other custodial types of care. There is a feeling that the use of psychotherapeutic methods is now widespread, and that increasingly drugs are used to control behaviour, but there is very little research evidence available to support this contention. This has meant that people have resorted to making vague accusations in order to voice a general feeling of unease and uncertainty.

For example, in an article in *New Society* in 1977, Steven Box alleged that:

English schools in urban slums and ethnically mixed areas are being transformed from places where children attend educational courses to places where they receive medical treatment. School children by the millions in America and tens of thousands in this country are being put on long-term programmes of drug-therapy simply because their behaviour does not fit in with the requirements of schools.

Dr Eric Taylor of the Institute of Psychiatry commented on this allegation in the *Guardian*:

> I would doubt very much indeed whether large numbers of children are being treated by drugs. Most child psychiatrists are very psychotherapy orientated and their use of drugs is not common.

The DHSS also commented and expressed the view that the increase in the number of children diagnosed as maladjusted, and their treatment by drug or psychotherapy, was due to 'new awareness of the problem and a corresponding rise in the number of child guidance clinics'.

It can be seen that there is no outright denial of Box's claims, rather a suggestion that he has exaggerated the use of drugs and mislabelled the recent developments in child-care which actually reflect a growing awareness of children's problems and a corresponding increase in the number of child guidance clinics to deal with the problem.

Against this practical background of day-to-day problems in schools lies the fact of educational failure: children of working-class origin continue to be under-represented in higher and further education and to score below their middle-class peers on tests of intelligence and attainment (Halsey, 1980). Faced with micro- and macro-problems of these dimensions, schools and education authorities can respond in one of two ways:

a. by coercion – increased use of courts and sanctions, or
b. by persuasion.

One of the methods of persuasion has been the reorganization of aspects of the curriculum in order to make it more 'relevant' to working-class children; this approach includes the development of teacher-training methods which stress the importance of 'relationships' and which, regarding the teacher as a 'significant other' in the child's life, encourage her to take the role of social worker or therapist towards the child – this is especially true when working with 'deprived' or culturally disadvantaged children. The work of Thomas and Lawrence (1971, 1972) on building self-concept in schools positively encourages this approach to schooling as therapy and expects teachers to act as counsellors and social workers as an essential part of their professional practice.

The link between the educational failure of working-class children and the rise of social-psychological theories and practice based on these theories has been made so well by Sharp and Green in the conclusion to their study on *Education and Social Control* that I can do no better than to quote from their observations. They commented on child-centred education that it had developed:

> as a reaction to what was held to be the rigidity of traditional educational structures which denied opportunity to the many; the progressive child-centred movement was impelled by a moral rhetoric which sought to re-establish the rights of the individual to freedom, self-development and individual expression, over and above the demands of society . . . Within child-centred progressivism, far wider ranges of the child's attributes became legitimate objects of evaluative scrutiny and explanatory variables in the construction of success and failure. Not merely intellectual but social, emotional, aesthetic and even physical criteria are often employed in the processing of pupils in educational institutions; the social control possibilities become enhanced. Moreover, the development of a quasi-therapeutic orientation to the educational task which we have suggested characterizes much of the 'progressive child-centred' thought impugns those who fail in ways which are non-threatening to established interest, thus 'cooling people out' and moving more and more people into soft-control areas. The incorporation of social and individual pathology views of certain categories of pupils has its counterpart in other substantive areas of social policy, in attitudes towards criminality, mental illness and so on, where increasingly social problems have come to be conceptualized in the same way. Such developments pose interesting questions for the sociology of knowledge regarding the institutional basis and support for these ideas and the established interest they serve.

The point they are making is that the problems and difficulties of contemporary schools are increasingly being seen as reflections of individual and family pathology of working-class people. If the problems of lack of attainment lie not within the structure of society and the schools it has provided for working-class children, but in the children themselves or in their families, it makes sense to try and change these children's attitudes in the hope that such attitude-change will increase attainment. Since compensatory education – the pouring of extra resources into Educational Priority Areas – has failed to make any real impact in reducing inequality, it is argued that the problem needs to be tackled on a new front and in a different way – hence the need for self-concept theories that will help to change the child's attitude towards his/herself. Thus the self-concept of the child becomes a legitimate interest of the teacher. These theories have not been lifted out of any political, social or economic context – they are as apolitical as the people who originated them. By ignoring the social structure and its reflection in the school system, these theories are potentially very damaging to the education of working-class and black children. Indeed, one could argue that they grow from a completely blinkered white middle-class point of view. Certainly they have little to offer in terms of an understanding of the development of self-concept in minority group children. In fact I would extend this criticism and say that these theories are inappropriate for an understanding of working-class personality and culture generally.

In this connection it is important to consider some related criticisms on the use of psychotherapy with working- and lower-class people. ('Lower-class' is used here to indicate the subsection of the working-class which suffers most from poverty and unemployment.) In many respects the aim of teaching for improved self-concept or self-esteem more closely resembles social work in its mental health guise, or psycho-therapy, than 'normal' teaching for academic or related goals. It seems appropriate therefore to consider this form of teaching as therapy, its aims and objectives being more closely related to mental health goals than academic or intellectually-oriented goals.

As early as 1938 an article by Davis drew attention to what he called the 'underlying cultural and philosophical' basis of the mental hygiene movement in America. He wrote:

Mental hygiene, being a social movement and a source of advice concerning personal conduct, has inevitably taken over the Protestant ethic inherent in our society, not simply as a basis for conscious preachment but also as the unconscious system of premises upon which its scientific analysis and its conception of mental hygiene is based.

Noting that those persons prominently associated with this movement were almost all middle-class professionals whose own achievements followed from sustained effort and delay of gratification, Davis further characterized the Protestant ethic as consisting in:

1. the belief in vertical mobility
2. competition
3. ambition
4. self discipline
5. 'wholesome' fun
6. prudence
7. rationality
8. foresight

Davis argued that this middle-class 'world-view' underlies the most widely held conceptions of mental hygiene, mental health and ill health in American society.

Twenty years later, in 1960, Gursslin, Hunt and Roach content-analysed twenty-seven widely disseminated mental health pamphlets from such sources as the National Association for Mental Hygiene, the New York State Department of Mental Hygiene and several large mental clinics. They found that approximately 60 per cent of the text of these pamphlets promoted essentially middle-class themes – the value of work, control of emotions, planning ahead, problem solving, sharing, adjustment and common participation. They commented: 'The basic conclusion to be drawn from a sizeable portion of the content under investigation is that the middle-class prototype and the mental health prototype are in many respects equivalent.' Like Davis they concluded that the mental health movement in America is unwittingly propagating a middle-class ethic under the guise of science. Schneiderman also comments upon the prejudicial effects of conceptualizing and conducting diagnostic and therapeutic work with working-class people from a middle-class perspective. He proposed a working-class ethic as the proper frame of reference for work with people of working-class background. He described this ethic as (1) an inclination to subject oneself to or to live harmoniously with what is viewed as given or natural in life, in contrast to the middle-class values of mastery over the physical and social environment; (2) an inclination towards relatively free expression; (3) spontaneity; (4) a non-development conception of activity and (5) a tendency towards greater orientation to the present rather than the past or future. He stressed the appropriateness and adaptability of this ethic for the realities of functioning adequately in the working-class environment.

No equivalent British critique of middle-class mental health values has been undertaken, although a few writers in the social work literature have argued against 'cooling out' working-class clients and have drawn attention to the inappropriate use of middle-class psychoanalytical terms and methods with working-class people. In education the development of teaching as therapy has been haphazard and disorganized, and has received little attention in terms of evaluation or scrutiny. In social work some clients are treated with mental health techniques when their problems are basically economic and environmental. In education, therapy functions on the fringes of the formal school structure – in withdrawal units, truancy centres, adjustment units etc., which themselves are on the fringe of the educational establishments. In a more general way, apart from its influence in the 'fringe areas', schooling as therapy has influenced general educational thought in this country, particularly as it relates to non-achievers and early leavers. In secondary schools this influence is more evident in the use of school counsellors, although it can also serve another function – the 'cooling out' of children with unrealistic ambitions. The 'cooling out' function of counsellors in American schools has been well documented (Clark) and is the process whereby 'non-directive counselling' is used to direct over-ambitious working-class children into 'suitable' jobs or training programmes. Clark looked at a school with an open door policy to higher education. All who wished to gain access to university or liberal arts colleges could, in theory, do so. But after two years of study there, Clark found that the school had deterred a large proportion of hitherto ambitious students from pursuing their original intentions. Cicourel and Kitsue's work also supports Clark's findings. In primary schools schooling as therapy is reflected in the 'progressive' philosophy of the post-Plowden era, with its similar concern with individual and family and a willingness to attribute educational failure to family background, not to any shortcomings in the school or the system.

This outline has highlighted the contradictions and conflicts underlying the issue of social class, self-concept and schooling. It seems clear that since schools reflect the dominant cultural values, children belonging to, or aspiring to belong to the dominant cultural group will have less difficulty in school. The fit between their own values and the school's will be much closer. For children of a different social class, there will be a gap between their own values and the school's. By introducing mental health goals of improved self-concept teachers appear to be ignoring the real power relationships involved. The fact is that the majority of research work on self-concept and schooling has been related to achievement or, for so-called 'disadvantaged children', lack of achievement in schools. It has not looked at the wider social structure. And so a number of teachers and theorists have become convinced that at least part of the explanation of working-class failure lies in negative self-image and poor self-esteem.

Influenced by a philosophy of education which stressed individual development and growth, and by the development of humanistic psychology and phenomenological sociology, teachers in urban schools became attracted to the idea of developing teaching based on these theories.

In many ways we have to regard their interest as reflecting a certain disenchantment with more orthodox approaches which aimed to improve academic attainment and promote greater social mobility and which failed to achieve either. A further complication is the personality of the teacher and particularly the job of teaching itself, whose stresses may well contribute to a certain degree of alienation from orthodoxy and imbue the new therapeutic theories with an attractiveness which they might otherwise lack. It is certainly a fact that many teachers in the urban areas find their job stressful and demanding and their working environment uncongenial. Self-theories therefore can offer an escape to the teachers as well as to the students they are seeking to help.

So far as West Indian children in Britain are concerned I shall argue that the major omission of the self-concept theorists and researchers has been their failure to take into account or to understand West Indian culture, particularly as this relates to formal education and schooling.

I shall also suggest that policy decisions, research recommendations and practical programmes aimed at more 'relevant' curricula for minority group children have failed to set this discussion within a historical frame of reference. They have ignored the development of education for the working classes generally. They have also tended to overlook the broader sociological perspective – the function of formal education in the provision of schooling for the majority of the working-class population.

In this country the Labour Party and the trade unions, especially the NUT, have long supported the demand for popular education in the belief that this would bring about equality of opportunity and social justice. But even in the beginning there was confusion about what 'education for all' meant and whether in fact it was worth having: the Labour Party seemed mainly concerned to extend the benefits of a grammar school education to working-class children. Milne-Bailey, in a memo to the Labour Advisory Committee on Education, made this point in 1921 when he wrote, 'the demand has been for the extension of the present so-called education received by children of the middle and wealthy classes to the workers' children without asking whether that education is worth having.' In 1923 Sir Fred Clarke, in his essays on *the Politics of Education*, commented on Tawney's *Secondary Education for All* (the document which put forward Labour policy on secondary education for working-class children): 'Unless I misunderstand, Mr Tawney seems to accept the present order of things in secondary schools and confines himself to the demand that all who are mentally fit should be submitted to its opportunities.' But, he added: 'The task of the Labour Party . . . is not merely to get children of the working man into the secondary school. It is to point us the way to a social order where, in and through the educative function itself, what was for the Greeks the special privilege of the few may become for us the common heritage of the many.'

In an article in the *Durham Educational Review*, J. R. Brook suggested that Tawney himself mirrored the inherent contradictions of Labour's educational policy – the desire to create an 'educated' labour force in order to bring about changes in the social composition of society and the desire to humanize the masses through education. This contradiction remains present in Labour's educational policy to the present day.

What is being suggested here is that in recent years formal schooling has failed to realize the paramount liberal objective of a more highly educated work force and hence more social mobility. Instead the second, and sometimes forgotten objective of 'humanizing' the working class, 'gentling the masses', has come more to the fore. Some researchers began to feel that the working class had been offered everything and still continued to lag behind and so other explanations had to be looked for. In America the Coleman Report (1966) supplied this explanation: working-class and black failure in school was a result of poor motivation resulting from bad family background and poor self-concept. In Britain the Plowden Report (1967) echoed this: the attitudes of parents and the home circumstances of the child were the most important factors influencing achievement in schools.

It was not a big step from making this connection to deciding that black children who were failing, not only relative to middle-class children but relative to other working-class children as well, must be failing for psychological reasons. It is clear that black children in England belong to a small minority group. As well as suffering from all the disadvantages of the indigenous working class, they also suffer racial discrimination, prejudice and rejection by the dominant group. The argument therefore was that they must 'introject' this view of themselves and that children in particular come to see themselves as failures and become non-achievers in the schools. This point of view has been put forward by Allan Little in his study of under-achievement in immigrant children in London (1975). Among his final comments on the relationship between achievement and self-concept of West Indian children he observed that 'the low economic and social status which New Commonwealth immigrants are frequently accorded in our society must affect the identity of these groups themselves and the self-concepts they pass on to their children.' Little argued that this negative self-concept in turn influenced the level of achievement the children are able to reach.

We will examine research findings on black children's self-concept which do not appear to support Little's conclusions. My own view, which is supported from research in many countries, is that achievement is basically related to class and not to self-concept. Consideration of the historical and sociological evidence leads one to the view that theories on self-concept and schooling develop in response to the consistent failure of the educational system to meet the needs of lower-class and minority group children. I would argue that the idea that middle-class schools and teachers can influence the self-concept of the majority of working-class or black pupils could only have arisen in a theoretical vacuum. Those teachers of working-class children who believe that they can provide an environment for 'growth', 'self-actualization' and the development of positive self-concept within schools, and without reference to the social structure which ultimately determines their pupils' role in society and thus their life chances, are operating within a philosophical tradition which says that the aims of education should include the free development of personality in a society which is hierarchically structured along fairly rigid class lines and where the schools are implicitly or explicitly charged with socializing children (of whatever social or racial background) into the cultural values of the dominant groups. It is hardly likely that institutions which have failed in their (apparent) primary educational purpose would be any more successful in achieving mental health goals. However, the situation in urban schools, pressure on teachers and children, rising numbers of absentees, and increase in violence and disruption may in fact be the real reasons behind the change in direction and willingness to try new methods seen in some schools.

Black Self-concept Compensation

In an analysis of the 'strategies of educational redress', Watson identified compensatory educational programmes as being of major significance. He argued that compensatory education strategies developed within the 'interactionist' theoretical framework which emphasizes the environmental impact and achievement. This perspective he contrasted with biological or genetic theories which stress the overriding importance of heredity in determining life chances (the theories of Burt, Jensen, Eysenck, and Herrnstein). Watson defined compensatory education strategies thus:

> compensatory education strategies involve an attempt to provide, in a school or formally arranged quasi-school situation, an 'enriched' social and cultural environment for children whereby the children can redress the alleged deficits in their perceptual skills, cognitive skills, linguistic and other interactional competencies which are an alleged corollary of living one's early formative years in such backgrounds.

Thus compensatory education can be seen as a form of 're-socialization'. The family and the social group is regarded as being (a) incapable or (b) unwilling to inculculate the collective social values into the young and organized social institutions have to assume this task. Compensatory education as 're-socialization' is directly related to this discussion because inevitably socialization is bound up with self-concept and self-image.

In Britain there is a widespread assumption among teachers and educationists that the children of West Indian people living here are particularly in need of 're-socialization'. This need is used to explain the 'educational failure' of these children. In America race has always been a central part of the debate on educational failure of working-class children – since, even within the working class, black children lagged behind in IQ scores and tests of ability and attainment in schools.

Although Leon Kamin has shown how the use of early IQ

tests in America was influenced to a significant degree by the
racial and political views of psychologists who developed them,
in Britain it is only within recent years that race, as a separate
factor, has entered into the IQ debate and is connected with the
arrival in Britain of immigrants from the Caribbean (other
immigrant groups – Asian, Cypriot and Irish – do not appear to
figure in this issue to anything like the extent that people of
African origin do) and the admission of large numbers of their
children to schools in England. Even before this there was
already creeping into educational literature the belief, or
suspicion, that it was bad families, uncaring parents and
deprived environments which contributed to working-class
educational failure (Douglas *et al.*). With the arrival of these
newcomers, who swelled the lowest ranks of the working class
and whose children presented to the schools as 'problems' from
the first moment of arrival, the explanation of failure as lying
within the individual and family pathology of certain groups of
people within the working class gained impetus. In America the
'search for explanations' had culminated in the Coleman Report.
This blamed poor families and particularly poor black families
for the failures of the American school system because, Coleman
argued, parental influence and pupil self-concept – confidence in
his/her own ability and achievement – enables the student to win
through and succeed against all odds. The Coleman Report
pointed the way towards social psychological factors to explain
working-class and black under-achievement in schools.

In Britain the Plowden Report of 1967 followed the trail and
reported in like vein: that it was families, parental influence and
expectations which ultimately exerted the most influence on
whether or not children succeeded in schools. Those children
who lacked parental support and encouragement were deprived.
Their parents were probably deprived as well, because they lived
in slums and their cultural environment was not such as to
encourage them to take an interest in their children's schooling.
The schools to which these children went contributed to their
'deprivation' and increased their 'disadvantage' – old buildings,
high rates of staff turnover, low levels of parental involvement.
The answer was to designate areas of 'educational priority' and
to intervene with a variety of strategies aimed at countering the
negative environmental factors. Although the Plowden Report

was concerned with 'Children and their Primary Schools', it exerted influence far beyond this age range – especially with regard to the use of social workers in schools. Together with the Newsom Report on the education of pupils of less than average ability, it established a trend in the direction of social, as opposed to educational goals, in schools for working-class 'slum' children, whose potentiality they saw as marked by 'inadequate powers of speech and poor home backgrounds' The Newsom Report had put forward many of the sam: proposals later echoed by Plowden, including special salary inducements and living accommodation for teachers to work in 'slum' schools, compensatory experience for children – access to the countryside, trips abroad, 'the experience of living together in civilized and beautiful surroundings' (if only for a week or so) – but its main recommendation was the raising of the school-leaving age to sixteen to prevent working-class children from leaving school at fifteen (which the majority of them would do, given the chance), to avoid waste of talent and to provide a 'generally better educated and intelligent labour force to meet new demands'. The significant feature of both these British reports is their stress on changing the attitudes of working-class pupils (Newsom) and parents (Plowden). For 'changing attitudes' is the business of psychologists and attempts to change attitudes must somehow link up with how people acquire attitudes in the first place. As a consequence, the desire to change attitudes to schooling implies an undertaking to change the psychological make-up (the attitudes) of sections of working-class pupils and parents:

> There is some evidence that the problem of deprivation in the home and its effect on education could best be alleviated by effecting changes in the behaviour of the families from which children come. *The school would then be presented with a pupil whose value systems were nearer its own* [my emphasis] (James Ruston, *Education and Deprivation*).

In the business of attitude change, as in any other business, some customers are more – how should we say – more gullible? Susceptible? At risk? And that means that they become 'target population' – those who will buy because of their gullibility, those who can be persuaded to buy because of your charm and those whom you can force to buy because they owe you money. So, in the educational game of attitude change, certain groups are 'most likely' targets: the groups who are 'problems', the truants, disrupters, educational failures for whom nothing appears to work. And to those desperate for solutions, the gospel of Coleman and Plowden must have appeared like manna from heaven: 'Change the attitudes of lower-class parents and children and all will be well.' When dealing with black children, a further proviso must be made —'attitudes to the self must also be changed as blacks hate and despise themselves and this causes them to fail at school and to manifest various behaviour problems.' Thus we arrive at self-concept and schooling.

Many teachers and educationists sincerely believe that if attitudes could be changed, black and lower-class children would achieve more in schools. In the case of black children they believe that one of the effects of racism has been to give the black child a negative self-concept and that part of the explanation of West Indian failure in schools is a function of that negative self-concept which tells the child that he/she cannot see him/herself as a success and thus he/she is unable to succeed. The trouble with this argument is that it does not explain the normal self-concept scores of most black people. It does not explain why, if this argument is true, black children in England and America have average-to-high scores on self-concept/self-esteem tests. In spite of contradictory research evidence, the belief in black low self-esteem persists, and along with it goes the parallel belief that schools can and should compensate black children for the negative social stereotypes which exist in the wider society. It is believed that courses in Black Ethnic Studies or Caribbean Cultural Activities, will promote a kind of 'cultural enrichment' which will lead to enhanced self-concept. As well as offsetting negative racial stereotypes this will also be a means of encouraging black children to achieve better in schools. To realize these aims some schools have developed special classes and programmes for West Indian pupils.

At the same time, the West Indian community (in evidence to the Select Committee on Race Relations, 1974) appears to attribute the low-achievement level of black children to the school system itself. The West Indian community papers (*West*

Indian World, Grass Roots, Tomtide) and newsletters deal extensively with education and related matters, an indication of the seriousness with which the matter is viewed by the community as a whole. Schools are seen as poor, teaching methods permissive and indulgent – the whole system operates to keep the black child in its place. What is its place?

The Bottom of the Ladder: The Sociology of Educational Inequality

In discussing the theories of cultural deprivation and the response to these theories in the form of compensatory education we have been considering one type of explanation for the educational failure of working-class and minority group children and of the persistence of educational inequality in Western societies. In focusing on the culture of the poor and on individual and family pathology these theories explain educational failure in terms that lie outside the social structure. As Bowles and Gintis have argued, if the illusion of equal opportunity is to be maintained, then students (and parents) must believe that they all start with equal chances and those who make it do so by their own efforts; likewise those who fail. It is for this reason that Bellaby, for example, has argued that the development of comprehensive schools might in fact serve to buttress the conservative ideology which supports the biological basis of racial and class superiority: if working-class children continue to under-achieve in comprehensive schools where 'equality of opportunity' is provided, it will be argued that they have failed because they are inferior to begin with.

Of course comprehensive schools do not provide equal opportunities, as Ford and Bellaby have shown. For the most part they simply mirror the hierarchical arrangement of the grammar schools which is based on the class structure of the wider society.

There are other views which seek to explain the existence and continuance of inequalities – both educational and social – in Western societies. We turn now to consider briefly the ideas of Raymond Boudon as outlined in *Education, Opportunity and Social Inequality*, in which he compares educational and social mobility in Britain, Sweden, America and France and also draws on some data from Russia. Boudon's work, subtitled 'Changing Prospects in Western Society', is concerned to explain why the rate of mass mobility has not increased with industrialization and why, in those societies which are most 'developed' and most committed ideologically to equality of opportunity, rates of social mobility have remained virtually static since the war.

Boudon begins by stating that since the war inequality of educational opportunity has decreased in Western societies but that there has been no corresponding decline in inequality of social opportunity. In the preface to this book, Boudon comments:

> After World War II, inequality of educational opportunity fell off steadily without noticeable effect on mobility. And this decrease in inequality of educational opportunity apparently had no effect on economic inequality. Indeed the educational growth witnessed in all Western industrial societies since 1945 has been accompanied by an increase rather than a decrease in economic inequality, even though the educational system has become more egalitarian in the meantime.

In Chapter 1, he considers the following problem:

> In the generally accepted view that industrial societies are largely meritocratic, level of educational attainment becomes one of the major determinants of status. From this, the temptation is great to conclude that educational attainment should be the major factor of social mobility. In other words, if educational attainment is actually a powerful determinant of status, the probability of an individual having a higher social status than his father should be greater, the higher his level of education. Conversely, the probability of an individual falling to a lower status than his father should be greater, the lower his educational attainment level.

Boudon examined the evidence and came up with the 'surprising' finding that 'this conclusion is neither empirically nor logically true or, rather, that it is only true under very special conditions that are not likely to be met.'

Thus he concludes that the distribution of social status has changed less rapidly than the distribution of levels of education. And moreover he suggests that a meritocratic society is actually likely to generate a low correlation between education and mobility:

> Except under very special conditions which are unlikely to be met, a highly meritocratic society will not necessarily give those who have reached a high level of education more chances of promotion or fewer chances of demotion than those whose level of education is lower. This apparent paradox derives from two circumstances. First, since those who obtain high levels of education more frequently have a higher background, they have to climb still higher in the hierarchy of social status in order not to experience demotion. Second, one consequence of the discrepancy between educational and social structure is that even under a high degree of meritocracy, people with the same level of education will reach different social status. Thus, even if a society has a strong tendency towards granting the best social positions to those who are better educated, education may have no apparent influence on mobility.

Boudon believes that inequality of educational opportunity is generated by a two-component process: 'One component is related to the cultural effect of the stratification system. The other introduces the assumption that even with other factors being equal, people will make different choices according to their position in the classification system.'

He explains this second component in an additional note where he argues that differences in behaviour may be explained by differences in utilities

> if X chooses a, while Y chooses b, this means, according to our scheme, that the utility of a is greater for X and smaller for Y. The 'value' theory says that the values people are committed to may cause them to behave against their interest (e.g. by not attending college, although college enhances the

probability of promotion). The present scheme, however, says that people behave according to the utilities attached to alternatives as a function of their position in the stratification system.

This is the basis of the 'structural' or 'social position' theory of educational choice which Boudon developed and relies on the cultural constraints on the individual and his family as well as the cost and benefits of staying on at school. This analysis leads Boudon to reject the idea that cultural constraints generate inequality of educational opportunity and restrict social mobility.

Boudon constructed a model to demonstrate how in a given society it is possible for a large degree of 'randomness' to be generated even though the society is characterized by a strong class bias and a strong credential bias in the labour market. This 'randomness' is in itself an outcome of systematic tendencies in the process, which rests on competition for the best education and the best jobs. In this 'race' there are handicaps:

1.   Individual children of the privileged are more likely to get the favoured school places and qualifications.
2.   The labour market favours, but does not always select, applicants with the best credentials.
3.   There is no necessary agreement between the number of people with credentials being produced by the schools and the demands of the labour market. Because of this there is usually a competition for jobs among equally qualified applicants in which the children of high social background often have to be satisfied with a less prestigious position than their fathers.

Thus a proportion of the middle classes is demoted and a proportion of the working class is promoted – but overall the relative position of the two classes does not change.

Using this model of analysis he constructs an ideal situation where reforms have completely obliterated cultural inequality: by the end of grade school all children, irrespective of their social background, are assumed to be similarly distributed as a function of school achievement.

He finds that even when (by assumption) the effects of

cultural inequality have been eliminated, the rates of disparity remain very nigh, albeit noticeably reduced.

He comments:

If we accept that the model as defined represents a realistic although simplified picture of the inequality of educational opportunity-generating process at work in industrial societies, we must accept that the secondary effects of stratification on inequality of educational opportunity are, other things being equal, probably more important than their primary (cultural) effects.

He goes on to show that beyond a certain level of achievement differences in social background disappear; whereas the effects of stratification do not die out, 'they assert themselves repeatedly throughout the life of the cohort'.

It seems therefore that even if the attitudes of working-class youngsters (and their parents) could be changed by self-concept enhancement or otherwise, the effect of this on their overall status position in the hierarchy would be quite minimal. The effect of the greater achievement would simply be the same (or less) for more – the same work, the same social position etc., for more hard work and greater school achievement – what Boudon called 'more schooling for the same rewards'. Is it any wonder that people exercise rational choice and decide to drop out of the system altogether? As Boudon puts it: 'People behave rationally in the economic sense of the concept', but 'they also behave within decisional fields whose parameters are a function of their position in the stratification system'.

Boudon came to the conclusion that since World War II most Western societies have exhibited weak decline in inequality of educational opportunity and, over time, stability of inequality of social opportunity and that this was largely due to the failure of these societies to bring about a steady decrease in economic inequality. A reclassification of occupational categories has created the 'new social classes' but has failed to effect any real modification of the social structure – class differentiation and distribution. And thus: 'no manipulation of the educational variables is likely to have more than a moderate effect on either inequality of educational opportunity or inequality of social opportunity.'

Put simply, introduction of 'relevant curricula' and teaching methods based on developing relationships with children, special units and specialist workers, together or separately, have little or no impact on reducing inequality and promoting more social mobility. I am arguing, however, that not only are they not effective in Boudon's terms, but that they may actually increase educational inequality through their emphasis on mental health goals – increased self-esteem – at the expense of academic achievement. The idea that low self-concept is to blame for black or working-class under-achievement is based essentially on theories which regard black and working-class culture as deficient and which assume the internalization of the negative views by these groups themselves. But Boudon has convincingly demonstrated that even if all cultural and social disadvantages were obliterated there would still be a significant degree of educational and social inequality. So even if the cultural disadvantage theory were well founded, it still would not answer the problems in a satisfactory manner.

Yet these views persist, and along with them go attempts to 'enrich' the culture of these disadvantaged groups, thus giving them a firmer basis for the development of a positive self-concept and high self-esteem. Swift (1978) writing on the influence of 'the environment' on the development of self-concept, has dismissed the cultural deprivation theory which says that ghetto working-class culture is deficient and, using the findings of linguists working in that field, has stated: 'From the sociological perspective, it can only be said that . . . the proposition that the dialect of ghetto culture is a coherent whole, well adapted to the needs of its environment and carrying the capacity for all forms of cognitive behaviour, is entirely congruent with any theory of culture.' The fact is that the operating of a particular social structure serves to select certain classes and groups for social status and reward on given criteria. Those who do not meet these criteria, whether on grounds of race or class, know this, and their culture equips them to make certain decisions, what Boudon calls 'choices' although the term 'choice' implies a more positive variety of alternatives than actually exists. Very often these decisions result in consequences which reinforce established class divisions and appear not to be in the interests of people who make them. As, for example, Willis's (1978a) sample of working-class boys whose style of life and method of coping with school resulted in the majority of them being socialized very early on into the 'sub-culture' of the shop floor.

Those who see black under-achievement in schools as due to 'alienation', 'isolation', negative self-concept, poor self-esteem and lack of identity are anxious about the consequences of this for the school system and for society in general. They believe that the school system must offer these children a chance to 'find themselves', to redefine their cultural heritage and to reassess their own individual worth. These aims are well-intentioned but will they make any difference even supposing they could be achieved?

As another French sociologist, Bourdieu, has written (1971), 'the school is required to perpetuate and transmit the capital of concentrated cultural signs . . . the culture handed down by the intellectual creators of the past. Furthermore, it is obliged to establish and define systematically the sphere of heretical culture.' Bourdieu argued that the school in contemporary society is invested with a function similar to that which the Church performed in early periods of history: to establish and define new doctrines and to defend old ones.

In this analysis the personality characteristics and lifestyles which are associated with cultural disadvantage or deprivation would be defined as forms of 'heretical culture' against which the legitimate culture (through the schools) must defend itself. One of the possible ways of defence may be to 'legitimize' certain aspects of the heretical culture – thus, for example, the incorporation of Creole dialects into the curriculum might serve this purpose – a similar process to the cultural legitimization of jazz music which Bourdieu cites as an example of such a process. Another response can be seen in terms of the compensatory model which explains aspects of the heretical culture as resulting from environmental causes including language deficit and attempts to 'compensate' the disadvantaged and thus to integrate them into orthodox culture.

Teachers in the 'micro-situation' of the classroom try to make sense of their own reality by responding to the needs of the children they teach and to their own needs for job satisfaction and their own interpretation of the wider social and political conditions in society. All this takes place against a background where, as Bourdieu puts it, 'the underlying affinities uniting works of learned culture . . . are governed by the principles emanating from the educational institutions.' This must mean that urban schools in Britain today are faced with a situation of great complexity: as agents of the orthodox culture they must preserve and enhance that culture and induct children into its value system. At the same time, schools are asked to accommodate themselves to the existence of other (foreign) cultures (or local sub-cultures) and somehow give them a degree of legitimacy in order to avoid alienation. It is a problem which educationists have not really dealt with; the ideas of compensatory education on the one hand and multiracial education on the other appear to be tackling aspects of the problem but this is more apparent than real, for the fundamental problem – of the role of the school in post-industrial society – has first to be seriously considered.

The role of the urban school with a majority of working-class and 'immigrant' children in what Daniel Bell has termed 'post-industrial society' has not been adequately discussed or examined by educationists or policy-makers. The term post-industrial society has been used by Daniel Bell to describe post-war Western society: 'industrial society is the co-ordination of machines and men for the production of goods. Post-industrial society is organized around knowledge for the purpose of social control and the directing of innovation or change'. Linked as it has been to theories of the development and management of scientific knowledge and state control of this knowledge to increase growth, Bell's analysis has been challenged of late as most Western industrial societies are experiencing a form of recession and a standstill or 'no-growth' in their economies. However, it remains true that we live in a 'knowledge' based society. Urban schools for working-class children developed out of the Industrial Revolution and the need for a skilled labour force. In post-industrial society, according to Bell, technology will replace manpower and 'knowledge', and in particular scientific knowledge will become more central. If Bell's analysis is only partly right, what are urban schools doing to educate working-class and black children for life in post-industrial society? Or is it intended that only a scientific elite should reap its benefits and be able to take a full part in it?

The presence of large numbers of immigrant children in British schools has heightened and thrown into relief many inherent problems which have been a feature of the British educational system since its inception: the nature of these problems has to do with the structure of society which, in spite of overall social and economic advance, continues to tolerate substantial minorities who are denied access to wealth and opportunity. Rutter, after a comprehensive review of the literature, concluded that it was 'futile' to search for causes, for the fact remains that inequality persists and schooling has done little to mitigate its overall impact. This suggests that Bernstein in his critique of the idea of compensatory education (1970) was right to conclude that 'education cannot compensate for society'. Tyler has suggested that any improvement in working-class attainment would have marginal effects in the job market. If black and working-class children achieve better at schools, the result would be a general forward movement of 'the escalator', to use Tyler's term, but the relative position would remain exactly the same. However Halsey *et al.* in their recent study of *Family, Class and Education in Modern Britain* concluded that although the impact of education on inequality has been marginal, there is now a situation developing where the advantaged (i.e. the middle class) are educationally saturated and therefore any further expansion in education must benefit the less privileged. The current massive cuts in education would certainly fit nicely into this analysis!

It will be clear, then, that I see the social structure as operating through schools to reinforce the low status of black pupils. The use of social psychological theories to 'explain' lower-class and/or black low-achievement in school I regard as an unwillingness to relate social psychological theories to the wider historical, sociological, political and economic factors operating in society, both in terms of working-class children generally, and of black children in particular.

While acknowledging the role of social structure in oppressing working-class people and minority groups, I do not regard people as passive, willing victims of an all-pervasive social structure. At the same time, I cannot accept that the subjective meaning which the situation has for the actor – the phenomenological view – provides a complete answer. My own position is somewhere in between the structural-functional and phenomenological extremes. The work of Levine on *Black Culture and Consciousness*, the theories of Negritude, Black Power, the Rastafarian religion – these are all definitions by actors of their situation, black people in a white world defining blackness as good and beautiful. But this action takes place within a social structure which largely ignores it and which can ignore it or oppress it, because ultimately it is power not self-concept that counts. The issue of real importance is that those who have the power can make their definition of reality prevail at any given time. To say that each individual's reality, subjectively created and uniquely defined, carries equal credibility, importance, sway, authority – is to deny the facts of life.

What we can say is that people can and do opt out of a system which oppresses them (at points where opting out is possible) and create alternative systems to sustain them and to give meaning and beauty to life, to make life – as apart from existence – possible. These systems would probably be defined as a 'sub-culture' but could also be regarded as alternative culture. It is to this alternative culture that most African people in the New World belong – it is this which has enabled black people to survive and to sustain feelings of self-worth and self-esteem.

Laurence Levine accused his fellow historians of distorting black American history; he called for a greater 'balance' not only in the amount but in the nature of the attention devoted to neglected groups. Of his own efforts to redress the balance he wrote:

> This book may dismay some because it abandons the popular formula which has rendered black history an unending round of degradation and pathology. The familiar urge to see in heroes only virtue and in villains only malice has an analogue in the desire to see in the oppressed only unrelieved suffering and impotence ... to argue, as this book does, that even in the midst of the brutalities and injustices of the antebellum and postbellum racial systems black men and women were able to find the means to sustain a far greater degree of self-pride and group cohesion, is not to argue that the system was more

benign than it has been pictured, but rather that human beings are more resilient, less malleable, and less able to live without some sense of cultural cohesion, individual autonomy, and self-worth than a number of recent scholars have maintained.

It is to this historical cultural material that sociologists and social psychologists should turn for an understanding of black self-concept, for they are certainly included among the 'scholars' who Levine accuses. We turn now to consider some of their ideas.

Black Culture and Consciousness

Socio-psychological theories and research built on them ignore the existence of black culture and consciousness. I suggest that an awareness of the historical role of black consciousness as shown in religious and political movements, in literature, poetry, music and song would lead researchers towards a better appreciation of black self-concept and self-image. Social scientists in Western society tend to operate in an ethnocentric trap where they (a) ignore black culture or (b) regard it as a pathological manifestation of white culture – Myrdal, Moynihan and Pettigrew exemplify this approach. The result of this is that even when in their own terms black children manifest positive self-concept and high self-esteem, social scientists explain it away either as the operation of an 'inflated mechanism' (Weinreich) or by reference to some other dubious 'theory'. One way of explaining positive self-concept in minority group children is to see it as a reaction to rejection, discrimination and marginal status. Here the group is seen as withdrawing into itself, developing its own standards of conduct, its members evaluating themselves against their own group criteria. This thesis was recently advanced by Louden to explain the increasing alienation and high self-concept of West Indian children in Bristol.

The concern with self-concept and self-esteem of black children relates to the fact that black children in America and in Britain are substantially represented amongst the disadvantaged and deprived in these societies. It is believed that this low status is related to negative self-concept which leads to poor motivation and consequent low attainment. Thus socio-psychological theories explaining the working of the social system in individual or family pathology terms developed within the mainstream European theoretical framework, reflecting the philosophy and ideology of the elite. The 'family-pathology' explanation, put forward by Daniel Moynihan, ties up with the individual pathology explanation in that the latter is the result of the former: bad child-rearing practice giving rise to various kinds of individual malaise. These theories, when isolated from those concerned with the nature of the social structure in industrial societies and the persistence of educational and social inequalities, may appear more convincing than they might otherwise do. Recent research (Gutman, 1978; Higman) challenges Moynihan's assumption that the black family was completely destroyed by slavery. Much of the research earlier reviewed failed to support the hypothesis of overall negative self-concept in black people in America and Britain.

Self-Concept as a Solution

These theories and ideas have to be related to the problems which the British school system faces in having to educate thousands of West Indian children who, as with blacks in America, are over-represented in the lower streams of comprehensive schools and in special schools for the educationally subnormal. A number of factors combine to make theories of low self-concept and self-esteem attractive to educationists and practitioners. These factors include: a commitment to liberal values which includes compensating the disadvantaged members of society; research reports which support the need for such compensation and the apparent failure of the instructional, cognitive approach to make an impact on measured 'intelligence' or attainment. These factors combine with developments in the sociology of education which stress concern for the individual and acknowledgement of the subjective experience of the actor as the basis for explaining the social world. These developments encourage classroom teachers to regard the building of relationships as one of the most, if not the most, important of their tasks. For the West Indian child in the classroom this will take the form of developing relevant curricula to build up his/her self-image and heighten his/her self-esteem. On another level, we see the development of large-scale national programmes which incorporate a 'social justice' compensatory approach to schooling but which also carry, implicitly, a commitment to promote individual growth and development.

A concern with the actors' own definition of their situation inevitably leads us to consider the West Indian community's response to the low attainment of their children in British schools. For this reason it is important not only to consider the role of schools and teachers in adapting to the presence of West Indian children, but also the role of the community in adapting to social institutions – of which the school is for many the most important. Thus, change and adaptation can be seen as a two-way process.

Theories which explain the West Indian child's low achievement as being due to poor self-image, family background and other social-psychological factors put the schools under increasing pressure to respond to these 'needs' by developing pseudo-therapeutic programmes. It seems important to understand as far as possible why some teachers think as they do and what the implication of this thinking may be for the education of black children in particular, although I would argue that it has implications beyond this group to other sections of working-class children who do not benefit from formal schooling – those children who in Hopper's typology are 'cooled out' by the school system, as opposed to those who are 'warmed up'. It is clear that in a society which is class-based and hierarchically structured and where success in life is linked to middle-class membership, a substantial proportion of bright working-class children need to be 'cooled out' and channelled into 'realistic' jobs. It is also clear that when such an out-group exists in such a system the important task of cooling out the 'unrealistic' ambitions of children in that group will fall to the school system. The fact that West Indian children have 'unrealistic' ambitions is well-known – 'they all want to be doctors'. Parents are also seen as being very ambitious for their children. At the heart of the self-concept and schooling issue lies the claim that better self-concept will lead to higher aspirations, better achievement and greater social mobility for working-class and black children. This claim has to be examined very carefully before it achieves widespread acceptance. The ideas on which it is based must be subjected to critical evaluation and close scrutiny before dubious practices are introduced into school curricula. It is at the outset of such innovations that research needs to be formulated: these assumptions and beliefs need to be examined before they become established doctrine (or dogma).

J. B. Thomas has made some observations on self-concept research and has offered advice to teachers. He wrote that:

> The gap between teacher and researcher has often seemed a widening one . . . because the results seem to reduce teachers to a feeling of helplessness in face of massive variables like social class, genetics and urbanization. But self-concept research is saying to the teacher: you are the backbone of the educational system, not the social scientist or the armies of advisers and petty officialdom. The teacher is a force in the classroom and in the field of self-concept he is a force for good, given he has the will to experiment and to succeed. Teachers can enhance self-concept through the provision of special curriculum materials, through encouraging . . . a supportive atmosphere . . . through developing experimental curriculum projects designed to enhance self-worth in children and in general through becoming more person-oriented in the classroom.

The desire to find solace in an atmosphere free from the realities of life can be very strong but before teachers, policy-makers and other educationists take this advice to heart the objective of 'person-oriented' teaching needs to be clearly spelt out, and its limitations fully appreciated. We begin this process with these observations:

1. Theory on self-concept and schooling has not been adequately formulated.
2. Perhaps as a result of the above, research results on self-

concept, race and class have been conflicting and contradictory.

3. There is research evidence which shows (a) no difference between disadvantaged and advantaged pupils; (b) disadvantaged pupils having higher self-concept scores than advantaged pupils (Rosenberg and Simmons); (c) no relationship between socio-economic status and self-concept scores (Rosenberg) and (d) an overwhelming relationship between achievement in school, high occupational and income aspiration and membership of the middle class (Bruckman and Sheni; Jackson and Marsden; Kahl; Rosen; Sewell *et al.*; Stacey; Swift, 1967; R. H. Turner).

4. Many theorists and practitioners persist in the belief that working-class and lower-class children generally have poor self-concept and black children in particular have negative self-images. Even those whose own research findings contradict this belief persist in holding to it and argue that black children would achieve better in schools if their self-concepts could be 'improved' or' enhanced'.

5. In formulating theories and research on self-concept of black and working-class children and the role of schools in 'enhancing' or 'improving' the self-concept of these children very little, if any, attention has been paid to:

a. the culture of the group being researched and written about; b. the role of the social structure of the society in which the group lives. Its relationships to self-concept have been almost completely ignored as in phenomenological theory, or given paramount importance as in the equation: social structure = black debasement and low status = black negative self-concept and self-hate (Kardiner and Oversey).

6. It is suggested that a policy which seeks to involve schools in programmes designed to achieve mental health as opposed to academic goals needs to consider the relationship of schools to the group from which their clients come. Thus we must know the role which schooling has played generally in relation to the working class in England, if we are suggesting that schooling could be made to have a particular role in relation to a section of the working-class. black children.

It is further suggested that the belief that achievement is related to self-concept is not generally supported by research evidence and that it is therefore misleading to have as an objective the aim of accelerated achievement or attainment for children taking part in 'cultural enrichment', 'ethnic studies', or any special education project of this kind. It would be simpler to have these projects as an end in themselves – surely the attainment of sound mental health is a worthy objective? – without clouding the issue by arguing that attainment in school will increase as a result of better mental health.

If one accepts the case for mental health as an end in itself, it still remains to be proven that there actually exists the need for this type of intervention. Do black children in fact have poor self-concepts? As I have already indicated, the research such as it is has been contradictory. Are schools and teachers the appropriate agencies for this work? It is against this background of unformulated and incomplete theory and contradictory research findings that my own study of the self-concept of West Indian children was carried out. In my research, the school-based projects relate to the theories of multiracial/multicultural education and to research based on these theories.

The community-based projects, and in particular the self-help ones, relate to community involvement in the schooling of children and the desire by a section of the working class to have some control in this area. Techniques for survival, for sustaining a culture and identity, are located in these groups. They reflect a process of adaptation which seeks to modify structures and resist efforts to exclude the group from having any influence on their own or their children's future.

The issues discussed in this chapter are of fundamental importance to the education of West Indian children in Britain. If society is so organized that there is built-in 'inequality' and if racial and class prejudice and the operation of 'interest groups' within society are such that black people and their children are consigned to the lower levels of this social and economic structure, what difference can self-concept make? Previous studies of self-concept, race and class do not usually consider these structural issues, but a critique such as this cannot acquiesce in this indifference to theories which are crucial to an understanding of the role of schooling for minority group children. Self-concept theorists and teachers who base their methods on these theories must face the fact that educational and social mobility are mediated by economic, social and political factors largely outside the control of individuals. A fundamental reassessment of these theories particularly in relation to the schooling of minority group children is needed. We turn now to consider the development of multiracial education and to examine the implications of this development for the schooling of West Indian children in Britain.

2. Black Self-concept: Theory and Research

Wylie's (1961) review and evaluations of self-concept research did not include one study of black self-concept. Her 1976 work mentioned twelve studies which appeared to be connected with black self-concept out of a total of some 1134 studies reviewed.

The tradition in American research has been to assume the existence of negative self-concept and poor self-esteem in black people. It was believed that since self-concept developed out of experience and since the black experience in America was one of emasculation and dehumanization then, inevitably, this would lead to group hatred and rejection and thence to self-hatred and rejection. The work of Moynihan, Radkhe *et al.*, Clark and Clark and Radkhe and Trager appears to confirm this view of black self-hatred as the obvious and logical result of inferior social status, racism and discrimination. The research of Franklyn Frazier extensively explored the pathology of the black middle class associated with that group's rejection of their black caste status. Indeed, Hare (1974) has observed that:

> Investigations of black self-concept and self-esteem have traditionally assumed that every aspect of black life is a reflection of the group's castle-like position, and that Black Americans are incapable of rejecting the negative images of themselves as perpetuated by the dominant white society.

Amongst the earliest pieces of research which established the belief in black self-hate and self-rejection was the doll study (Clark and Clark) which found that a large proportion of black children, when faced with a choice of a black or a white doll, preferred a white doll and frequently identified a white doll as being similar to themselves. The reliability of the degree of mis-identification produced in the Clark study (where 33 per cent of the children in response to the request 'Give me the doll which looks most like you' picked the white doll) has been challenged by Greenwall and Oppenheim who increased the range of choices by adding a light brown doll and found that then only 15 per cent of children mis-identified.

The American research on black self-concept and self-esteem has been adequately reviewed by Coopersmith. It is clear from his review that severe criticisms of the content, methods and conclusions of research on black self-concept have been widely expressed by sociologists and social-psychologists.

Writing on the self-esteem of the black child, Coopersmith observed that:

> On the basis of the common view of Negro life in America there are many reasons to believe that the black child would have low self-esteem. He is, after all, a member of a group that has a minority status in American society and has suffered frequent insult, discrimination and rejection. For many, if not most, Blacks there are only limited opportunities to gain the economic security and physical comforts that they see widespread in the broader white society. Lack of status, economic insecurity, social isolation, public disrespect and limited horizons are the hallmarks of black life in America, and all of these conditions presumably lead to personal feelings of powerlessness, rejection and isolation. If ever conditions existed that would produce low self-esteem they presumably occur in the life of the American Black.

He went on:

> While the preceding description corresponds with what we know of the 'black experience' in America it is based more on logical grounds than on a direct assessment of black attitudes, beliefs and self-esteem. In a very real sense much of what has been written about black self-esteem is based on inferences made by white psychologists concerned with suffering and human dignity and willing to accept those inferences without direct investigation. Viewed in historical perspective the direct examination of black self-esteem is a very recent event and almost all of the studies before 1960 were descriptive and impressionistic in nature.

He quoted Kardiner and Oversey's conclusions on the personality of the American Negro, which state that the Negro's 'self-esteem suffers because he is constantly receiving an unpleasant image of himself from the behaviour of others towards him.' Coopersmith then referred to Pettigrew's summary of knowledge regarding the personality of the American Negro and reaches similar conclusions to those of Kardiner and Oversey. He concludes that 'the personality consequences of this situation can be devastating – confusion of self-identity, lowered self-esteem, perceptions of the world as a hostile place and serious role conflicts.' After reviewing earlier research on black self-concept Coopersmith decided that it had been impressionistic and mainly based on the commonsense notion that blacks should have low self-concept. Increasingly recent research findings have challenged this commonsense notion by showing blacks as having average or high self-concept. But Coopersmith continues with the idea that logic and intuition would lead us to expect differences to exist between black and white self-esteem. He suggests four possible reactions to the evidence that differences do not exist:

1. Previous reports of lower black self-esteem were inferential rather than empirically based. This position he says has strong support from direct studies of black self-esteem.
2. They are a recent development reflecting changes in the socio-economic and political life of America including marked improvement in the life of black Americans.
3. Test results reflect the limitations of test instruments in that these tests may not detect defensiveness, response sets and nuances of meaning particularly and specifically related to racial affiliation.
4. The fourth possibility is to see the self-reported lack of difference between black and white self-esteem as 'valid' . . . accepting that similar levels of self-esteem may stem from different individuals and groups.

Having decided to adopt the fourth position, that is, to see self-reported normal self-esteem of blacks as valid, Coopersmith goes on to consider the concept of 'psychological defences'. He says that these defences may be 'conscious or unconscious' and may involve strategies for coping or evasion. He suggests that it is important to know what part 'defence' plays in personal response style: 'If we speak of defence then something must be defended . . . If we speak of threat, then what is being threatened? . . . If we speak of pain, then what is being injured? His reply is that defence is to protect our 'self-image'. 'The threat . . . is to the self-image we hold of ourselves and the pain is an expression of the disparity between that image and the events we experience in our private thoughts and public actions.'

It is clear then that whilst accepting normal or high self-esteem scores in blacks as 'valid', Coopersmith sees this not as part of a dynamic historical process, but as psychological defence mechanism: to avoid pain. Therein lies the difference between a creative and reactive response to the same structural conditions.

Pettigrew postulated that the 'real tragedy' of the Negro is that, having been forced to play the servile, passive, inferior role, he came to believe it as a reflection of his self-image. He argued that black Americans internalized the negative views which the dominant society held of them, so that in the end they themselves came to be as they were thought to be.

Deutsch also lent support to the view that black self-concept suffered from a negative attitude; he suggested that Negro children generally had more negative self-concept and were more morose, more passive and more fearful than their white schoolmates. Rainwater focused on the Negro family's central role in transmitting values and attitudes of and towards society. He believed that the life patterns of the Negro as the 'crucible of identity' mean that black lower-class children develop strategies for coping which work against their own long-term interests.

Pettigrew, Deutsch and Rainwater bring to their analysis of black identity and self-concept a narrow, culturally-bound, ethnocentric approach which characterizes writing and research in this area.

In his review of the research on race and self-concept in children, Zirkel noted that although earlier studies had purported to show that blacks had negative self-concept, recent (post-1960s) research increasingly demonstrated that 'there is no significant difference between the self-concept of negro and white students' and that there is even some evidence that 'the self-concept of Negro children may surpass those of their white counterparts'. Rosenberg and Simmons also used the theory of 'defence' and 'inflation mechanism' to explain why there was only a small difference in self-esteem scores of academically unsuccessful and academically successful black school children.

Reference Group Theory

Social scientists have found another possible explanation of positive black self-concept in Reference Group Theory, which explains differential evaluation not as a form of compensation or defence but as a consequence of a different value system which takes as its point of reference not (as in the Rosenberg study) the school or the teacher's evaluation or more generally the 'dominant' society's view of a child but that of the group to which it belongs. It will be clear that the antecedents of self-esteem for a child coming from such a cultural background will be different from those for a child from a middle-class white Anglo-Saxon background. If this is taken into account as an important and crucial factor in the development of black self-concept then it will be seen that high self-concept need not be a defensive mechanism, designed to compensate the disadvantaged individual but a perfectly realistic, adaptive and, given the milieu, reasonable response to reality.

British Research on the Self-concept of West Indian Children

Most British research on black children's self-concept and self-esteem has followed the ethnocentric, 'race relations' model as established in America. It has been concerned not with black people or children in their own right but has largely attempted to make comparisons between black and white self-esteem or self-concept. The theory upon which most of this research is based is also mainly American and no British writer or researcher has begun to develop theories which take account of British conditions or the peculiarly West Indian experience in

Britain. It is to be hoped that before any more research is undertaken, some attempt at constructing a coherent theory of the development of self-concept in minority group children which takes account of the historical and cultural background of present-day lifestyles will be made.

I want now to look at some of the research on black self-concept and self-esteem which has been undertaken in Britain, all of which is of recent origin, taking place from 1970 to the present day.

Hill (1970) measured a variety of evaluations of the self and others by means of the semantic differential technique. Based on Osgood's research the semantic differential is a form of self-rating combined with aspects of word association procedure. The technique is based upon the use of a number of, usually, seven-point scales defined by opposing pairs of adjectives. Hill's sample included English and West Indian children attending schools in the West Midlands. He found that West Indian adolescents did not devalue themselves in comparison with their English peers, although they were more likely than English subjects to see their home and parents in negative terms; conversely, they saw school in a more favourable light. Hill found that his West Indian sample expressed a 'tremendous desire' for whiteness, both for themselves and in their future friends, neighbours and boy/girlfriends.

Pearson, in a study of Leicester, found what he called a 'notable lack of cohesion' within the West Indian community and observed that 'individualism' was a central feature of adaptation. He concluded:

It has been shown that individualism has often been seen as a psychological phenomenon which centres on an 'individualistic personality' which encourages self-hate, marginality and negates the formation of meaningful group identities.

Dove studied 545 adolescents of various ethnic groups attending three London comprehensive schools. She found that West Indian adolescents showed much more confusion over ethnic identity than Asian or Cypriot adolescents. Dove believes that this confusion over racial identity will diminish over time, especially for those born in Britain whose experience of racism will clarify any remaining problems of racial identity.

However, Hill, in a later study of Birmingham adolescents (1975), found that longer residence in Britain led to greater neuroticism in West Indians as measured by the Eynsenck scale, in comparison with their English peers. Bagley and Coard undertook a study of 'cultural knowledge and awareness of identity' amongst West Indian school children in London schools.

Bagley and Coard's Research

The subjects in this study were a 1:7 random sample of white and black (West Indian) children in three multiracial schools in London – an infant school (ages 5–6), a junior school (ages 7–10) and a junior high school (ages 11–14). Two interviewers were involved in the study, one black and one white, and responses were tape-recorded and analysed later.

Because of the sensitive nature of the body image enquiry, these questions were not put to the subjects in the junior high school. Black subjects in all three schools did complete, however, a test of 'cultural knowledge', asking forty questions concerning West Indian heritage. ('Have you heard of Paul Bogle; Toussaint L'Ouverture; Henry Christophe; Angela David; Africa? What are slaves? Were any people in the West Indies slaves a very long time ago? What is/are shango; the West Indies Federation; Anansi stories; Yorubas? etc.') A score of one was given for each item correctly identified. A check on the scores of children tested by the white and black interviewers revealed no bias due to the race of the tester.

Bagley and Coard found that, 'Although scores on the cultural knowledge test increased as we moved from subjects in the infant school to black children in junior and junior high school, the total level of knowledge concerning the West Indies and Africa was disappointingly low'. Only 3 of their 58 subjects had ever heard of Paul Bogle; none had heard of Toussaint L'Ouverture; 4 had heard of Marcus Garvey but 24 knew of Martin Luther King; 13 knew some Anansi stories, and 16 knew about calypso. They observed that, 'Overwhelmingly, the black

Table 2.1: Comparison of Skin Colour Preference in Black and White Children

	White children N=73 %		Black children N=43 %	
Wanting to change skin colour, unequivocally	3	4.0	10	24.0
Equivocal	6	8.5	8	19.0
Do not want to change skin colour	64	87.5	24	57.0

Significance of difference between the two distributions $p < 0.01$

Source: Bagley & Coard, 1975.

children in our study thought Africa was a poor and backward country. The physical affinity between Africans and West Indians was seen primarily as an embarrassment. Five-year-old Philip, for example, said, 'It's a big country. Some of the people are black and some of them are white. Some are nice . . . the whites. The blacks are (embarrassed pause) . . . I don't know.' Bagley and Coard concluded that:

1. A sample of West Indian children in three London schools display a disappointingly low level of knowledge concerning the cultural heritage of the West Indies.
2. A substantial number of black children interviewed rejected their ethnic identity (skin, hair and eye colour) in favour of European characteristics. Such self-rejection was not found in a sample of white children in the same schools.
3. There is a significant tendency for children who have poor cultural knowledge to reject their ethnic identity.
4. There is a tendency for children who reject their cultural identity to be seen as having behaviour problems in the classroom.

They called for the teaching of 'Black Studies' which they said
would almost certainly be a beneficial addition to the curriculum
of multiracial schools. They added the caution that such
teaching (which should be paralleled by shared curriculum in the
cultural background of European and other cultures) should
begin early on in the child's school career. Their final comments
include the hope that: 'In multi-ethnic classrooms, children
should learn not only to be secure in, and magnanimously proud
of, their cultural heritage but also to know and respect the
cultural heritage of their fellow pupils'.

Comments on Bagley and Coard's Conclusions

1. Bagley and Coard in their conclusions say West Indian
children 'displayed a disappointingly low knowledge of cultural
heritage' yet in a sample of 58 black children nearly one-third
were between the ages of five and six, i.e. infant school pupils.
Would a corresponding number of five- to six-year-old English
working-class children display cultural knowledge about
Nelson, Waterloo, Charles Dickens, William Shakespeare? To
ask a West Indian child, 'What is/are slaves . . . Shango . . . the
West Indian Federation?' etc. must be seen as the equivalent of
asking English children about Wesleyan religion and the rise of
Methodism, about factory legislation and the conditions of the
working class in Britain.
2. 'A substantial number of black children rejected their
ethnic identity' – yet if the figures are examined closely, nearly
60 per cent of black children did no such thing and nearly 20 per
cent were 'equivocal'. If these two groups are put together
nearly 80 per cent of the black children did not reject their ethnic
identity. If the conditions of life for black children in London
are examined – a minority group discriminated against,
experiencing appalling housing and environmental conditions
and generally 'stigmatized' status – this is indeed an encouraging testament of group loyalty and cohesion.
3. The case for poor cultural knowledge and rejection of
ethnic identity has not been substantiated by the author's own
research.
4. The 'tendency for children who have poor cultural
knowledge to be seen as "behaviour problems by teachers" '

Table 2.2: Number of Black Children in Infant and Junior School Wanting 'White' Skins

Preference	Number	% of 42 in total sample
Wanting to stay black	24	57.0
Equivocal	8	19.0
Wanting to be white	10	24.0

Note: 'Wanting to be white' indicates a clearly expressed preference for a 'white' or 'pink' skin. 'Equivocal' indicates responses such as 'yellow', 'I don't really know – I don't like brown or black'.
Source: Bagley & Coard, 1975.

could be explained in a number of ways and the assumption that increased cultural knowledge would reduce 'behaviour problems' needs closer scrutiny and more rigorous testing than is given here. Therefore, the authors' call for the teaching of Black Studies 'as a beneficial addition to the curriculum of multiracial schools' should not be accepted on the basis of the evidence given in this study.

Milner's Research

Milner studied 300 children drawn equally from the West Indian, Asian and English groups in the schools in two large English cities both with a substantial 'immigrant' population:

Four aspects of the children's attitudes towards racial groups were investigated, each via a separate group of questions. Every question involved the same basic situation, namely that the child was required to make a choice between two dolls or two pictures, in response to a question put by the interviewer. In each case, one figure represented the child's own racial group while the other figure represented the other principal racial group in the child's immediate environment. *The children were clearly engaged by both the dolls and the pictures and needed no encouragement to respond to them as though they were real people* [my emphasis].

Milner later conducted a follow-up study to test the degree of misidentification over time. It entailed:

a second series of identification tests with *some* of the West Indian children tested in the original study, after a period of one year. Other tests were also repeated, but it is the identity tests we are concerned with here. The picture that emerged from these tests showed a remarkably close correspondence to the predictions that follow from the interpretation of misidentification proposed in this chapter. Half of the sample maintained the same choice of figure from the first test to the second; the other half changed their choice from the first to the second test; some in one direction, some in the other.

Table 2.3: Consistency of Choices over Two Identity Tests

Identified with blacks on both tests	black to whites	white to blacks	Identified with whites on both tests
31.25%	6.25%	43.75%	18.75%

Source: Milner, 1975.

Milner concluded that:

The 'black to white' group contains those children who identified with blacks on the first occasion and white on the second; the 'white to black' group contains those who made the reverse change between the two occasions. In so far as these repeated tests give a better identification of the child's enduring notion of his identity, it does seem that there are two groups who are consistent in their identifications (with either blacks or whites) and a central group whose choices are much more unstable. And the extreme groups are also distinguishable in terms of their Preference responses, a much higher level of white preference being found among the consistent outgroup identifiers. It cannot be said on the basis of this further study that our interpretation of the significance of misidentification is proved; however, it is certainly true that the data from the two studies taken together are entirely consistent with that interpretation.

Some Observations on Milner's Research

1. The socially desired response is somewhat played down – the tendency for people to respond in a socially desirable way (and do what they think is expected of them) has been well documented. This is especially true in personality-type research, and its effect cannot be ignored.

2. The researcher effects should have been examined more carefully in terms of the above.

3. Commonsense explanations for doll choice in terms of availability and general acceptability of dolls of different colours in shops and markets could have been noted – it is possible that many of those black kids had never actually seen or played with a black doll before.

4. Racism and racial stereotyping in children's literature have recently received increasing attention (Dixon) and on the basis of how black dolls are depicted in children's literature and on television it is not surprising that children should respond to black dolls in the way Milner reports. The difficulty comes in trying to establish whether these feelings, attitudes etc. also accurately reflect feelings about real people – oneself and one's racial group.

There were once three golliwogs who were most unhappy in the nursery cupboard. None of the other toys liked them, and nobody ever played with them, because their mistress,

Angela, didn't like their black faces (Enid Blyton, *The Three Golliwogs*).

5. Milner said that the children needed no encouragement to respond to the dolls 'as if they were real people' – yet dolls in fact are not 'real people' and any inferences to be drawn from children's (or adults') behaviour with dolls (or other toys) should bear this fact in mind. It is not simply a matter of detail.

6. In his follow-up study, Milner re-tested 'some' of his original sample – he does not give precise figures. If this was a typical primary class, with children away ill, some moved away, a few truants etc., over the interval of a year it is possible for 15–20 per cent of children to have changed class. It is extremely difficult without precise information to know how far the follow-up study was testing the original children in the first study.

7. Milner's research, more perhaps than any other, fits Levine's thesis of the 'pure victim' theory, which explains black personality in terms of self-hate and racial mis-identification, and which ignores completely any other explanations or interpretation of the evidence.

Further Research on Self-concept and the Black Child

Lomax used a sentence completion test to examine the self-concept of girls in a large secondary school which was two-thirds West Indian. Although mostly in the lower streams of the school these black girls had significantly higher self-esteem than their white peers. In keeping with Hill's (1975) findings, girls born in Britain had poor self-concept compared with girls born in the Caribbean.

Louden used Rosenberg and Simmons' measure of self-esteem in a study of 375 adolescents from various ethnic groups attending school in the Midlands. Louden found that, in general, the higher the concentration of blacks in a school, the higher the self-esteem levels of black pupils although it was the group of West Indians in schools with medium concentrations (between 30 and 50 per cent West Indian) who had the highest levels of self-esteem.

Louden suggests that:

a whole variety of factors in the school may influence self-esteem in various ethnic groups, including the degree to which minority groups are insulated from various types of white racism. Broader social forces have operated to place the great bulk of minority group adolescents in a racially insulated environment, and this environment establishes certain barriers to assault upon the feelings of personal worth. This is one reason why the self-esteem level of black adolescents as a group is not as low as one might otherwise expect . . . In many cities in this country most black adolescents live their daily lives in essentially black worlds and actually have little exposure to white adolescents.

Jones noted that West Indians are often successful in sporting activities and examined the hypothesis that success in sport would be associated with higher levels of self-esteem in black pupils. The subjects of his study were 1612 English and West Indian adolescents attending London secondary schools. The measure of self-esteem he used was the 23-item measure of general self-esteem, derived from the Coopersmith scale. First Jones found that both West Indian males and females had significantly poorer levels of self-esteem than their white peers. Jones found that the following items in the General Self-esteem Scale showed West Indians (male and female) as having significantly lower self-esteem than English pupils: 'My parents expect too much of me'; 'I can't be depended upon'; 'I'm pretty happy'; 'Things are all mixed up in my life'; 'I often feel upset at school'; 'No one pays much attention to me at home'. On the items, 'I often get discouraged in school' and 'I'm a failure' West Indian boys had lower self-esteem than English boys. On the item 'I'm proud of my school work' West Indian boys and girls had significantly better self-esteem than their white peers. West Indian boys had significantly better self-esteem than white boys on the items: 'I often feel ashamed of myself' and 'I spend a lot of time daydreaming'.

Jones observed too that the West Indian pupils were much more likely than whites to use the sporting and social facilities of the school in the evenings, using the school rather than the home as a focus of activity. Although West Indian pupils were much more likely than whites to be included in school sports teams, and to excel in sport generally, this success in sport was not correlated with self-esteem levels. Although English pupils who excelled at sport had higher levels of self-esteem, this was interpreted as being a function of their generally higher stream level. Blacks, even those excelling in sport, were generally in lower streams and this stream membership rather than sporting success was seen as the most powerful influence on self-esteem. Those West Indians who were in a higher stream tended to have levels of self-esteem which were equal to those of their white peers in the same stream. Jones suggested that these high achievers among the West Indian population came from rather different family situations 'than the usual rather authoritarian setting of the average West Indian'.

Bagley, Mallick and Verma added further to the already confused research findings on pupil self-esteem in their study of thirty-nine schools.

The studies of self-esteem and related concepts in minority adolescents in British schools have produced interesting but sometimes contradictory findings. In part this could be due to the different methods of measuring self-esteem. It could also be due to specific factors within school and community which influence self-esteem in particular ways. Our own studies, looking at levels of self-esteem in West Indian adolescents aged 14 to 16 in 39 schools in London, the Midlands and the North of England, may be particularly valuable in obtaining a more comprehensive, overall picture of black self-esteem, in which local and situational factors are randomized.

The results are as follows: a higher score on the General Self-esteem Scale indicating poorer self-esteem; the score on the GSE scale for West Indian girls is 18.67, SD 10.39; for the English female controls, 18.94, SD 10.13. The mean GSE score for West Indian boys is 22.35, SD 10.62; for the English male controls 17.65, SD 9.74. A comparison of means using the t-test indicates that West Indian boys have significantly poorer self-esteem than the English controls, at the 1 per cent level of probability. The difference between West Indian girls and the English controls is not significant however. West Indian girls have significantly better self-esteem than West Indian boys (at the 5 per cent level of probability). This effect, for black girls to have better self-esteem than black males, runs counter to the trend in a number of other studies of self-esteem in white, English subjects, in which males have better self-esteem than females.

Weinreich's research is concerned with what he calls 'identity diffusion'. His frame of reference is basically Freudian, being grounded in psychoanalytical theory as modified by Eric Erikson. His work is with English and immigrant adolescents; he takes the tasks of adolescence to be 'to resynthesize all the childhood identifications in some unique way and yet in accordance with the roles offered by some wider section of society' (Erikson). Failure to achieve these tasks according to Weinreich leads to identity diffusion: 'Clinical features of identity diffusion are described as consisting of tissue confusion, self-consciousness, role fixation, work paralysis, bisexual confusion, authority confusion and confusion of values.'

In the belief that 'immigrant' adolescents experience greater dysfunctions between the values of home and wider community Weinreich hypothesized that 'immigrant' adolescents will exhibit greater identity diffusion than will indigenous adolescents. He adopted a case study approach together with a modified form of Kelly's Personal Construct method which he sees as being based on the value system of the individual and therefore appropriate for use with children of any language or culture. For each individual his own constructs were presented to him on rating sheets which enabled him to construe the facts of his own self-image alongside significant individuals and groups of people from his own social world. Weinreich's sample consisted of adolescent school leavers at Bristol schools, 32 West Indians, 13 Asian and 37 English. Weinreich found that Identity Diffusion was greater for West Indian girls than for West Indian boys and English boys and girls. Thus West Indian girls, as measured by Weinreich, show 'realistically' low self-esteem, but West Indian boys show defensively high self-esteem – he deduced this from the fact that there was no difference between the level of self-esteem in West Indian and English boys. It seems rather pointless to use instruments which are 'based on the value system of the individual' if the researcher can then turn around and place his own interpretation on findings which do not fit his model. Weinreich's West Indian sample was very small and it is doubtful whether any reliable conclusions could be drawn from such a small study within a theoretical frame of doubtful relevance to the West Indian group under study.

It is not surprising that Louden's research on West Indian children should use the language of 'inflation mechanisms' and that Weinreich should also write in terms of 'defensively high' self-esteem in West Indian boys. Within their theoretical perspective it would be difficult to draw any other conclusion. The major study by Milner which has been very influential with the NFER and the Schools Council is also open to serious reservations – for instance, outgroup preference in his West Indians could be explained by the fact of a white researcher asking black children which dolls they preferred. Milner was sensitive to this and allowed that it could have influenced the results. On a more fundamental note – can choice of dolls really indicate race preference in a child? – watch television and see the dolls being advertised, Cindy, Mandy and so on. Is a black or brown doll ever shown? Are dolls the same as people? Do children regard dolls in the same way as they regard people? Is it a realistic and valid inference to make that choice of doll indicates how children feel about themselves and their race? Or is it a function of fashion, of the marketplace and what is being offered generally to children in their everyday lives? I have serious reservations about the implications that have been read into the doll studies and the interpretations that have been placed on a choice of doll. I think that there are equally plausible explanations for choice of white dolls as against black or vice versa which may have nothing or very little to do with how one values oneself and one's racial group.

Bagley and Young reporting on their recent research on the self-concept of black West Indian children in London said that West Indian children in the schools where over half of the pupils were black, had 'significantly better levels of self-esteem' than black children who were a minority in school and that this did not have an adverse effect on the self-evaluation of white children in these classrooms. They go on to say that this finding, if replicated, has important implications for the concept of multicultural education.

Ideally the school should transmit to ethnic minority children effective and cultural skills which enable them to cope successfully in the wider society. But at the same time the school should transmit to all of the ethnic groups in the multicultural school . . . an intimate knowledge of, and a magnanimous pride in, the language and culture of their traditional society.

This approach, they argue, would promote true 'integration' and would reflect a move towards community schools which, reflecting neighbourhood integration, would include a considerable minority, and often a majority, of black and Asian pupils. The authors regret that 'this ideal model of multicultural education is far from implementation in British schools'.

There are many contradictions and dilemmas facing the liberal education reformer. The idea of community schools reflecting the multiracial/multicultural make-up of society is appealing and appears to resolve many of these contradictions. Gerald Grace in his recent excellent study of urban education and teacher ideology commented that the ideological appeal of the community school is considerable because it appears to offer a mode of working within 'the system' while at the same time offering critical opposition to it. Merson and Campbell have attacked the very idea of community schools as a solution to the problems which working-class people and their children face and have argued strongly that 'socially relevant' curricula will disqualify working-class children from the realms of political discourse and thus from the ability to deal with the political oppression which the authors identify as the major factor affecting working-class lives. Merson and Campbell do not regard the development of community schools as a radical innovation, but as a potentially dangerous and limiting exercise which may add to the oppression of working-class children by cutting them off from 'the mainstream of social and political discourse'.

It is a feature of the discussion of the schooling of West Indian and other minority group children that theories and research, and practices based on them, appear to take no account of ideas and theories in mainstream education. Black children are a section of the working class in Britain and whatever is true of the working class generally, is also true of West Indian children. Since historically the school system in Britain has had a particular role *vis à vis* the working class, it is sheer folly to expect that a section of the working class can change this historical role of urban schools.

As to the research discussed here, it is generally inconclusive and contradictory. Hill finds no difference in self-concept or self-expression between West Indian and English children. Weinreich finds a difference between West Indian girls and English girls and boys. Louden found no significant difference between Asian and West Indian adolescents. Bagley and Coard found misidentification and cultural ignorance amongst their sample. Milner also found a high degree of misidentification and out-group preference. Lomax found black girls having significantly higher self-concept scores than their white peers. Dove found more identity confusion among adolescent West Indians than Asians or Cypriots. Pearson believed West Indians to have 'individualistic personalities which encourage self-hate'.

It will be seen from this review that there is no coherent body of research or theory on the development of self-concept in minority group children in Britain. The research methods vary with virtually each study; no study has been replicated.

However, most studies call for changes which they hope will improve the situation. Milner's study has been extremely influential: the Schools Council and the NFER *Education for a Multiracial Society* project includes many of the recommendations made in Milner's research. Among the recommendations which gain support from many liberal teachers and educationists is the call for Black Studies made in many of these research reports. It is felt that Black Studies will have the effect of 'equalizing' the situation for both black and white students. In America the call for Black Studies came originally from militant student activists not from social scientists working in race relations. What meaning has this call for Black Studies in the context of British society?

Black Self-concept and Schooling

> No child should be expected to cast off the language and culture of the home as he crosses the school threshold, nor to live and act as though school and home represent two totally separate and different cultures to be kept firmly apart.
>
> Bullock Report, 1975

In criticizing the 'conventional paradigm' of educational sociology, David Gorbutt described its history in these words:

> The primary focus of attention within the sociology of education has been to establish and explain the differential performance of working-class children as compared with middle-class children in educational institutions. The explanations given have been overwhelmingly in terms of the cultural background of the children. By and large they boil down to a theory of cultural discontinuity between home and school: the working-class child brings to school values and attitudes, language patterns and cognitive styles which are not consonant with those of the school or his middle-class peers. Underlying this explanation is a notion of cultural deficit which implies that working-class culture is not only different but deficient and inferior.

It is clear that the Bullock Report and the views of the conventional sociological paradigm represent two views of the roles of schools from different points of view. The Bullock views are the most recent and appear to ignore the earlier critique of Bernstein (1964) and other sociologists whose work demonstrates that in practice for the working-class and middle-class child the school and the home are 'two totally separate and different cultures'. If this is true for the native working-class child, it must at least be equally true for the foreign, culturally and racially different child.

The Parliamentary Select Committee on Race Relations and Immigration commented on Black and Ethnic Studies in its report of 1974, stating:

Like the phrase 'black power', Black Studies appears partly to symbolize a search for identity among some members of minority groups who feel that 'white education offers inadequate education to black people' . . . In as much as Black Studies is merely seen as the resolution of a confrontation between black and white it would be partial and divisive.

It also rejected the idea of black teachers teaching black children in separate classes and recommended instead the setting up of a fund to meet the educational needs of a special kind of non-white children.

The Case for Black Studies

The claim for Black Studies is based on the need to redress the balance as Sam Morris argued in his pamphlet:

The black child goes to a white school, he is taught by white teachers, he sees pictures of white persons, he uses books written by white writers, he uses equipment made by white craftsmen, he hears and sings songs about white people, he learns poems about white people . . . the primary purpose of Black Studies is the adjustment of this imbalance.

And the Black Studies syllabus of one London comprehensive school demonstrates this approach in its preamble:

The purpose of a 'Black Studies' course is to provide both black and white peoples with a means of compensating for inadequacies of understanding, lack of identity and poor self-image, sheer ignorance, the holding of myths and prejudices, feelings of superiority and hostility so that a degree of understanding and humility may lead to mutual respect.

This may be utopian but no more so than many syllabuses in various subjects. The difficulty is that the course would entail virtually the rewriting of world history from about the beginning of the seventeenth century. Further, it would make it necessary to take a look at the influence of that history upon the related subjects of geography, literature etc.

Fortunately, there has been in the last few years an increase in the production of textbooks which provide this kind of analysis.

The following syllabus is designed to cover a two-year course and is aimed more at schools with mainly West Indian originating children. It will be necessary therefore to be both selective in parts and expansionary in others. Throughout 'black' is meant to include all non-white, since there is a growing realization that the shade of colour of skin is relatively unimportant.

It is essential that in a study of this kind, care is taken not to lean over backwards to compensate, perhaps subconsciously, for the past, but to present a true picture, warts and all, of both whites and blacks. 'Black is beautiful' but not all black is beautiful: 'Papa Doc' in Haiti, General Mobutu in the Congo, could hardly be called liberals during their infamous regimes. Since some of the material will necessarily be controversial, it would be useful to have outside speakers coming in to give different points of view and to stimulate thought.

Bernstein (1970) asked, 'How is black "culture" to be defined and classified by the school system – Reggae music? Steel bands? Patois speech?' Let us briefly examine some schools which tried to cater for what is defined as black culture.

Schools in Conflict

School 'X' is a London comprehensive boys' school of some 2000 boys and about 100 staff, including some black teachers. In response to the perceived needs of the 60 per cent West Indian children in the school, a programme of cultural activities was introduced – this included a steel band which was scheduled to run during class time. As many of the West Indian boys were already engaged in non-academic activities (mainly sport) which took up a lot of their time, some of the teachers (mainly black but including one or two others) protested to the Head about the timetabling of the 'cultural activities' within the normal school day. They felt that these activities should be carried out after school hours. They felt that the West Indian children were being further disadvantaged (as in most London schools, blacks were mainly in the lower streams) by being encouraged away from regular school work. The Head and others were at a loss to understand the objections of the black teachers. They were, as far as they were concerned, doing their best to encourage West Indian cultural forms in the school; since West Indians performed best in sport it made sense to encourage them to succeed in an area where they were competent. To the black teachers it was simply the school confirming the old racial stereotype: 'Music and sports, that's all we're good for' was the way one of them put it to me. They saw black children being seduced into activities which were immediately rewarding but carried no prospect of future advancement, and to them it was ironic that this was done in order to give the black children identity and improve their self-esteem through their own cultural form. Another factor which the Principal and others in the school hierarchy completely missed – but which was of enormous importance to the West Indian teachers – was that of mobility. The teachers argued that the black children were being educated by the school system for unemployment and that steel bands and other 'cultural' activities were simply to keep them happy, whereas the black teachers saw the children's futures in brighter terms – they could return to jobs in their homelands or migrate to Africa or other parts of the Third World. They were not trapped in the way that the English working class was trapped and a bright West Indian child who worked hard could succeed and get to be 'internationally' mobile. This tendency by teachers to encourage children to look beyond a bleak future on the dole in this country was very marked among the teachers in the Community schools I studied – there were posters advertising jobs for engineers and doctors in different parts of Africa and this was put to the children time and again as something for them to work towards. This is a feature of the education of black children which completely escapes many educators and teachers, who do not appreciate that mobility, moving away in search of jobs and better prospects, has always been a feature of Caribbean life. I would argue that one of the reasons why there is no West Indian middle class to speak of in this country is this very fact – successful people and their children simply move on 'back home', or to North America and increasingly parts of Africa, Nigeria, Tanzania and Ghana.

To get back to the discussion of the school in conflict, these teachers were bitter and frustrated and felt completely demoralized; they were accused of being too 'middle-class' and not appreciating 'their' own culture. It made for a very tense and unhappy situation.

Below are the two opening paragraphs of an article which appeared in a community magazine *Stepping out* in Ealing, West London under the heading 'Steel Bands in our Schools', which puts another school's policy very neatly. The issues are very similar to those examined in the first school but this time there was no conflict with teachers and no problems are referred to.

Steel band music is a fascinating and authentically Caribbean art. Interest among the general public here in Britain has been further encouraged recently by several television programmes in which steel bands have figured.

Why steel bands in our schools? Their contribution in terms of education and community relations is clear: developing a positive self-image for many West Indian children and providing yet one more positive contribution from the Caribbean heritage to the life of the school and its community. This can be at the level of full participation or of appreciation. But the inclusion of the steel band in the curriculum of the school is based on sound musical principles: music-making in groups like this is an important social force; steel music involves a high degree of musical memory and ear training; it requires co-ordination and skill and relates to dance and movement. It may provide a useful innovation in the metalwork departments of secondary schools. Its history and development links with carnival, the 'national theatre' of Trinidad, makes an interesting study in itself.

The rest of the article dealt with the practical details of setting up a steel band in a school.

This brief outline serves to illustrate the difficulties that can ensue when schools try to meet what they define as the 'cultural needs' of black children. One must ask the question – is it possible, given the school role in society at the present time and given the position of black parents and children in that society, for schools to meet the cultural needs of black children?

Another example, a more happy one this time, came from a school where one teacher had met with a group of West Indian boys to run a class on the Rastafarian religion. Again it was in a London boys' comprehensive school, with roughly the same racial composition of 50–60 per cent West Indian children. The Religious Education teacher was black; he had been teaching World Religions to his fourth-year boys. After the session on the Rastafarian religion, a group of West Indian boys approached him and asked if he would tell them more about the Rastas – could he include more sessions on them perhaps? The teacher told the boys that the class was Religious Education and the subject World Religions and not everyone in the class would want to devote two or three more sessions to the Rastas, but he agreed to run a series of classes after school for anyone who was interested. The boys took up the offer and met for several weeks to study the Rasta faith.

This group of boys is included in my research sample and will be discussed in greater length at a more appropriate time. It seemed important to make the point now that schools can be, as it were, a point of contact for many children who can then follow up what they have learnt through groups in the community or informal learning situations. But, in general, the ways in which schools can contribute towards the development of cultural awareness in minority group pupils are severely limited.

Raymond Giles has apparently been converted to the idea of Black Studies for West Indian children in British schools (1977) but in his American research (1975) he was led to a very different conclusion. Having discussed the relevance and importance of providing Black Studies and various alternative programmes in American schools, Giles concluded:

> Another very real possibility is that black children whose parents would like them to develop a black consciousness or awareness of self-based concepts of Negritude or other philosophical or religious precepts might find that release time from school – the equivalent of religious instruction, for

which there is a precedent – would be a more appropriate and effective approach. The one difference between the demands of black students and community groups and those of other minority groups is that in no case have Chinese, Japanese, Indians, Puerto Ricans, Mexican Americans, Jews or other ethnic groups come to school expecting middle-class value oriented teachers, white or otherwise, to discuss with members of those minority groups what it means to be Chinese, Japanese and so on.

My own views are that, given the overall structure of English society, and given the role of the schools in that structure in relation to working-class culture generally, it would be quite unrealistic to expect schools to cater to the cultural needs of a black minority of the working class when they have demonstrated their inability or unwillingness to cater to the cultural needs of the majority white working-class culture. Programmes such as the NFER Schools Council Project appear to develop without any real understanding of their implications for the majority of children in 'multiracial' schools. The history of formal education in this country has not generally reflected the culture of the mass of the people; the culture which is assumed to be superior is the 'high culture' of the middle and upper classes. When therefore the English working-class child is asked to respect other people's culture he is being asked to be super-normal. In seeking to develop programmes, whether steel band, reggae music or Black Studies to bring about an improved self-image or more positive self-concept in black children, educational theorists and practitioners appear to be ignoring the role which the education system has traditionally played with respect to English working-class culture and self-image. Underlying many of these programmes, ideas and theories are the assumptions that schools have a duty to fulfil every conceivable task in relation to children and adolescents in Western society (Musgrove; Illich; Wardle). Take as an example Yvonne Colleymore's strictures against a relevant Home Economics curriculum (quoted in David Hill, 1976):

How can a West Indian girl with African hair, looks and

colour relate the information on hair care and make-up to her own complexion, skin and hair texture? Surely at this point she must realize that she is different and the teaching irrelevant?

There are many points to be taken up. 'She must realize that she is different' – did she not know that before? Would the English girls find a Home Economics class on Afro hair care more relevant? Or does it matter? Why should schools have to teach young women how to look after their hair? I have been such a girl with 'African' hair, looks and skin colour. I was educated in the Caribbean by completely black teachers; nobody from outside my family ever thought it necessary to teach me how to 'comb hair'. Hair braiding is a communal, social matter amongst most African women and girls who learn it in the society of other girls and women. That's how I learnt it. That's how most West Indian girls still learn it today.

I give the following example as a contrast to the one provided by Hill.

A West Indian girl has been recently admitted to a Senior Girls' Community Home School (formerly an Approved School). Staff discuss how she is settling in.

Senior House Mother: 'I know Cheryl is settling in all right as she was having her hair braided by Donna when I last saw her upstairs.'

General discussion about hair braiding amongst West Indian girls and all staff agree that this is a social activity, and that if a black girl is excluded from it and can't find anyone to braid her hair, then she would be in a very desperate situation indeed (Stone, 1976).

As Kenneth Richmond has argued in his book, *Education and Schooling*, and as Ivan Illich and others of the de-schooling movement so ably demonstrated, 'there is a danger of confusing all "education", that is, the process of understanding and learning, with "schooling", which for some people may have very little to do with learning in any meaningful sense.' Hair and body care are the kinds of education that one traditionally acquires in the family. It is questionable how far it is necessary for schools to take over this function for any group of pupils. For many children schools are not doing the job they are meant to be doing very well. It might be better not to extend their area of influence and avoid doing worse.

This has taken us away from our central concern but not very far because hair care, food, eating habits etc. are all part of a people's 'culture', i.e. 'way of life'. Quite apart from the fact that there is no clear evidence to support the view that black children as a whole have significantly poor self-concepts, if schools seek to influence people's feelings about themselves (as the schools perceive these feelings to be) by incorporating aspects of people's cultures into the school timetable they may be creating more problems than they solve.

Black Culture, Consciousness and Self-concept

Culture is more than the sum total of institution and language. It is expressed as well by something which the anthropologist, Robert Redfield, has called 'style of life' . . . This argument applies with special force to the West African cultures from which so many slaves came. Though they varied widely in language, institutions, gods and the familiar patterns, they shared a fundamental outlook towards the past, present and future and common means of cultural expression which could well have contributed the basis of a sense of identity and a world view capable of withstanding the impact of slavery.

Laurence Levine, *Black Culture and Consciousness*

Wade Nobles has drawn attention to the fact that all American and British theories which seek to explain the development of self-concept in human beings are grounded in a Western philosophical tradition which ignores the explanations derived from other cultures and in particular African culture. As much of the research and writings on self-concept since the 1960s have, in America and increasingly in Britain, included studies of black self-concept, it would seem important to look at some of the recent social, political and religious movements within black society which have a direct bearing on this subject.

Africanity and Self-concept

Nobles' criticism of theory and research on black self-concept, suggested that Africans and people of African descent see the self as a consequence of the group's being. He contrasts this with the Western orientation which views the group as depending mainly on individual ingression. He says:

> The African world-view suggests that 'I am because *we* are and because *we* are, therefore I am': in so emphasizing this view it makes no real distinction between self and others. They are in a sense one and the same: 'One's being is the group's being, one's self is the "self of one's people" ', one's being is the *'we'* instead of the *'I'*. One's self-identity is therefore always a *people* identity, or what could be called an *extended* identity or *extended self* [author's emphases].

Accordingly, he suggests, the African world-view requires that when focusing on the self, one should not be bound 'to the examination of distinct, separate individuals but, rather, one should examine the dynamics of the "we" or the feelings of belonging to as well as being the "group".' He feels that, unlike Western conceptions which examine independent and individual selves, research involving the African world-view cannot make a critical distinction between self (I) and one's people (we). He argues that it is not necessary to make an explicit distinction between Western (white) and African (black) conceptions of self but simply to note that many, if not most, peoples of African descent living in America operate in everyday life from an African perspective. He cites Billingsley, Dubois, and Herskovits who stress the existence of an extended African self. He concludes that, 'the African self is one's people or tribe. The two – oneself and one's people – are more than simply inter-related, they are one and the same.'

Even before Levine's massive historical study of *Black Culture and Consciousness* in which he reviewed black culture as reflected in 'folk thought', other scholars, notably the French historian Roger Bastide, had already noted that persistence of African thought and culture amongst people of African descent in the

Caribbean and the Americas. The Jamaican social anthropologist, M. G. Smith (1965), has also documented this in his studies of various Caribbean communities:

> It is of crucial importance to establish the existence of a separate black culture amongst Africans living in the new world: this culture, whether it is seen as the residue of the original African culture or as a mixture of the Afro/American, Afro/Caribbean or Afro/Latin American, hardly matters: what matters is the acceptance of the idea of a distinctive African world-view, a way of thinking, or regarding oneself and one's people, which is different from people of other cultures.

Those American writers who gave birth to the traditional view of black Americans and who have influenced all British work in this area, took the view that blacks had no culture worth speaking of. In 1946 Myrdal wrote: 'In practically all its divergences, American Negro culture is not something independent of general American culture. It is a distorted development, or a pathological condition, of the general American culture.' The research and literature on black self-concept both in America and in Britain reflects this view of black people as marginal, without culture, obsessed with being something other than themselves (most usually being white), pathologically accepting other people's negative views of themselves as realistic, even though, as Gordon and Gergen have convincingly demonstrated, most people will only accept credible sources as realistic reflections of their own self-concept. These researches will be examined in more detail in a later chapter. I want to close this discussion of black culture and consciousness with a further quotation from Laurence Levine's study of black American culture. In the Introduction he wrote:

> This book may dismay some, because it abandons the popular formula which has rendered black history an unending round of degradation and pathology. The familiar urge to see in heroes only virtue and in villains only malice has an analogue in the desire to see in the oppressed only unrelieved suffering and impotence. The ideal construct – the

pure victim – is no more convincing by what we know of human psychology and history than the ideals of pure hero or villain.

It is central to the thesis of this book that one must attempt to understand and take account of people's definition of their own world. This, if you like, is the phenomenological part of my argument, and includes a concern with the history, culture and contemporary experience of West Indians living in Britain. But it is only one part. We have then to consider the constraints on the actors, and one of the main constraints for the black child is living in a society which sees his culture as non-existent or at best inferior. Within this context it is interesting to note the Working Draft of the NFER/Schools Council Project, *Education for a Multiracial Society*:

> *Criteria for the Selection of Learning Experiences*
> 2. Other cultures and nations have their own validity and should be described in their own terms. Wherever possible they should be allowed to speak for themselves and not be judged against British or European norms . . .
> 5. Because people and cultures of African descent have been undervalued by Western writers and historians, it is reasonable to correct this imbalance by showing black characters in positive roles and by selecting for study a variety of African societies.

It seems, then, that the NFER and the Schools Council are charging schools with restoring the imbalances which have existed in Western society for centuries. The admission that 'Western writers and historians' have undervalued African cultures is welcomed – but is it realistic to expect schools to change this? It has been the purpose of this discussion on black culture and consciousness to argue that, whether undervalued or ignored by Western historians and social scientists, African culture survived and still survives and that part of that survival has been the development of different criteria for self-evaluation and a process for the development of self-concept which stressed the group, what Nobles termed the 'we', far more than Europeans or Anglo-Saxon Americans do. This development is carried to its logical conclusion by the Rastafarian use of the term 'I and I' for 'we': true 'Brethren' grass-roots Rastas never say 'we' because 'we' are part of 'I' and thus 'we', the other part of 'I', do not exist as a separate entity but as 'I' and 'I'.

As the Negritude movement forms an important part of the historical background we are discussing we turn now to consider briefly its major emphasis and its contribution to African culture.

Negritude – The Belief in a Distinctive 'African Personality'

The concept of Negritude first arose in the West Indies in Haiti; it was basically a reassessment by a small group of black writers and poets of their African heritage: 'The African Personality or Negritude: the distinction is unimportant. Each concept involves the other' (Mphahlele).

Negritude claimed the whole of the black world. Historically it laid emphasis on the arts – the great names in Negritude writings are the poets Leopold Senghor and Aimé A. Cesairé and the West Indian novelists Rene Maran and Leon Damas. Negritude was foreshadowed by the Harlem Renaissance of the 1920s in the United States. The Harlem Renaissance is the term used to describe the flowering of poetry and arts which took place amongst blacks at the time. The works of these writers were known to Senghor and Cesairé and exerted great influence on them.

> In France as well as in Germany, before the close of the Negro Renaissance, Harlem's poets were already being translated. Leopold Sidar Senghor of Senegal and Cesairé of Martinique, the great poets of Negritude, while still students at the Sorbonne, had read the Harlem poets and felt a bond between themselves and us . . . The Harlem poets and novelists of the twenties became an influence in far-away Africa and the West Indies – an influence still today in the literature of black men and women there. To us, 'negritude' was an unknown word, but certainly pride of heritage and consciousness of race was ingrained in us (Langston Hughes, *The Twenties Harlem and its Negritude*).

The most important concept to grasp about Negritude is that it was international – it was an idea about black African personality and culture which involved people of African descent everywhere. It never made an impact beyond narrow intellectual circles, black and white. It could be seen as the philosophical aim of the cultural nationalism movement which began with Du Bois, an American, had Marcus Garvey, a Jamaican, as one of its most eloquent prophets and included the West Indians George Padmore and Edward Blyden, who first spoke about the 'African personality' in a lecture delivered in Sierra Leone in 1893.

The Negritude movement is important mainly as an historical landmark. It was a black intellectual movement aimed at asserting African values and culture and insisting on the existence of a distinct and unique African personality. Critics of Negritude include many contemporary African writers, Mphahlele for example, who accuse the Negritude writers and poets of romanticizing the African personality and of giving credence to 'the noble savage' estimation of blacks by their unwillingness to see the 'whole' person, faults and shortcomings included. The Senegalese novelist, Senbane Ousmane, has dismissed Negritude as an intellectual abstraction with no relevance to the mass of African people: 'Negritude neither feeds the hungry nor builds roads'. But Senghor (1967) writes, 'Negritude is the cultural heritage, the values – and above all the "spirit" of Negro-African civilization'.

The central core of Negritude doctrine and belief in African personality rested on the belief in the cultural unity of all black people, Africans, Afro-American and Caribbean blacks alike. Cesaire has written time and time again (1945, 1956) that the black West Indian, despite the traumatic experience of transportation, slavery and the manifold forms of enforced acculturation, remains, in his innermost being, an African, an African who has 're-interpreted' his ancestral culture in the light of a radically different socio-economic situation. He does not deny the influence of slavery and of colonialism upon the culture and personality of the black West Indian, indeed the whole Negritude movement was in part a defence against the attack of colonialism and colonial cultures upon the 'authentic' African personality.

The fact is that Negritude never set out to feed the hungry or to build roads – it was basically a cultural movement, stating truths it felt needed to be stated. It had the shortcomings of its time and place but still, for all that, it exerted great influence on black writers and thinkers of the time and as at least a counterbalance to the all-prevailing colonial culture, it fulfilled a necessary task. Certainly many of the slogans of contemporary blacks, including the defiant 'Black is Beautiful', have echoes of the poems of Senghor which glorify blackness and black beauty.

Black Identity and Black Power

The Head said that several children in the school talked about Black Power and Black Identity, but they were just making noises. I asked if their parents could sustain this attitude as much as white parents who had anti-black feelings could amongst their children. She felt to some extent that black parents could, 'providing that black children go on being disadvantaged as they get older, then this is just adding fuel to the Black Power fire'.

R. Giles, 1977

The English 'model' and ways can still play an important part in West Indian psychology, and this can lead to rejection of all that is West Indian. Such rejection has also been enhanced, in the past, by the use in West Indian schools of material which emphasizes the 'white' image; portraying white heroes and generally glorifying a light coloured skin. Conversely . . . a dark skin is deemed to be of inferior status.

D. Hill, 1976

Like Negritude, the concept of Black Power also had an international or pan-African flavour from its beginnings. Unlike Negritude, it was, to begin with, a particularly American response to identifiable racial, economic and social problems. Of the phrase 'Black Power', Martin Luther King said: 'The phrase had been used long before by Richard Wright and others, but never until that night had it been used in the Civil Rights

Movement.' 'That night' referred to the occasion in June 1966 when, during a Civil Rights march, Stokely Carmichael, then Chairman of the SNCC (Student Non-Violent Co-ordinating Committee) raised the cry, 'We want Black Power'.

Stokely Carmichael and Charles Hamilton in their book *Black Power*, defined Black Power as the means whereby black people will 'exercise control over our lives, politically, economically and psychologically . . . We blacks must respond in our own way, on our own terms, in a manner which fits our temperament. The definition of ourselves, the roles we pursue, the goals we seek are our own responsibility.'

Black Power became, as it were, the political arm of Negritude, the means whereby the 'African personality', unique and distinctive, would make its presence felt. It is clear that Carmichael accepts the basic ideas of Negritude:

> We are an African people, with an African ideology, we are wandering in the United States, we are going to build a concept of people in this country or there will be no country.

And again:

> It seems also that the motherland has a responsibility to safeguard the humanity of Africans where they live outside Africa. They also need cultural organizations that will begin to revive and place the culture of the African back on the pedestal where it belongs.

This demand for reviving cultural organizations and emphasizing the importance of African culture was one of the major influences of Black Power on the educational institutions of America, where in schools and colleges throughout the land students began first to demand courses in African History and Culture and then Afro-American courses and finally Black Studies courses. The demand for culturally relevant education for black students and school children sprang directly from the Black Power movement and ideology as outlined and developed by Carmichael, Hamilton, Newton etc. in the Black Power Manifesto of 1967.

To recapitulate, we started our analysis with the mainly intellectual movement of Negritude which idealized and romanticized the African and asserted a belief in an 'authentic', unique 'African personality'. This lasted until the mid-fifties and was never a popular movement in any sense of the word, but it was a pan-African movement and involved people of African descent in the New and Old Worlds of America, the Caribbean and Africa. We then moved on to consider the contribution of the Black Power ideology to the black consciousness movement. Again, like Negritude, Black Power was international – it identified Afro-Americans and others in the New World as 'wanderers', African people living in a colonial-type situation in societies which seek to oppress and dehumanize them. It appealed to all people of African descent to unite in fighting common oppression. Unlike Negritude, Black Power was always an activist movement appealing for people to take action to re-define their position and to develop alternative forms of resistance to colonialism.

Although Negritude started in France and Black Power in America, West Indians or people of West Indian origin from the French or British West Indies have made major contributions to both the intellectual doctrines of Negritude and to the Black Power ideology, and it therefore makes sense that Black Power ideology should have exerted influence on Caribbean people living in Britain. It is most important at this point to establish that the connection exists – for many West Indian families in London, America is not a remote place, many people have relatives living there. Until the United States brought in restrictive immigration laws in the 1950s, the United States was the place most West Indians emigrated to. Within the black community in London contact with America through visits to relatives, letters and literature is a continuing feature of life. Movement has always been a feature of Caribbean life and people accept this with its benefits and limitations.

As shown in the quotation from Raymond Giles's book *The West Indian Experience in British Schools*, the ideas of Black Power carry some force amongst black school children in London schools. Whether they are 'just noises' or whether they have become something more significant is an issue which cannot be ignored. David Hill (1976) has written a guide for teachers in multiracial schools and in it he put forward the received wisdom on black non-identity: blacks love white, blacks hate black. His solution is a multiracial curriculum which teaches respect for one's own culture and for other people's. Yet, by completely ignoring West Indian cultural forms which speak clearly and with pride of a black identity, he himself does not set a good example in the movement towards respect for other people's culture.

However, the form in which West Indian cultural identity has chosen to express itself and which is of the most contemporary importance for schools is the development of the Rastafarian religion and social movement amongst black youths in this country in the past ten years. We turn now to consider the significance of this movement for the black self-concept debate.

Rastafarian Religion

> By the rivers of Babylon, there we sat down, yea, we wept, when we remembered Zion. For they that carried us away captive required of us a song; and they that wasted us, required of us mirth, saying, sing us one of the songs of Zion. How shall we sing the Lord's song in a strange land?
>
> *Psalm 137*

Black Moses: Garvey and the Return to Africa Movement

Garveyism was another branch of the Pan-African movement which included Negritude. It was started by Marcus Garvey (1888–1940), a black Jamaican, who preached that Africa was the homeland of all black people and that black people could only get justice and freedom when we return to Africa. Garvey has been made a national hero in Jamaica and he is a central figure amongst black people in the Caribbean and America who are part of the black consciousness movement.

Garvey was not a Rastafarian, in fact he appeared not to be very religious. He wrote:

> Black men the world over must practise one faith, that of confidence in themselves, with: one Cause! one Goal! one Destiny! Let no religious scruples, no political mechaniz-ation divide us, but let us hold together under all climes and

in every country; making among ourselves a RACIAL Empire upon which the sun shall never set (quoted in Cronon, *Black Moses*).

Garvey's dreams never came true and he died in obscurity in London in 1940. However, the seeds of his ideas had taken root amongst the poor people of Kingston, Jamaica. For Garvey, unlike the intellectuals and others of the Negritude and Pan-African movement, actually went amongst the poor people and preached about black pride and return to Africa as the homeland of the black race. He founded the Universal Negro Improvement Society in America and the Black Star Line which he intended to use to transport people back to Africa.

For the Rastafarian brethren, Garvey is a major prophet – he is reported to have said: 'Look to Africa, when a black king shall be crowned for the day of deliverance is near', and to have prophesied the redemption of the African people in the 1960s (Smith *et al.*)

Arising out of Marcus Garvey's insistence that black people should look to Africa for redemption and in particular the prophecy that the crowning of a king would mark the beginning of the new era, the people in the ghettoes and shanty towns of Kingston, going back to their Bibles to find a basis for this belief, found it in *Revelation 2*:

And I saw a strong Angel proclaiming in a loud voice, 'Who is worthy to open the book, and to loose the seal thereof?' . . . And one of the elders saith unto me, 'Weep not, behold the Lion of Judah, the root of David, hath prevailed to open the book and to loose the spirits of God sent forth into all the earth.'

Structure of Beliefs of the Rastafarian Religion

1. Haile Selassie is the reincarnation of Christ.
2. Marcus Garvey was the Prophet sent like Moses to lead the sojourners back, but his task is unfinished.
3. The black man is the re-incarnated ancient Israelite who at the hands of the white man has been exiled to Jamaica.
4. Repatriation to Africa is inevitable and is the only way of redemption for the Western black man.

5. Jamaica, the land of their birth, is Babylon (Babylon means evil).

6. The soul of the Rastafarian is present in all blacks – it is simply a matter of self-discovery.

7. It is a sin for a black woman to straighten her hair.

8. It is a sin to practise witchcraft.

Practice

Drawing on the essential belief system, the Rastafarian brethren maintain a strict code of practice as a way of living out their faith. The essential code of practice includes:

1. Correction of all ways of life which they consider to be alien or non-African.

2. Members practise a code of ethics based on the notion of Peace and Love. (A common fraternal greeting when meeting or departing are the words 'Peace and Love'.)

3. Adherents of the faith do not believe in the practice of birth control; this they hold is a form of genocide.

4. Material possessions are considered superfluous and not vital to life.

5. Christian marriage is considered to be a part of European culture with no meaning for the black man (Barrett, 1968). Though the woman holds a subordinate position in family life, she is regarded very highly and known by the male as his African Queen or 'Rasta Queen' in a faithful, concubinage relationship.

6. Although Rastafarian Brethren subjugate material possessions, they hold highly moral standards of family life and child-care.

7. Work is good, but alienated labour is simply a perpetuation of slavery.

8. Pork and shellfish are forbidden; so is alcohol.

9. Only I-tal food, that is, naturally grown food, is eaten by devout brethren.

10. Most Rastafarian youths wear the Ethiopian colours of red, green and gold on the head and as scarves.

This summary of Rastafarian beliefs and practices draws on the work of Garrison and others researching in the field.

On 30 November 1930, Ras Tafari, Regent to the Throne of Ethiopia, was crowned King of Kings, Lord of Lords, Elect of God, Emperor of Ethiopia, by the Patriarch of the Ethiopian Orthodox Church. This was seen by Garvey's followers in Kingston as a fulfilment of his prophecy; Haile Selassie was seen as the second Christ, a Black Messiah who would lead his people to freedom. It was after this that the Rastafarian religion really took root in Jamaica and it has developed slowly ever since, to the point where its followers and adherents include all sections of the community. It is the only really indigenous religion, faith and sect in the Caribbean. Beginning in the slums and shanty towns it has spread through Jamaica and the Caribbean and also to England where it is finding an increasing band of supporters amongst young people.

Rastafarians in England

> *Babylon*
> Babylon's patrolling the street,
> Always squatting at a nigger's feet,
> You try to fight back,
> But you're outnumbered,
> Cause they bring the fleet,
> The day will come when we'll be strong,
> To fight the Babylon back.
> Rise up you niggers and face the facts
> You'll always be harassed because you're black.
> > Janet Morris, July 1975

This poem, written by a black London schoolgirl, caused great offence to the police, who are, of course, 'the Babylon' referred to. The poem is an illustration of Rasta thinking and influence on black youth in England. It has been harnessed as part of an alternative culture, a political protest movement, a musical, poetic art form, a language which speaks of black experience, in exile, and looks forward to redemption and return to Mother Africa. Len Garrison in 'The Rastafarians: Journey out of Exile', has analysed the use of reggae music as a call to dispossessed black youth in Jamaica, or London, or Birmingham to seek spiritual and cultural Salvation within their African consciousness.

To many young black people born in Britain the Rastafarians' religious and social movement offers them an alternative to the dispossessed, marginal, alienated non-status position offered by the dominant white society. It represents a total rejection of white social values and way of life. Barry Troyna, at the Centre for Mass Communication Research at Leicester University, has investigated the patterns of friendships and the leisure pursuits of third- and fourth-year boys in two areas of Leicester and Tottenham. A questionnaire was used to determine media use, peer group and leisure activities. He found that there were more ethnic friendships in the upper streams than in the lower streams. Amongst West Indian subjects, interest in reggae music was seen as evidence of a growing political awareness in young blacks –'following the sound' and travelling outside their areas to get records of the music being a major preoccupation of the group. Troyna comments; 'The language of reggae has been transferred to a situation here of policemen being "weakhearts" and "Babylon".'

The poem of Janet Morris quoted earlier, which caused such offence to the Metropolitan Commissioner of Police, also clearly reflects this view of society, as does the reggae song of Junior Curveh, *Police and Thieves*, which reflects black bitterness against the police and general discontent. Dick Hebdige in 'Reggae, Rastas and Rudies', has provided a most penetrating analysis of the development of the Rastas' faith, and reggae music and its significance for black culture. He argued that the movement is a displacement of material problems on to a spiritual plane and that, given the fact that Christianity still permeates the West Indian imagination, it was natural that the 'displacement' should take a religious form. He writes:

Christianity still permeates the West Indian imagination, and Biblical mythology continues to dominate, but at certain points in the social structure (namely amongst the unemployed, young and deviant adult population) this mythology has been turned back upon itself so that the declared ascendancy of the Judaeo-Christian culture (with its emphasis on work and repression) can be seriously scrutinized and ultimately rejected. Instrumental in this symbolic reversal were the Rastafarians.

He continues:

> The Rastafarians believed that the exiled Emperor, Haile Selassie of Ethiopia, was God and that his accession to the Ethiopian throne fulfils the prophecy made by Marcus Garvey – 'Look to Africa, for the day of Deliverance is near'.

But the religious milieu in which Rastafarianism was evolved demanded a specifically Biblical mythology and this mythology had to be re-appropriated and made to serve a different set of cultural needs. Just as the 'Protestant Ethic' in Western Europe had performed its own re-appropriation of the original Judaeo-form, so by a dialectical process of redefinition, the Scriptures, which had constantly absorbed and deflected the revolutionary potential of the Jamaican black, were used to locate that potential, to negate the Judaeo-Christian culture. Or, in the more concise idiom of the Jamaican street-boys, the Bible was taken, read and 'flung back rude'.

The development of the Rastafarian religion and social movement amongst young blacks in Britain has been adequately explored in other recent works (Hebdige, 1979). My main concern here has been to establish that an alternative view of black culture and self-concept exists and has always existed within all contemporary societies in which African people live. This phenomenon has been completely ignored by social scientists in writings on black children, self-concept and schooling, whether they be negative or positive. In this context, is white society a 'credible source' of information to the black child or adult? Would its views largely accord with the views blacks have of themselves?

> To argue . . . that even in the midst of the brutalities and injustices of the antebellum and postbellum racial systems, black men and women were able to find the means to sustain a far greater degree of self-pride and group cohesion than the system they lived under ever intended for them to be able to

do, is not to argue that the system was more benign than it has been pictured, but rather that human beings are more resilient, less malleable and able to live without some sense of cultural cohesion, individual autonomy, and self-worth than a number of recent scholars have maintained.

Laurence Levine looked at folk culture in order to gain some idea of black culture and consciousness in America. It is necessary to look at other sources of information on black personality – because I believe that during the time that social scientists have been busy 'proving' that black people have negative self-images based on white stereotypes, blacks have been busy living in accordance with their own 'world-view'.

This view has been variously articulated:
1. by black intellectuals as Negritude;
2. by radical activists as Black Power;
3. by poor and dispossessed Jamaicans as the Rastafarian Faith.

I want to consider these ideas in so far as they contribute to an understanding of the self-concept of black children living and going to school in British society today.

Black Culture, Self-concept and Schooling

It has been clearly established in Chapter 1 that many practitioners and theoreticians on self-concept and education believe the school experience to be of crucial importance in the development of the child's self-concept. At the same time, schools are also viewed as having the function Durkheim attributed them with, of transmitting cultural values. If a section of a society is culturally different, how can the school be true to all these ideals? I.e. how can it:
1. transmit the culture of the dominant group;
2. enhance the self-concept of the child and also
3. 'promote in pupils respect for and more positive attitudes towards their own and other national ethnic groups' (Schools Council Project, *Education for a Multiracial Society*)?

We have also to remember that schools fulfil a vital economic role of selecting and 'processing' future workers. The future of the majority of workers of West Indian origin now at school in this country (if they continue to live here) is one of low wages or unemployment. An article in the *Guardian* (21 October 1977) estimated that over 60 per cent of West Indian school-leavers would remain unemployed. With the recent severe cuts in projects which create work for the young unemployed, this figure must now be seen as an underestimate.

Durkheim claimed that each type of people has its own education which is appropriate to it and that this education is part of its social structure; thus education as a function of social structure would mirror the overall arrangements of the total social structure. If, therefore, that social structure includes within it groups which are discriminated against and ascribed inferior roles and status, it seems clear that the formal education system will reflect this arrangement. There are those, especially in the area of 'Race Relations', who view the role of schooling optimistically, and regard formal education as determining, rather than determined by the social structure. The work of Stenhouse for example and the ill-fated NFER project belong to those schools of thought.

However, schools operate against a historical background and social facts which cannot be ignored. As we examine the ideas of black consciousness – Negritude, Black Power and the beliefs of the Rastafarians – we must not forget the historical background against which these developments occurred. The West Indian historian, Walter Rodney, in the conversations with his 'brothers' (*The Groundings With My Brothers*) described the black experience in these words:

Now we have gone through a historical experience . . . by all accounts we should have been wiped out . . . The documents are there. White slavemasters used to conduct a discussion. They said, look we have some blacks, what do we do with them? Is it better to let them grow old and work for us over an extended period of time or work him so hard and let him die and buy a fresh slave? And the consensus of opinion was this: take a prime African black, work him to death for five years and you make a profit. We survived . . . the Black people in the West Indies have produced all that we have . . . Black people who have suffered all these years create.

It is suggested that an important part of that survival was the development of a positive sense of self mediated through a form of language (to which the elite had little access and no control), of religion, literature and music – that is to say, a culture. To understand the self-concept of West Indians and their children living in Britain today and how they see themselves in relation to British social institutions it is necessary to have some appreciation of the meaning of this culture and its relationship to black self-concept. In looking at the contemporary situation in Britain, where the descendants of the slaves have come to live amongst the descendants of the slavemasters, we now look to see something of this process where they adapt to one aspect of the structure of that society – the school system. We see the school system as having, within the total structure, certain 'meanings and norms' which are generally accepted by the different classes which make up that society. The school system is also vested with power to enforce the 'norms and meanings' which have been arrived at.

What happens when a new set of 'actors' enters this scene? They bring with them a history of survival in the most appalling conditions ever known; this experience of slavery has left its mark – it has been called the 'Mark of Oppression'. But structures (even slavery) do not only constrain, they also enable. Within contemporary urban British society the West Indian community is faced with a school system which traditionally has offered a second- or third-rate service to working-class people, and traditionally English working-class people have accepted that service; at best making the most of it to get out and move up, at worst simply accepting and suffering what was offered. Without wanting to exaggerate the importance of the Saturday school movement out of all proportion, it can certainly be seen as a reaction to aspects of the social structure which are regarded as (in the main) having a constraining and limiting effect. This can be seen in relation to the 'high expectations' and 'unrealistic ambitions' which many teachers, head teachers and careers officers regard West Indian parents as having for their children. The West Indian community has reacted by providing children with additional schooling. Based on their own experience 'back home' in the Caribbean they know that schooling/education can be provided other than in the formal school system and they have started to organize and run such schemes. Clearly the schemes vary in sophistication, effectiveness and style but the fact is that the existence of Saturday schools is an expression of the enterprise and initiative of the West Indian community, and demonstrates an unwillingness unquestioningly to accept whatever is offered them in established educational channels.

Background to the Present Study

Anthony Giddens has written that 'the sociological observer cannot make social life available as a "phenomenon" for observation independently of drawing upon his own knowledge of it as a resource'. This has relevance to my research because I have constantly 'drawn on my own knowledge' of West Indian life to understand certain processes – for example, mobility – in terms of West Indian working-class life. 'Mobility' here means not simply moving up on the social ladder but moving on (to another country if need be) in order to move up the social scale. The Headmaster of a school in the East End of London is incredulous when black teachers tell him that West Indian kids can be 'internationally' mobile. He is naturally sceptical of this since, as he says, it is something of a social revolution for an East End family to migrate to Basildon in Essex. What he has forgotten to take into account is that most of these children or their families have already travelled many thousands of miles in search of jobs and opportunities. As a West Indian myself, I can understand the roots of the Saturday school system and the high expectations and 'unrealistic' ambitions of parents who know that, whatever they do, their children are almost certainly destined for a place at the bottom.

The question of objectivity and bias arises inevitably in social science research. This problem can never be satisfactorily resolved. But certainly the idea of the researcher as a resource can be seen as a positive asset in social science research, especially where that research attempts to explain, clarify or interpret a process of social interaction. However, the research design, by including the collection and analysis of objective empirical data, should offer some control on any tendency towards bias or subjectivity. It is interesting to note in this connection that although being West Indian had certain advantages in the Community groups I visited, mainly in being permitted access in the first place (although this was not always the case and I was refused access to a number of projects), within the school system this could (and I think did) work the other way in terms of what was said to me and what was made available to me. What this amounts to essentially is that the researcher is a subject, the 'objects' of her research are subjects, and in this sense the 'research act' in social science is a unique and critical process unlike anything in the natural or physical sciences. From this perspective and mindful of the criticisms which have been advanced here and elsewhere, it seemed imperative to have a research design which, in its use of objective empirical data and field methods, would avoid the worse excesses of both.

Full details of the research questionnaire and method of analysis are provided in the Appendix at the back of this book.

For the purposes of my research a sample of 264 West Indian children aged from ten to fifteen years old living and going to school in the Greater London area was taken. The children were all drawn from Inner London and Outer London Boroughs known to have above average concentrations of West Indian children in their schools.

The DES *Statistics of Education* (1973) giving the breakdown of immigrant pupils in schools in 1972 are reproduced in Table 2.4.

Table 2.4: Immigrant Pupils by Origin in All Maintained Schools (January 1972) and Percentage of Total Immigrants

COUNTRY	NUMBERS	%
Australia, Canada & New Zealand	2,455	0.9
Cyprus (Greek)	9,504	3.4
(Turkish)	4,461	1.6

COUNTRY	NUMBERS	%
Gibraltar, Malta	1,252	0.4
Kenya (Asian Origin)	17,340	6.2
(African Origin)	1,385	0.5
Other Commonwealth Countries in Africa	14,444	5.3
India	56,193	20.1
Pakistan	30,629	10.9
Other Commonwealth Countries in Asia	8,008	2.9
West Indies (including Guyana)	101,898	36.4
Non-Commonwealth Countries:		
Italy	12,009	4.3
Poland	1,958	0.7
Spain	3,275	1.2
Other European Countries	5,980	2.1
Rest of World	9,081	3.2
TOTAL	279,872	100.0

Source: DES (1973), *Statistics of Education, 1972.*

It will be seen that West Indian children are 36.4 per cent of the total number of immigrant pupils – providing by far the largest single minority group. It should be noted that these figures cannot be regarded as completely accurate for a number of reasons, including the definition of 'immigrant child' used by the DES: children born abroad, and those born here to parents who have lived here for ten years or less. However, we can for the purposes of this research accept the figure as showing that West Indian children constitute a high percentage of children defined as immigrant by the DES.

Another set of statistics also of interest is the breakdown on London Boroughs with populations of 50,000 or more provided in Table 2.5

Table 2.5: New Commonwealth Immigrant Children in London and County Boroughs with Populations of 50,000 or More Where they Exceed 10 per cent of All Pupils in Maintained Primary and Secondary Schools

January 1972	% Primary and Secondary
Inner London Boroughs:	
Hammersmith	15.7
Kensington & Chelsea	13.6
Camden	11.7
Westminster	14.0
Islington	20.7
Hackney	22.3
Tower Hamlets/City of London	10.5
Lewisham	14.0
Southwark	12.8
Lambeth	19.8
Wandsworth	16.6
Outer London Boroughs:	
Brent	25.2
Ealing	21.6
Haringey	26.5
Newham	17.3
Waltham Forest	11.2
County Boroughs:	
Bradford	11.4
Birmingham	9.4
Derby	6.4
Huddersfield	12.4
Leicester	14.4
Wolverhampton	12.7
Warley	10.5
Preston	11.0

Source: DES (1973), *Statistics of Education, 1972.*

It will be noted that in the Inner London area Hackney with 22.3 per cent, Islington with 20.7 per cent and Lambeth with 19.8 per cent have the highest figures and are followed by Wandsworth with 16.6 per cent and Hammersmith with 15.7 per cent. In the Outer London Boroughs Haringey has 26.5 per cent, Brent has 25.2 per cent and Ealing has 21.6 per cent. These are figures for all immigrant pupils but we know from Peach, recent ILEA and ERC publications that West Indians predominate in Inner London. Thus, the figures for the five Inner London Boroughs represent areas of West Indian concentration. The Ealing figures represent a mainly Asian population (Southall) although in Acton and Ealing (town) itself there are West Indian populations.

West Indian immigrants to this country have gone as 'replacement' populations into the decaying inner city areas of large conurbations – more than 89 per cent of West Indians live in these urban areas.

In 1967 three important documents were published:

1. *Race, Community and Conflict: A Study of Sparkbrook* by John Rex *et al.*;

2. The Plowden Report on *Children and their Primary Schools* and

3. The Population and Economic Planning (PEP) Report on *Racial Discrimination in Britain.*

These three studies confirmed that the West Indian population was concentrated in urban areas, received poor and inferior education and was discriminated against. There is no doubt that the vast majority of West Indian children in this country come from homes which under the Registrar General's Classification would be classified as Classes IV and V. Thus, although it was not possible to gather details of socio-economic status of my sample population this was not considered to be a major handicap. What I felt to be of more importance was to have a widespread geographical sample ranging from inner city to suburban type areas. The difficulty of achieving this geographical spread and also meeting the primary research condition of special projects or classes for West Indian children proved enormous and in the end reduced the total sample by about one-third.

The sample was divided into four main groups:
1. School MRE;
2. Community (Official);
3. Community (Self-help);
4. School Comparison Group.

The fourth group comprised children who were not receiving any attention in the form of compensatory or supplementary education.

1. *School MRE*: N = 76

This group consisted of children in three schools which were involved in running special classes, projects, studies or programmes for West Indian pupils or where West Indian history and culture formed part of the normal school curricula. One school supplied two groups: the first was part of a World History course which included studies of West Indian history, including slavery and the plantation system; the second was a group which had studied the Rastafarian religion in their spare time and included some recent Rasta converts. These two groups were separately coded in the analysis.

2. *Community (Official)*: N = 53

This group was comprised of projects which were officially funded from local authority or central government funds and were usually under the control/direction of the local community relations officer. It was assumed that there would be major differences in the way official projects would be run compared with voluntary or self-financed projects, but this belief was not supported. The way the projects were run appeared to depend on the parents rather than on the project workers or financing body. The projects were meeting the needs of parents for extra education for children and people voted with their feet – so the official and self-help projects turned out to be more similar than I had anticipated. There was one major difference – the official projects were better equipped both in terms of educational equipment, chairs, tables etc. and in terms of their accommodation and facilities. They were simply nicer places to be in (although the overall standard of housing and equipment was fairly low in all the community groups).

3. *Community (Self-help)* : N = 46

As the name suggests, these were voluntary self-financed groups
run on the proceeds of jumble sales, fêtes and voluntary labour
by teachers and parents. These groups received no official
backing and were free from formal controls, but they did not
differ greatly from Group 2 in the way their schools were run
except that they had less professional involvement. Their aim
appeared exactly the same – the provision of basic schooling.
They just seemed to depend less on aid and more on self-help.

4. *School Comparison Group* : N = 89

The final group comprised children from three schools in which
there were no programmes for enrichment and this group
served as a comparison group for the study. There were children
from a boy's comprehensive, a girls' comprehensive and a final
year primary school class. The girls' comprehensive and the
primary school were in an area of London with heavy
concentrations of West Indian people and the schools reflect
this, with West Indian children being over 60 per cent of the
school population in the girls' school and around 80 per cent in
the primary school.

Observation, Interviews and Documentation

I observed as many classes and projects and interviewed as many
teachers, parents and project workers as was possible and details
of these observations appear under the report for each class or
project. These interviews/discussions were informal and took
the form that the teacher or project worker decided, rather than
the form the researcher wanted or what was best for the research
– as the workers and teachers always pointed out, the research
was not the object of the classes and projects, and I had to make
the best of the conditions I found. The object of observing
projects and classes and of talking to the people involved was to
get some idea of what the aims of the class or project were and
how the teachers/workers saw themselves within the wider
education/school context, and more than anything why they felt
that it was necessary to have these special projects/classes for
West Indian children. The answers to these questions, I felt,
would give some clue as to how the workers viewed the school

system generally and the specific issue of West Indian children within it. There was no formal access to parents of children in schools and access to parents of children in the community groups was through informal contact, mainly 'hanging around' and grabbing people as they came in and if they were willing to talk. I was also present when parents came and asked for children to be admitted to the projects and I observed the 'formalities' of the admission procedure on those occasions.

This was very helpful to me in clarifying the reasons why parents sent their children to the Supplementary schools – this will be reported in greater detail at a later time – but for the moment it can be said that on each occasion where I observed parents question workers about the project before asking whether their children could join, their overwhelming concern was with 'educational' criteria: 'Do you teach maths?', 'Will he/she get help with English?', 'She's not doing too well with her reading – can you help with that?'. Those were the sort of 'problems' the parents looked to the Supplementary schools to solve – bread and butter day-to-day basic problems of English, maths and reading. They did not seem politically motivated, nor were they looking for 'positive experiences' for their offspring – they were simply trying to make sure that their children had the extra help they felt they needed in basic subjects. I never heard of a child being sent for 'cultural reasons' in the sense that parents wanted their children in an all-black environment – although it seemed to me from all that I heard and saw that parents believed that these teachers took more care and trouble with teaching and were more interested in helping the children.

The teachers in the schools and project workers in the community certainly appeared dedicated and one could not but be impressed by their enthusiasm – very often in unhelpful (school) environments and with poor (community) facilities. There was certainly 'political motivation' amongst most of the project workers. The teachers tended to have a naïve view of what could be done 'to help' black children – they tended to believe in 'compensation' for poor social and family backgrounds and for racial prejudice and discrimination. They saw themselves trying to build up 'good relationships' with the children through showing respect for their culture and being generally tolerant. They worried that black kids were mainly in bottom streams but felt that this was partly a function of teacher-expectation and low self-concept. Thus they saw themselves as trying to break down prejudice in the schools and also offering the children a chance of building different self-concepts. These are general impressions; more specific details will be included in the description of each class or project.

The project workers tended to be more cynical about what the formal education system had to offer black kids. There was a general feeling that if any black child succeeded it would be in spite of, not because of, the school system. They tended to have a more 'political' outlook whether or not they were officially or voluntarily funded. The general belief seemed to be that if black children were to have a chance of success in the school system they would have to receive more formal teaching than they got in schools. The issue of self-image had to be posed to them – they concentrated far more on practical issues of teaching and education. Cultural and social issues were included automatically in the activities of these community based groups but they were regarded as 'perks', 'treats' or 'outings' and not the *raison d'être* of the projects. Whatever the motivation of the project workers, it was clear to me that acquiring basic educational skills was the basis of what actually went on in the Supplementary schools and was the reason why parents sent their children to them. This kind of insight would never have reached me through analysis of my questionnaire material.

I collected syllabi and written material, including students' work, from teachers and project workers where available, and where they were willing to part with them. This kind of information provides useful background material and details of the stated aims and objectives of teachers and workers in the projects.

3. Multiracial Education

Theory

The role of multiracial education falls within the scope of the compensatory education model which essentially attempts to compensate educationally 'disadvantaged' children through the development of special education projects. Research and discussion about the 'problems' of West Indian (and other immigrant) children in British schools invariably includes a request/demand for more and/or better multiracial education. A society of teachers exists to promote the aims of multiracial education, the National Association for Multiracial Education. The Schools Council project, *Education for a Multiracial Society*, sought to promote MRE through the development of new curricula and teaching methods. Two of the teachers involved in this small research project have since gone on to become Advisers on Multiracial Education in different local education authorities. And yet no one really has any clear idea of what multiracial education is or what function it could usefully serve, although it can be regarded as a part of the development of professionalism and specialization within the teaching profession. The setting-up of research and development centres for MRE in London and Birmingham confirms this view of a professional expansion concerned as much with career advancement as with extending curricula.

Although this approach may be described as falling within the compensatory education model, this can also be a matter of convenience and 'politics' on the part of some teachers who recognize that this is the only way they will be allowed to do anything 'positive' (as they say) for black kids. So they have to sell it with that label, even though they may profess to find the liberal ideology which inspires compensatory education and theories of cultural deprivation abhorrent. However, a more

generally accepted view of multiracial education is that which
M. Rogers and J. McNeal expounded in their study of *The Multi-
Racial School*. They outlined four factors which affect the
teaching situation in these schools:

1. varied languages and range of competence in each;
2. cultural differences between pupil and teacher, teacher and
parents;
3. race relations – a complex set of factors involving not only
group relations within school but *every minority child's view of
himself* (my emphasis);
4. deprivation of housing, income and environment leading
to deprivation of family experience and affecting the whole
development of the child.

The contributors to Rogers and McNeal's book describe their
various attempts (all successful) at multiracial education. One
multiracial primary Head described the transition to teaching
for 'an international, multiracial school'. Another told how he
abandoned streaming in his secondary modern (as was then) and
introduced a two-unit remedial department for non-English
speaking children and those with 'dialect' difficulties. Yet
another described the breaking down of barriers between black
and white parents which followed her attempts to build up a
community school.

Thus the multiracial education movement has influenced
curriculum development, with its claims for social justice and
relevant education for minority group students. It developed in
direct response to numbers of black and brown children in
British schools. Critics of the school system argued that the
school system itself was guilty of increasing the 'disadvantage'
of minority group children since it did not reflect their cultures
or their existence. They argued that the curriculum was racially
biassed and needed reform to reflect more accurately the fact
that present-day Britain is now a multiracial society. The NFER
has been very active in promoting and encouraging MRE.
However, its sponsored research is presented in an uncritical
way and its own working party has become bogged down in a
dispute over details which appear (from published material) to
be somewhat irrelevant.

There is an unexamined assumption that MRE is 'a good thing', not dissimilar to the assumptions about progressive education in the early seventies. Any real concern about MRE has to face the problem that so far the only criticisms of it have come from the right-wing, which has encouraged a certain complacency and consensus among its practitioners. I want to suggest that MRE is conceptually unsound, that its theoretical and practical implications have not been worked out and that it represents a developing feature of urban education aimed at 'watering down' the curriculum and 'cooling out' black city children while at the same time creating for teachers, both radical and liberal, the illusion that they are doing something special for a particularly disadvantaged group.

Many of the ideas of MRE draw upon the social-pathology analysis of the black personality, lifestyle and family arrangements. Although explicitly rejecting labels of inferiority it argues instead for 'difference' – meaning exactly the same thing. In interviews with teachers who were working in MRE projects it became evident that they saw themselves as an enlightened minority desperately trying to hold back the engulfing waves of prejudice and racism both among their pupils and also (very much) among their own colleagues. It is easy to see how, faced with situations where such feelings are entrenched and children are presenting problems, some schools and teachers can come to believe that MRE will solve all their problems.

1. It will help minority group children to develop pride in their identity and in their group.

2. It will encourage white pupils to see their black classmates in a more positive light.

3. It will encourage teachers to examine their own attitudes to minority group children and change these attitudes where change is needed.

4. It will reduce alienation of minority group children – especially West Indian pupils.

5. By developing new curricula and new teaching methods it extends the concern of the school into home and the community and thus makes schooling more relevant to groups which are hard to reach.

6. The new curricula will also be more successful in

motivating minority group pupils and in promoting positive attitudes to school and teachers.

It will be seen that these objectives are vague and undefined and totally ignore the issues of power and control in the school system. They simplify and idealize the developmental aspects of schooling. They ignore class and they treat race and culture as a social psychological abstraction. As to the claims of MRE to represent the culture of minority group pupils, what I want to suggest here is that West Indian and other minority group children are, in so far as they are working-class, part of the continuing problem of urban schooling. The school system has never 'reflected the culture' of the majority of children in this country who are working-class. Why then this concern to reflect the culture of small sections of that class? Whatever role the school may have, it certainly represents a form of socialization to which most children are exposed for significant periods of their life. Inevitably this process of socialization prepares children for various roles in adult society, among the most important of which are work roles. The reality for most black children is that they are meant for a wageless existence or low wages in unpopular or menial jobs. What has MRE to say to this fact? It says that by presenting black children with other images of themselves they can encourage a positive self-image which in turn creates higher aspiration, higher achievement and an opportunity to break out of the 'cycle of deprivation' through such innovations as Black Studies classes or calypso music. But no attempt has ever been made to see what effects these innovations have. Such work as is done is usually aimed at improving MRE, extending or developing it. Given these facts the question arises as to whether MRE represents anything more than a misguided liberal strategy to compensate black children for not being white? It is certainly misguided. Indeed the kind of stuff published under the MRE label is so patronizing and ethnocentric that it probably has the effect of encouraging the very attitudes it seeks to change.

MRE is seen as a cure-all to the problems which minority group children present in schools in Britain. Great claims are made as to its efficacy – but these claims are unsupported by any evidence. The factors which determine a person's economic and social role in society have little to do with self-image. The DES report on teaching in primary schools stated that teachers in urban schools did not stretch their pupils. Many of these children are West Indian and the reason why they are not stretched includes an increasing reliance by teachers on personality and other social-psychological theories which stress individual and family factors as being responsible for failure of certain groups to achieve. This means that teachers are encouraged to act as social workers to these children. MRE is very much part of this development. It rests on claims to improve individual and group relationships and encourages schools to intervene in areas of culture and personality in a way which may be detrimental to both. The aims of multiracial education are tied in with the cultural deprivation theory which aims to compensate working-class children for being culturally deprived (of middle-class culture) and black children for not being white. Again it takes schools and teachers away from their central concern which is basically teaching or instructing children in the knowledge and skills essential to life in this society. It effectively reduces choice and creates dependence on experts and professionals which undermines the individual's own capacity to cope. Matters of individual personality and group culture should not be primarily the concern of schools but of the family and the community. It does not really matter very much if schools develop what they term multiracial education projects since, as will be seen from the research reported on later in this book, such projects have a very marginal impact. What really does matter is the substitution of the traditional school curricula either partly or wholly with new curricula which are of doubtful value. We will return to this discussion more fully later on.

We turn now to consider four of the school-based self-concept enhancement MRE projects. The approach of the teachers in these projects broadly resembles that described in the recent publication, *Teaching in a Multicultural Society* (Cross, Baker and Stiles). This approach appears to accept the reality of inequality but suggests ways in which the teachers in the classroom can avoid devaluing the culture of minority children or emphasizing their 'deviance'. These classes demonstrate attempts by teachers to value minority group children and their culture by (1) use of dialect, (2) use of historical material which is culturally diverse, and which relates to children the part their own group played in historical events and (3) examines the religions of the various cultural groups including African and Caribbean religious forms.

The reports on these projects are based on contact with the teachers and the three schools concerned over a three-year period. This contact has included prolonged discussions and more formal interviews about the nature of the projects, their objectives and methods of teaching. In all but one case ('Black Images') I have sat in on classes. This was not in order to carry out any formal process of observer participant research, but simply to get the feel of the classroom, to enhance my own appreciation of what was involved for the teachers, the pupils and the school generally. In the case where I did not observe classroom activity, the teacher felt that the situation in the school was so fraught and her own position with the Head so precarious that she did not feel able to ask for me to be allowed in her classroom to do further research.

It is important at this stage to mention some of the problems connected with doing this type of research in schools. Very often a group of teachers agree to carry out a particular project in their department; people outside the immediate circle of involvement might not know much about it. If it is connected with minority group or 'difficult' pupils, teachers are allowed a fair degree of freedom. Heads do not always know the details of what is happening in their schools and one can be told officially that there are no special projects or classes for black kids in a school only to hear, unofficially, that there are 'things going on'. This made it very difficult to know the extent and range of different projects – there was an air of sneakiness about them – which meant that it was only through informal contacts and word of mouth information that I managed to locate four projects where teachers, the school and the LEA were willing for me to carry out research.

It may appear contradictory or confusing to suggest, on the one hand, that schools are increasingly using therapeutic and other psychological methods to 'solve' the problems which minority group and other children present, and then to say that these kinds of groups operate in a cloak and dagger world of undercover secrecy. The fact is that this area of school life and activity has not been much opened up to investigation or research – it is something of a secret world. The unwillingness of some Heads to become involved is not necessarily through hostility to these ideas – it is that they would rather not know too much about what is happening as long as it works, i.e. keeps the teachers happy and controls the children. Sieber has drawn attention to the role of innovation and change in co-ordinating and controlling clients and employees of the school system. In some schools Heads choose not to know too much about these developments. In other schools, Heads give active support and encouragement to 'group work' of various kinds. It appears to depend on personal inclination and how willing or otherwise the Head is to acknowledge that the school has 'problems'. Acceptance of group work and other kinds of special projects for children in a school implies the acceptance of 'problems' – the children's problems usually, which they bring to the school and which the school has 'to do something about'. Many Heads are reluctant to have their school labelled in this way.

In setting out these profiles of the different groups and writing about the schools in which they were located, I drew on a variety of sources of information about the schools, from informal community contacts, from teachers working in the schools and pupils attending them, parents in the area, contacts in the different LEAs – in fact any accessible and willing informant. This helped to build up a picture of the school and to place the projects within this overall framework.

In terms of a phenomenological appreciation of what these innovatory school programmes mean to the individuals taking part, both teachers and pupils, it is necessary to take note of the fact of 'strangeness' (Schutz): the teachers are strangers to the West Indian culture they are trying to appreciate; they may be kindly, well-intentioned strangers, but they are strangers nonetheless. As strangers there are facts and areas of knowledge about West Indian culture which they can identify and regard as important for children to know in order to help them combat racial and other stereotypes. But these same facts and areas of knowledge may carry for the West Indian children and the community an entirely different meaning, and may have attached to them 'values' which the teachers can never share, even if they wanted to. One example is the way in which West Indian boys in school-based history groups reacted to the showing of the TV film *Roots* which dealt with the history of a black American family through slavery to freedom. The teacher told me that for weeks after the showing of this film (which had been discussed in class) the black boys constantly answered him 'yes m'sa, no m'sa' and when spoken to (about anything) would reply 'don't beat me m'sa, please m'sa' in a grovelling manner. He said it was all he could do to keep from showing his annoyance and he was glad when it wore thin and stopped. Thus, innovatory projects of this kind have to be aware of their 'vulnerability to the schools' social environment' (Sieber), where TV plays an important part and where, irrespective of whatever happens in school, children have experience as individuals and members of groups which may lead them to attach to school-based knowledge, meanings and interpretations which are quite different from anything which might have been intended or foreseen.

Group A: On the Buses West Indian Style

This is a mixed comprehensive school (previously a secondary modern) of just over 1000 children with a high proportion of West Indian students. Exact figures are difficult to come by but most teachers agreed that between one-third and one-half – 30–40 per cent of the students – were from a West Indian background. The Headmaster has made various efforts to 'meet the needs' of his immigrant pupils including in-service training for teachers on aspects of West Indian culture and history etc., and the teacher responsible for this class has also been on an exchange visit to Jamaica as part of the school in-service training programme. The school premises are used for a Saturday school which was originally set up by this same teacher with the help of some parents over five years ago, and is now run by the local Community Relations Council as a completely independent venture. The school has close links with groups in the local community and has been the venue for exhibitions, Caribbean evenings and other cultural events which the school has supported by offering premises and other facilities, and which have been well supported and patronized by the Head and other teachers at school. I think this school would be described as providing a good multiracial/multicultural environment for the children who attend. The atmosphere inside the school appears relaxed and friendly, but the general feeling I picked up outside, in the community, was that the standards were low and that not much was expected of the children who attended there.

The particular project I want to describe now was part of the third-year English syllabus, but was an optional subject on Caribbean literature. The teacher told me that when the optional class first started there had been about one-third English to two-thirds West Indian children in it. At the time I visited the school and during the period of the research the class composition was 100 per cent West Indian. The teacher explained that the white children had been coming for social reasons, because of friendships and that, as these friendships broke up, they had no more interest in the class and dropped out. In a situation such as this some teachers may actually prefer an all-black class. It seemed to me that even though the English kids may have come for social reasons to begin with, one would have imagined that the content and presentation of the lessons might have proved intrinsically interesting to at least a couple of them. There may be, for some teachers, a certain prestige in being the only white person in such a group – that person can then be seen as the 'expert' who 'understands the problems' and to share this with any other outsider, even white students, might result in a lessening of this kind of prestige. This is my impression, and does suggest some possible explanation why a particular teacher would not necessarily view a development such as the loss of one-third of her option subject class as a reflection on her teaching ability or professional skill.

My general impression of the class after three sessions was of mild indiscipline amongst the pupils and of great tolerance or indulgence on the part of the teacher. For example, one boy used the tape-recorder in the classroom to listen to taped music and, with a few of his friends, spent an entire session listening to reggae. At the second session I realized that the tape-recorder was used for recording classroom discussion and drama sessions when members read bits of their own work. But during this first session the tape-recorder was used solely for playing music by this small group of boys.

Another group of boys played cards and one girl plaited her hair, all this whilst the teacher was delivering a talk on Caribbean dialect which was connected to a creative writing project they were doing. The only way that 'order' was maintained was through the teacher making no effort to insist on attention or interest from the students who were otherwise occupied. It was as if a bargain had been struck whereby the teacher would be allowed to teach if certain pupils were allowed to follow their own interests. In a class of twenty to twenty-five pupils this group accounted for five or, at the most six pupils and the teacher stressed to me on several occasions that they did not normally behave like that, that some were 'playing up' to my presence and 'showing off'. Whilst accepting a certain degree of 'playing up' and 'showing off', it would appear that the normal classroom procedure must have been, in any case, somewhat lax for pupils to turn up equipped with cassette tapes of music, playing-cards and other diversions. Many teachers have to come to this kind of arrangement with certain pupils; in order to avoid constant friction and conflict in the classroom they 'accommodate' those kids whom others exclude as disruptive by allowing them a certain degree of freedom. Reynolds called this a 'truce' arrived at by teacher and pupils with the aim of reducing conflict and avoiding stress.

However, there were pupils who were interested in what was being taught and these were by far the majority. It was fascinating to watch this English teacher teach West Indian children how to speak Caribbean dialect; many of the children seemed embarrassed, giggled and made remarks such as 'My gran speak like that'. The class had been looking at the use of dialect by West Indian playwrights and each pupil had been asked to write a short playlet using West Indian dialect –the teacher read out from these scripts and pointed out the errors (which were many) in them – and then demonstrated how a West Indian would really speak. The teacher spoke the dialect with the greatest ease and facility but whenever one of the student group attempted to read from his/her work it was a slow and painful process, punctuated with much laughter and clowning about.

I sat at the very back of the classroom and I could hear a small group of girls discussing the playlets. There was general agreement that the teacher was 'good' but one girl said her Mum wouldn't let her speak like that in the house —'even though she does' — and others commented that it was the older people who mostly spoke like that. They seemed to think it 'quaint' but not of great importance. I did not manage to hear any of the boys' views on the class as they sat well over to the right, were greatly outnumbered by the girls and were more highly represented in the 'uninterested' group who were playing records and cards amongst themselves.

The second time I was with this group the pattern was more or less the same except that more boys took part — each person being directly called upon by the teacher to speak, read or comment on a piece of work. But there was an overall arrangement whereby small groups followed their own interest joining in from time to time when inclined to or when called upon.

The third time I was with the class almost the entire session was devoted to a script which one of the class members had produced, *On the Buses*, and this was by far the most 'successful' class, securing the most group interest and participation. The entire script was read through, discussed and the final fifteen minutes of the session was spent in small groups, each group planning a play.

My notes on this session read:

> The class was quieter today and seemed to be making more of an effort . . . The play reading was stilted and listless . . . The children kept on 'correcting' the dialect and substituting standard English phrases which the teacher had to 'correct' back into Caribbean dialect. Yet when the children talk amongst themselves they are free and easy in their speech and can talk dialect . . . The group I sat with agreed to write their play in English first and then translate it into dialect for the class. This suggestion came from one girl after the group had spent some time talking about how exactly to set about writing in dialect.

The discussion which follows very closely resembles the one

which took place that morning. This recording captures the atmosphere of the group with such authenticity that although these girls, Audrey, Eleanor, Sonya and Meryl are a completely different set of girls, their treatment of the issue of West Indian dialect represents almost exactly the opinions which were expressed by the group that day. This transcript appeared in the Community publication, *Stepping Out*, and is reproduced by kind permission of the Commonplace Workshop.

Transcript of a Taped Discussion on West Indian Dialect

Audrey: I don't think it's bad anyway, because they use it a lot over the West Indies.

Meryl: You think it's a good thing, do you?

Audrey: Yeah, 'cos that's the way people talk over there.

Meryl: But do you think it's right for in England?

Audrey: No really, no.

Meryl: So you'd rather have English speaking books?

Audrey: Yeah.

Sonya: Yes, but the English talk posh, the Chinese talk Chinese, Indians talk Indian so why can't West Indians talk West Indian?

Meryl: So you agree with it?

Sonya: Yes.

Meryl: You think it's a good thing?

Sonya: Yes. But I don't think parents approve it so much because they think you're trying to act bad. (*A lot of agreement from the others.*)

Meryl: What do you think, Eleanor?

Eleanor: I don't really think that how they talk . . . I think it's just naturally how they talk . . . if they can't talk proper English it's not their fault. If I'm talking to a white person you have to sort of put on, you know. But when you're at home or anything you just talk normal how your parents talk and things, you know.

Meryl: So you think it's a good thing?

Eleanor: Yeah. Some people just can't help speaking it. I mean you know, when I come to school I go all . . . (*she makes a posh sound and everyone laughs*).

Meryl: Do you think your mother would agree with you reading books like that?

Eleanor: She doesn't really mind, you know. It's true how they talk – how they write it is how they talk.

Meryl: But don't you think she'd sort of think, er, well you're in England, forget all that seeing as you were born in England anyway?

Eleanor: Well, anyway, well I only pick it up because my sisters and them when they came over they was quite young, you know and we sort of pick up the words from them because if they never came in England we would talk really posh you know – not posh but Englishy, Cockney like, you know. Otherwise I don't think it's a bad idea.

Sonya: I think English people get a laugh out of West Indian people talking West Indian.

Audrey: Some of them even learn it.

Sonya: What do you think, Meryl?

Meryl: I think it's a good thing. I don't think there's anything wrong in it . . . West Indian dialect.

Sonya: Would you bring up your children speaking it?

Eleanor: Yeah, it's homely you know when you see your friends and you can understand what they're saying and you don't have to keep saying what, what?

Meryl: If my mum heard me talking like that she'd bust my little ass. Your mum would as well?

Audrey: Yes, she'd say 'You're in England now, so talk English'. My dad's really got the Jamaican accent.

Meryl: If you were to say 'What a rass hole' and all this stuff at home, would your mum start . . .

Eleanor: But this is swearing isn't it? I mean if you're just talking properly like 'day' instead of 'they' you know, there's nothing wrong in that but if you're swearing and shouting you can understand them being angry and frustrated.

Meryl: When you say 'day' and 'tree' and all that instead of 'three' and all that, don't they say it's not 'tree' it's 'three'?

Eleanor: No, because they know what I'm talking about, they're used to it. The majority of families say 'tree' instead of 'three'. I can't help saying 'tree' instead of 'three' because it's just, I don't know, it's just natural.

Meryl: My parents talk like that but when I do it they try and stop me.

Eleanor: Well, I don't see why they should stop you because it's natural. There's nothing wrong with it.

Meryl: No, there's nothing wrong with it.

Eleanor: Well, I don't know . . .

Sonya: Maybe they think if I, maybe the parents think that if my children go around speaking like that, then all the other people will think bad of them.

Eleanor: Maybe the only disadvantage of it is when you're coming for a job.

Audrey: Yeah, you've got to talk all posh. You can't really talk West Indies to them because they wouldn't know what the heck you're on about. They'd do what, what?

Eleanor: Anyway, I think West Indian dialect is very good. I like it.

The point is that these girls have identified the kinds of situations in which 'dialect' or 'talking posh' may be appropriate. Without saying that dialect should never be formally used in schools, I would argue that it is the job of the school to enable children to function with ease in the standard language. By the same token it is the job of the home, family and community to keep the dialect alive. The use of dialect in the classroom may obscure the basic role of the school, confuse the issues and create further contradictions.

Although the girls (both in the recording and in the classroom I visited) were able to have a sophisticated and intelligent discussion on the use of dialect, the general atmosphere in the classroom was not of this level. From the three sessions I spent with this group my impressions were that most of the children did not take the class very seriously. However I had no way of knowing whether this was a general attitude or specific to this Caribbean Literature class. There were a number of confusing or contradictory things going on; the children seemed unable to read dialect, talked about it as what 'the old people speak' and yet amongst themselves they too could lapse into dialect with ease. In order to write in dialect they first had to write in standard English and then translate it into dialect. The playlet, *On the Buses*, was written before my involvement with the group and I do not know what process of composition it underwent, but unlike the TV series it was certainly not a comedy. The teacher explained to me that the class had discussed different TV comedies and one girl had commented that, although London Transport has over half black conductors and drivers in some places, the TV series dealing with life on the buses did not include one single black face. The teacher suggested that the class could put this right by writing a West Indian version and the girl who first made the comment undertook the task. When the class talked about this play no one complained about it not being funny; everyone agreed that it was true to life – and that seemed most important.

Dialect in Culture and Schooling

Should I create a Black curriculum? Should I put Creole on the time-table? Over my dead body; and the majority of my parents would cheer me to the skies.

Max Morris, Headmaster of a London Comprehensive school with over 80 per cent 'immigrant', mostly West Indian, pupils.

Seen from a cultural perspective and in terms of black consciousness and self-image, the development of a distinctive dialect can be regarded as part of the process which African slaves were involved in when creating an alternative reality for themselves based on what they brought from Africa and what they learnt from their masters in America and the Caribbean. In this language a means of communication and a definition of self and others existed without reference to the dominant society. If the institution of slavery could be likened to the colonial situation, the masters as colonists and the slaves the colonized, it will become apparent how great the need is for the colonized to create an alternative language and mode of communication in order to sustain a viable sense of identity and worth, for in the colonist language they are at best invisible or worst sub-human. On the question of the relationship of language to culture, imperialism and identity, Ngugi Wa Thiongo the Kenyan playwright and novelist had this to say: 'if you learn a people's language, and you adopt their culture, you are more likely to see yourself in terms of their world outlook.' In American and Caribbean societies, Black English developed both as a means of communication and as a form of resistance. Analysis of 'cultural imperialism' such as that offered by Fanon in his *Black Faces White Masks* virtually ignored the language of the mass of Caribbean people and concentrated exclusively on the bourgeois and petit-bourgeois who aspired to join the French colonialist elite culture, hiding their black faces behind white masks. In recent times the importance of 'folk speech' as a language in its own right has been acknowledged and the implications of this for the schooling of black children in America, the Caribbean and Britain have been widely discussed by scholars in departments of linguistics and education. Labov has offered the most comprehensive analysis of black language in America and its existence as a distinct and separate form of English, with its own internal logic and grammar. Baratz and Shuy have also investigated the role of dialect in *Teaching Black Children to Read*.

In the Caribbean, Craig and Carrington and their associates at the School of Education, University of the West Indies, have investigated the role of dialect in teaching Caribbean children to read and understand West Indian English. Le Page (1968) has also been involved in a study of the problems involved in 'the use of English as the medium of education in the Caribbean'. Cassidy and Le Page have produced a *Dictionary of Jamaican English*. In Britain the issue of language, education and social class has been dominated by Bernstein and has been almost completely restricted to a discussion of the differences between middle-class and working-class speech. With the presence of West Indian children in British schools the issue of dialect and its influence on literacy and comprehension has received some attention. Le Page (1973) argued for the need for teachers to understand something of the structure of West Indian dialect so that they can help children to function more adequately in standard British English. Wight advanced essentially the same argument and more recently Edwards has suggested that dialect may influence the understanding of standard English to the extent that West Indian children, when matched for age and social class and reading ability with English children, appear behind in understanding the meaning of standard British English.

There are, therefore, the pedagogical issues, but there are also the cultural issues. The researchers at the Centre for Applied Linguistics (Labov, Baratz & Shuy) argue that black parents (who generally oppose the use of dialect in schools) would be converted when they saw that their children actually learned to read and write better standard English. This is also the argument which Craig, Carrington etc. at the University of West Indies School of Education use to counter parental and other opposition. It has also been suggested that some black intellectuals and academics oppose the elevation of dialect to the status of a language because it threatens their own elite status. It would seem, however, that the development in linguistics has not been paralleled by similar developments in sociological and educational thinking which could clarify the fundamental issues of power and control in relation to the use of dialect in schools. If we are living in (or moving towards) a post-industrial, technological, knowledge-based society, where does Creole or dialect figure in terms of the structure of that society? In terms of culture, can dialect be seen purely in technical terms? Language functions for the preservation of values as well as communication. What implications has the 'legitimization' (Bourdieu) of dialect (or aspects of dialect) for the cultural homogeneity of the minority group? To regard dialect as a matter relating simply to linguistic competence in relation to standard English is to ignore the development and persistence of the use of dialect in preserving for the minority aspects of cultural identity and coherence and the consequences which ensue from undermining these features.

This discussion on dialect, black culture and schooling relates to the West Indian literature class above. What we found there wasn't a teacher being helped to understand some technical detail of the dialect so as to enable children to function more adequately in standard British English; on the contrary the teacher herself was an accomplished dialect speaker. She was trying to enable the children to appreciate the full potential of their own first language, for drama and literature, in a way which they had not thought possible. The message of this approach is one which links what linguists have been saying (in terms of black dialects being languages with structure, logic and possibilities for abstract thought and reasoning) with self-esteem enhancement ideas – so that the black child can gain increased self-esteem from seeing her first language used to create literature and drama in the same way that standard English is used. This approach ignores the historical fact that dialect has functioned as a source of self-esteem and the basis of an alternative value system from the times of slavery. It also assumes that the process of legitimization, through the acceptance of dialect for use in schools, is itself an enhancing process, which shows that the language is 'good' and has teacher's approval. What it does not take into account is that the audience for this 'legitimization' may resist it, and react by modifying and adapting the original dialect, inventing new words in a continuing counter-action against absorption.

The issue of black culture, dialect and schooling has therefore to be seen in terms of:

1. *History* – where dialect as a language of resistance functioned as an alternative to the language of the elite, which essentially debased the slave and offered no possible basis for the development of positive attitudes to self and group.

2. *Pedagogy* – in terms of the influence of dialect on children's ability to use and understand standard English.

3. *Sociology* – where, as in contemporary British society, schools as agents of social control may begin to legitimize aspects of the dialect in order to promote self-esteem and reduce alienation, and conversely dialect users (especially young blacks) may respond by developing and adapting the dialect, thus making it more inaccessible to control and maintaining its illegitimate status as the language of an out-group.

So far, discussions of dialect have centred largely on the pedagogical issues; increasingly, sociologists and educationists will have to take account of other factors which relate to the role of dialect in culture and schooling. Lawton (1968) warned against a 'sentimental attitude towards working-class language', arguing that the working-class socialization processes (of which language is a part) are preparing its young members for a world which is disappearing. Lawton writes that 'in the near future routine manual jobs are going to disappear and jobs which will become available in industry or in bureaucratic, welfare or distribution spheres will require a much higher level of symbolic control'. An interesting and contrary view of the role of dialect in industrial societies is represented by Steinberg who sees the persistence of dialect in Western European societies as a direct reaction to the pressures towards a 'mass culture'. Noting that most Western European people speak at least one dialect (and often at least one foreign language) as well as their own 'standard' language, Steinberg suggests that what he terms the 'Confusion of Tongues', i.e. the variety and number of dialects, will continue to flourish because they are linked with culture and identity in ways we do not begin to understand.

It is interesting that discussions on West Indian dialect and schooling are carried on without reference to regional and other dialects and their relationship to schooling. In a paper entitled 'Dialect in School – An Historical Note', Brian Hollingworth described the tensions which have existed between schools and dialect in the North East of England. West Indian dialect can thus be regarded as one in a variety of dialects sharing in common the problems and possibilities of other dialects in the community.

Bearing in mind this discussion of the role of dialect in culture and schooling we now return to Group A, the West Indian dialect group.

I administered the test to the group on my fourth visit to the class, towards the end of the term. On that day there were 20 children present – 14 girls and 6 boys.

The registered number attending was 30 but the teacher said that average attendance was 20–5 and girls outnumbered boys by 1:5, so the day of the test was a fairly typical one.

The class was used to my coming and sitting quietly at the back. The day I introduced the test was the first time I actually spoke. I introduced myself, explained the research project, agreed to answer any questions at the end of the class and followed the instructions outlined in the Piers-Harris manual. (The teacher had told me that the class was very curious about me and wanted to know more about what I was doing.) The class co-operated beautifully; they settled down to the questionnaire with real keenness and twenty minutes into the session most of them had completed it. This was in stark contrast to most other testing sessions and was not what I'd been anticipating from their earlier class sessions.

Teaching Style

The teaching style adopted by this teacher was one based on 'relationships' and concern for the growth and development of children in the group. She tended to evaluate her performance and the class progress in terms of relationships, rather than in cognitive, instrumental terms related to achievement or attainment on an academic level. There was a clear, stated commitment to 'valuing' the speech and culture of the West Indian children, which was seen as devalued in the wider society and in most of the school. Bennett has discussed teaching styles in terms of formal and informal classrooms. He defined informal teachers as those who stress the importance of self-expression, enjoyment of school and the development of creativity; formal teachers stress academic aims. Eisher has made a similar distinction between expressive and instructional objectives in teaching – expressive corresponding to informal and instructional to formal teaching styles. In this analysis the teacher of the West Indian dialect classes used an informal/expressive teaching style.

This was an examination class; the children were working to a CSE Mode III Syllabus.

Self-concept of Group A

Here are some examples of the answers which Group A (aged 14–15 years) gave to the sentences below designed to indicate their self-concept.

(a) NOW AND AGAIN I REALIZE...
(b) WHAT I LIKE MOST ABOUT MYSELF...
(c) SOMETIMES WHEN I THINK ABOUT MYSELF...

Boys
(a) I can do what I want to do and have what I want to have
(b) nothing
(c) I wonder if I can be changed

(a) that I does wrong and stupid things
(b) is my character and the way I get on with people
(c) (no response)

(a) that I am really fed up
(b) is that I am smart
(c) really good

Girls
(a) long for wishes to come true
(b) everything
(c) I say God – how lovely I am and lucky

(a) have been wicked or mean
(b) I like my eyes, hair, face and personality
(c) wonder what I have done with my life

(a) that I am growing up. But do not have as much freedom as people my own age
(b) my eyes, my voice. But only since people told me about it I noticed myself
(c) I wish that I was dead. But then I wish I could have a good life when I grow up

Attitudes to School of Group A

Eleven (7 girls and 4 boys) responses (55 per cent) included Intellectual reasons for liking school. Four girls (20 per cent) gave Physical and Manual reasons, the same number gave 'support from adults' and 11 (9 girls and 2 boys) mentioned Social reasons for liking school.

Fifteen of the 20 children gave as their reasons for disliking school the attitudes of teachers, general dislike of teachers and especially the power of teachers. Four (20 per cent) mentioned a particular subject and two (5 per cent) mentioned bullying and disruption. The sentences below are examples of what the children wrote about school in response to the stems:

(a) WHAT I LIKE MOST ABOUT SCHOOL . . .
(b) WHAT I DISLIKE MOST ABOUT SCHOOL . . .

Boys
(a) English and Social Studies
(b) Some teachers

(a)   Is the friends I meet and the subjects and teachers
(b)   Is the way some teachers treat you like little kids and later
tell us that we are adults

(a)   the friends, the learning and the fun
(b)   the boring hours of class work like TD and art

Girls
(a)   I like school because that is way you get to known your
friends and meet and talk during the day. I like to get out of
the house at times
(b)   I dislike Biology. I think it is a bore. I sometimes feel to
take a whole week off and do nothing.

(a)   is not going and when they ask you where you were don't
tell them
(b)   teachers that thing they are smart and clever and know
everything. And be nosey

(a)   is my friends and the people who like and help me, and
lunch and break times
(b)   is the boring hours when people, especially teachers, make
me do things I don't like

Aspirations of Group A

Only 3 out of the 20 children in the group hoped to end up in a
profession/semi-profession, such as nursing. If the categories
Success and Money (I want to be rich and famous) and Self-
fulfilment (I want to be happy . . . do anything I want to) are
added together we find that this General Expressive category
accounts for the aspiration of just under half the group (9
responses: 45 per cent) and hopes for Marriage and Family bring
the total to 12 responses (60 per cent of the total). In terms of
future jobs the girls seem to have a clearer idea of what they want
to do. Few specific jobs were mentioned by boys and the
remaining answers express the hope that some day they could
'stay home' from school.

SOME DAY I WOULD LIKE TO . . .

Boys
. . . drive, make children and work
. . . be my own man and do what I like
. . . have cars, house, a good job

Girls
. . . become a nurse and then if I am good enough I would like to
    become a physiotherapist
. . . be a social worker, visit the world
. . . be a telephonist and lead my own life
. . . be happy sing my very own song before a large audience
Even where girls were expressing more general hopes and
desires they were couched in terms that seemed realistic and
achievable:
. . to go back to my homeland Jamaica without my parents to
    watch me
. . . get married to a respectable man who would never leave me
    and love our children. That we are in good jobs and can look
    after our children

Group B: 'Black Images' Modern Languages Class

Group B came from a mixed, purpose-built, three-year-old
comprehensive with some 800 pupils of which (in 1977) the
third-year were the most senior group. The school had a
reputation for being 'tough'; many incidents of violence
involving teachers and pupils had been reported. Levels of
suspension and expulsions were reputedly high, especially
amongst the West Indian pupils who formed roughly 35 per cent
of the school population. There were a small number of
teachers, who could be variously described as 'left-wing', who
had taken a particular interest in black kids in the school. The
Deputy Head of the Modern Languages Department was one of
these and she had developed and led the MRE project in the
school. My contact with this teacher and some of her colleagues
was very productive, but I had no direct contact with the
children apart from the actual administration of the test.

However, the project itself was well documented by the school staff as part of their efforts to have it accepted as a Mode III CSE Examination course.

The teachers felt that MRE was in constant jeopardy from the Headmaster and other senior staff. The Head of the Modern Languages Department had left to take up a job as Multiracial Education Adviser in another LEA and the Department was currently without a leader. This increased the insecurity of the staff and their worry over what would happen to their multiracial educational projects. This tension was added to by the fact that the Deputy Head of Department was not being promoted, even temporarily, to the Head of Department's job. It would appear that the 'credibility' of the department was lost when the Head of Department left.

To begin with, the staff saw the Headmaster as being somewhat indifferent, but over a period of time his attitude changed to one of hostility to the project. He argued that 'West Indian parents come over here to get their children a British education and that is what we should give them'. Many West Indian children in his school were wearing the Rastafarian colours of green, red and gold on woollen hats and scarves which they refused to remove. Teachers were in constant battle (literally) with kids to remove their woolly hats in the classroom; many children defied their orders. The teacher who ran the project believed that the children would become more hostile if they were forced to remove their Rasta hats and that it would be better to respect their culture and not provoke further hostility and conflict in the school. On the other hand the majority of staff and the Head regarded it as a discipline problem and felt that they must insist on appropriate standards of dress and behaviour from all pupils, regardless of racial or cultural background. A minority of the teachers felt that this was a narrow and hypocritical view to take at a time when all the values of the educational system were under question anyway.

This school had by far the most extreme conditions of the three schools contacted, but there were other schools which I also visited and maintained contact with over two to three years, and it is my impression that this school was not exceptional so far as schools in the London area went. Teachers at the school recorded incidents in an Incident Book: after five 'incidents' pupils were suspended – incidents could range from giving 'cheek' to tripping up a teacher in the hallway (apparently a common 'sport'). The extreme conditions in this school could be explained or understood by a consideration of several factors.

1. It was a new school.
2. In three years it had three Heads: (a) Head 1 left after less than one year; (b) Head 2 was on temporary appointment of Deputy Head until post was filled; (c) Head 3 (present Head) had been there just over one year.
3. It was a 'neighbourhood' comprehensive in an almost exclusively working-class area of London.
4. After four years it was still an incomplete school – the third-year being the top form.

The Use of Photography in the Study of 'Self-Images'

The course in this school made use of the media and photography to help children realize their concrete physical identities, how they 'present themselves' (Goffman) and the realization of this as a social process. This project on Black Images was part of an overall course on 'The Study of Images' (Milhum) which included a section on 'The Study of Racial Images' (Pines). The approach to 'image study' followed by these teachers corresponds roughly to the description of their work by the Half Moon Photography Collective given in an article in *Screen* (published by the Society for Education in Film and Television) and I quote from this article:

> *Creating an Alternative 'Reality'*
> Many of our projects revolve around the collection of material and analysis of images from printed mass media, but concurrent with this was the production of images and writings of and by children themselves and about how they experienced the world. Very often the first photographs produced echoed the attitudes and postures of those featured in the media, but this gradually diminished as soon as there was an involvement in projects revolving around their own identity.

The 'Collective' go on to observe that:

> The view we have of ourselves is dependent on feedback from other people both in their treatment and description of and to us (not forgetting our mirror image of course) which dictates to us how we ought to look, behave, speak, conduct ourselves etc . . . It must be obvious however that if we are receiving a biased, partial or totally negative and distorted view of ourselves from others, then our self-image will probably contain the same biases and distortions and we may learn to be ashamed of what we apparently lack. Long before children understand language explicitly they will have assimilated the posture and body language of the adults with whom they live. In addition the educational system and other institutions clarify and reinforce such views and present them alongside portrayals of other apparently more successful and highly idealized individuals and groups.

What is needed, therefore, is to help the children to create for themselves an 'alternative reality' based on their own experience and view of the world. As this article is meant to provide a guide to teachers who have started or are interested in starting an Images course, it seems helpful to conclude with something on the practical aspects of organizing such a course. Teachers are told to . . . evolve a good filing system so that everything is retrievable and not easily damaged. A system which allows original matter to lie flat is better than an upright one. Perhaps several teachers either within one school or at a local Teachers' Centre could share a central bank of images. We feel that the categories used . . . of sexism, racism, ageism and classism are useful starting points. Images can also be filed under general subject headings such as Families, Men, Women, Children, Babies, Black, Love, Sex etc . . As material increases, it is useful to break it down further into 'positive' and 'negative' images. In this way it is possible to set out recurring themes and establish some of the dominant 'norms' in printed media. Stereotypes such as the 'Happy Family', the 'Sexy Female', the 'Independent Male' and children who fall into neat packages according to the sex, will soon emerge.

A comparison could be made of a variety of magazines

depicting the Black experience, ranging from the idealized lifestyles of *Ebony* to *African Woman, Soul and Blues*, to those dealing with African Nationalism.

The articles go on to suggest various topics for project work:
1. *Identity*: who am I? Who are other people?
2. *Faces*: what do we really look like?
3. *Visual Life-lines* and personal histories.

All these topics were included in this class on Images. It was interesting to see three photographs which showed one black girl in the Identity project. In photograph 1 she was 'I myself'; in photograph 2 she was 'I as I would like to be seen'; in photograph 3 she was 'my idea of beauty'. Photograph 4 was of a girl Rastafarian who created her 'ideal' self by painting her face even blacker and thus heightening her African 'image'. After hours of viewing the material of the whole Images course it was clear that the guidelines given in the *Screen* article had been closely followed. It seemed to provide a striking contrast to what was being done in other groups both in method and in content.

Teaching Style

This teacher was convinced of the need to form relationships with children and to value each individual child as a person. Many of the West Indian children in her Images class had out-of-school contact with her; she visited homes, helped with problems and was generally a friend or social worker to children and their families. Not having observed her classroom manner, I cannot comment in any direct way on her teaching style, but having spent many hours in interviews and discussions with her, it was clear to me that her approach to teaching was fundamentally expressive; she appeared to get most satisfaction from the relationships she had developed with the children. Even so she was critical of lax teaching methods and acknowledged the need for children to be able to perform at an acceptable level. From the beginning of the course she worked for it to become a CSE Mode III examined subject; she achieved this aim just at the time when the course first came under threat of closure.

Self-concept of Group B

This group of 13–14-year-olds had average scores on the self-concept and self-esteem tests. Here are some examples of what the group wrote about 'self':

(a) NOW AND AGAIN I REALIZE THAT I . . .
(b) WHAT I LIKE MOST ABOUT MYSELF . . .
(c) SOMETIMES WHEN I THINK ABOUT MYSELF . . .

Boys

(a) I am very bad tempered and hard to get along with
(b) is that I know I can do something if it is very important to me
(c) I think will I ever be able to make it in life

(a) I have fell in a blunder
(b) personality
(c) I feel regretful

Girls

(a) that I have done a lot of things wrong
(b) I am good at some things
(c) I smile

(a) I change my mind about some things that I'd like to be when I grow up
(b) I like about myself I am kind-hearted
(c) I think that I am horrible to people sometimes. And cheeky

Attitudes to School of Group B

The largest number of responses (10:71 per cent) fall under the Intellectual function of school. Social/Friendship comes next with 8 responses (57 per cent). This group has a number of children who see school as a route for Advancement (4:28 per cent). In common with the rest of the sample, these children mention teachers as being what they dislike most about school – the attitude of teachers and their power over the children were the features most mentioned as causing dislike.

(a)   WHAT I LIKE MOST ABOUT SCHOOL . . .
(b)   WHAT I DISLIKE MOST ABOUT SCHOOL . . .

Boys
(a)   the games lessons and meeting my friends
(b)   the way some of the teachers treat us like morons

(a)   I like to get away from home and meet people
(b)   the work is getting harder and I can't take much more

Girls
(a)   because I learn something in it when I leave school I can
       get a good job
(b)   is that some of the teachers are wicked, the school uniform
       and things

(a).   is my friends and the good company I have and what I learn
       too
(b)   is sometimes the teachers pick on me

Aspirations of Group B

There is a slight sex difference. Girls are clearer about what they
want to do in life – with the exception of one girl who some day
hopes 'to go to heaven'! Girls always wrote more than boys so
there were 12 responses from 6 girls and only 8 from 8 boys. It
was hardly ever necessary to double code a boy's response (see
Table 3.1).
SOME DAY I WOULD LIKE TO . . .

Boys
   . . be an important man in the eyes of the earth like Henry
      Kissinger
   . . not have to go to work
   . . . be somebody who helps people and people help me, love
      and be loved
   . . . become an Architect or a Surveyor or Electrician

Girls
   . . . have my own shop doing hairdressing

. . . be a secretary working for a barrister, a private secretary

. . . be a good actress

. . . be a secretary and have a lot of A levels and degrees. And be
a film star.

Table 3.1: Aspirations of Group B (N = 14)

Statement Category	Total Response		Girls		Boys	
	No. %		*No.* %		*No.* %	
Success and Money	4	29	2	33	2	25
General desire to 'get on'	—		—		—	
Travel – General	1	7	—		1	13
Travel to the WI	1	7	1	17	—	
.. America	—		—		—	
... Africa	—		—		—	
Occupation: Doctor	—		—		—	
.... Teacher	—		—		—	
.... Nurse	—		—		—	
.... Scientist	—		—		—	
.... Skilled/Semi-skilled	5	36	3	50	2	25
.... Manual	1	7	—		1	13
.... Entertainment	4	29	4	66	—	
.... Football	—		—		—	
Marriage & Family	—		—		—	
Self-fulfilment	2	14	1	17	1	13
Other Professional	1	7	1	17	—	

Groups C and D: Roots and Rastas

This boys' comprehensive school (ex-secondary modern) was
noted for its efforts in the area of multiracial education. There
seemed to be a constant stream of visitors from London and
further afield doing a pilgrimage to this school. And these
children seemed to take my presence for granted in

a way those in the other schools did not.

Because the school placed emphasis on MRE, multiracial courses were an integral part of the history syllabus throughout the school. But underlying the courses was a belief that the black children had something special to gain from the content of these lessons. There was an assumption that their own self-concept would improve and that their view of the role black people have played generally would become more positive. It was felt that English children in these history classes stood to gain from exposure to knowledge about the history of other groups which now make up 'multiracial Britain'.

The methods, organization and teaching in Groups C and D were very impressive, and the level of discussion seemed to indicate general interest in the class during the sessions when I was present.

Teaching Styles

The teaching style adopted by both teachers was formal and instructional. Both the History and RE syllabuses were taught throughout the school to 'O' and 'A' level. Although the underlying commitment to multiracial education, valuing minority group culture and offering the children the opportunity through knowledge acquired in school to build a positive self-image, was the same as in the earlier groups, the methods seemed somewhat different. Operating within mainstream education in established subject areas, having the support and co-operation of colleagues and external agencies – the other teachers, the Resources Centre and their LEA policy – the conditions under which these teachers worked contrasted sharply with the isolation and fringe status of the teachers in Groups A and B.

Roots – World History (Group C)

The History Department of this school teaches West Indian history as part of its World History syllabus to all third-year boys. During the time I visited the class they were examining the slave trade as the basis of the West Indian history unit. I sat in on two sessions of this group and I was impressed with the teaching of the master and with the interest and attention the subject received. The History master had a rather charismatic personality and would probably have made anything sound interesting – but as well as this he had a sound grasp of his subject and the lesson was very well prepared. The level of discussion was very high, most boys speaking easily and commenting without any prompting from the teacher. It just seemed to me to be a straightforward History class, which was lucky to have a good teacher. It did not strike me as the kind of 'knowledge' which a child was likely to incorporate into himself and have his self-concept influenced by.

The course was essentially an academic course, encourag-ing critical thinking, the ability to deal with primary source material and to relate history to contemporary world and local situations. The teaching was of a high academic standard and was intended to lead to 'O' and 'A' level work in the fifth and sixth forms of the school.

Rastas Group (Group D)

This group started out as part of a regular RE World Religions class which included a number of sessions on the Rastafarian religion. The teacher told me that a number of West Indian boys in the class became very interested and came to see him with requests for more classes and more information. Out of this there emerged a once-a-week lunch-time session which this teacher ran – other West Indian boys, mostly friends of the original group, also joined it, and there were twenty-five boys in the group. The teacher who ran this class was the only West Indian teacher in any of the MRE groups. I was unable to attend any of the sessions of this lunch-time group. However, I did attend three classroom sessions of the RE World Religions class. These were conducted in much the same way as the World History class described earlier. It was a formal classroom situation: knowledge was presented and appeared to be absorbed. There was much less discussion and classroom interaction between teacher and pupils than in any other school-based group I visited. I was not present during any of the sessions dealing with the Rastafarian or any African religion.

It must be said here that not all West Indians share Barrett's views on the Rastafarian religion and some parents actually object to their children being taught about the Rastas whom they regard rather in the same way as, say, hippies or 'Flower People' were regarded in the sixties by mainstream British or American society. The same analysis of attempts at 'legitimization' discussed in relation to dialect in schools applies with equal force to religion; the implications are virtually the same.

Self-concept of Groups C and D

The 42 13- to 14-year-old boys in the two groups had average-high self-concept and self-esteem scores in the sentence completion test below.
(a)   NOW AND AGAIN I REALIZE THAT I . . .
(b)   WHAT I LIKE MOST ABOUT MYSELF IS . . .
(c)   SOMETIMES WHEN I THINK ABOUT MYSELF . . .

Group C
(a)   that I will fail myself in my lessons and be without a job when I leave school
(b)   my face and my ability in sport and in my lessons
(c)   I wonder what going to happen when I grow up. And if I'm good looking

(a)   that I say things I really don't mean
(b)   is that I'm kind and like having friends
(c)   I think that I could improve on the whole

(a)   I loose my temper too much
(b)   is that I'm black
(c)   I wish that I was working

Group D
(a)   that I am quite stupid compared to other kids
(b)   is that I aint bad
(c)   I am over wight

(a)   I need to improve my work
(b)   is being a christain
(c)   I think that I should be more correct in what I do and a bit more ability

(a) I am kind to people
(b) I like myself because everything I do I do it good
(c) I think I am a lucky person

Attitudes to School of Groups C and D

It seems best to bring this descriptive material together for both groups since there are no sex differences to report from this single-sexed school. Of Group C 11 (or 55 per cent) saw school as likeable for Intellectual reasons, the corresponding figure for Group D being 9 (or 50 per cent). Group D gave the highest percentage of Physical responses, 9 (40 per cent) liking sport, games and related physical activities. The response to this among Group C was also quite high at 6 (30 per cent). Sixteen Physical and Manual responses combined give a total of exactly 50 per cent for Group D but still only 6 (30 per cent) for Group C. Group C also regard school as important for Advancement: 4 (20 per cent) mention this. In Group D only 1 boy mentioned this. Social reasons/ Friendship account for the overwhelming number of responses in Group C at 13 (65 per cent) whereas the Rastas Group had 6 responses (27 per cent) in this category.

These boys found no difficulty in stating what they disliked about school – bad teaching was mentioned by 2 boys in each group (9 per cent). In the Roots Group 9 respondents disliked the attitudes of teachers; 2 disliked teachers' power and 2 disliked everything. In the Rastas Group, 4 (18 per cent) mentioned bad teaching, 9 (40 per cent) disliked teachers' attitudes and 4 (18 per cent) disliked everything about school.

(a) WHAT I LIKE MOST ABOUT SCHOOL . . .
(b) WHAT I DISLIKE MOST ABOUT SCHOOL . . .

Group C
(a) that you learn something useful
(b) that it isn't any stricter

(a) Games, Break and home-times
(b) nearly everything

(a) friends and some lessons
(b) some teachers

Group D
(a)   to do some work I like
(b)   some teachers think they are superior to the pupils

(a)   meeting my friends and to learn something from good teachers for a job
(b)   teaching system is stupid. They don't teach you nothing about when you leave school

(a)   I like sport
(b)   a lot of teachers

Aspirations of Groups C and D

Of the 42 West Indian boys, the highest percentage of 30 per cent (13 responses), see their future in terms of achieving Success and Money. In terms of specific ambitions, Entertainment (singing mostly) with 4 responses (9 per cent) and Football with the same number emerge as the most popular choices of career.

There are no would-be doctors, teachers or nurses, but one scientist, 'Other Professionals' being one would-be computer operator or electronic engineer, one architect and one musician. Among the two groups differences were mainly on Marriage and Family and Self-fulfilment: 5 respondents in Group C mentioned future hopes for Marriage and a Family, only one mentioned a general wish for Self-fulfilment, 'being happy'. In Group D the situation was reversed; none mentioned Marriage and Family and five mentioned 'being happy, free, doing what I want' etc.

SOME DAY I WOULD LIKE TO . . .

Group C
. . . be a computer operator or an electronic engineer
. . . be a famous person or a footballer
. . . get a job and get married
. . . visit a nudist camp and have a night out with the prettiest black woman in the world
. . . own my own house and car
. . . bust the teacher's head

Group D

. . . be a successful football star for Arsenal

. . . be a cricketer or an electrician

. . . stick to all my lessons and pass the test to get the job I want

. . . be a musician

. . . be an architect because I am good at drawing, I like drawing

Summary

Self-concept

All the children tested in the three schools can be regarded as having self-concept scores within the average range on the Piers-Harris self-concept test, with high scores on the Ziller self-esteem item and average on the sentence completion items. There were no apparent differences between the four groups in terms of the teaching styles, that is to say, teachers who adopted relationship-based, affective teaching styles with the emphasis on individual growth and development in terms of self-concept and self-image enhancement, did not appear more effective in having higher self-concept scores. The lowest scores on the Ziller self-esteem item were in the 'Black Images' group with a mean score of 12.5, out of a possible full score of 18. The teachers who adopted a more instrumental, cognitive approach to their teaching had pupils with similar self-concept scores to the affective-style teachers. There were no apparent sex or age differences in the children studied.

Attitudes to School

Just over half (41:54 per cent) the children gave reasons for liking school which we can classify as falling into the Instrumental/Intellectual category (see Chapter 5 for details of analysis): this means that there were 41 individual statements which mentioned some factor connected with the intellectual, cognitive, learning aspect of school as something they 'liked most about school'. Just over half (11:55 per cent) the children in the West Indian dialect group (A) made statements which fitted this category; the 'Black Images' group (B) had 10 such children (71 per cent). The figures for the History group (C) were 11 (55 per cent) and 9 (40 per cent) for World Religion (D). Thus the group with teachers who adopted a less instrumental approach to teaching, in terms of their objectives which emphasized growth and personal development of pupils, had pupils who were marginally more positive to school, but in interpreting this data it should be remembered that boys generally express less positive attitudes to school than girls (this was true for all groups) and it is possible that these slight differences could be due to sex rather than teaching styles.

Social reasons and Friendship combined account for the next category of 'likes' (36:47 per cent). Advancement is mentioned by 9 (12 per cent), Physical by 20 (26 per cent) – 15 of these being in the boys' school and all reflecting a concern with games, sport and PE. Three of the four references to 'support from adults' occur within Group A, the other coming from Group C.

Attitudes to Teachers

Teachers are seen as being powerful and exercising authority in an arbitrary fashion. Forty-eight (63 per cent) of statements deal with the resentment which children feel against teachers. There is no real difference between groups in terms of attitudes to teachers generally; it is purely a matter of emphasis. Some mention attitudes of teachers, others specifically mention the power of teachers, but the negative feelings expressed are the same. The seven statements which express dislike of 'everything' are all from boys. Two girls and one boy dislike 'nothing'. Bullying, being 'picked on' and disruption are disliked equally by boys and girls, but receive only 7 mentions by children in this group.

Attitudes to teachers do not appear to be related to attitudes to school in any direct way – children who express positive attitudes to school in terms of what school offered by way of intellectual stimulation and advancement did not express more positive attitudes towards teachers generally.

Further discussion on these and other findings follows in Chapter 6.

Aspirations

The categories which receive the most mentions are Success, Money and Self-fulfilment (34:44 per cent). These children appear to see the future in vague, but rosy terms; they hope to be happy and successful, to be rich and self-fulfilled. When they express particular aims they are either fairly mundane in terms of skilled or semi-skilled work (12:16 per cent) or very ambitious in terms of acting or singing careers (10:13 per cent). Ten express hope or desire for a 'professional' type career: one girl hopes to be a nurse, one boy hopes to be a doctor and another (boy) to be a scientist. The 'other professional' category includes an army officer, a pilot and an architect.

Attitudes to Parents and Family Life of the MRE Groups

Parents

Feelings, wishes, desires are concentrated in the Expressive category. Twelve (14 per cent) responses identify the giving of help and support as a function of parental roles. Love and kindness received mention 25 times (33 per cent). Fourteen responses (18 per cent) mention parents as Guardians/Protectors. On the negative side, restrictions on freedom got the most mentions at 12 (16 per cent), mostly from girls. Cruelty was mentioned 5 times, being bullied or humiliated 4 times, as was a feeling of being rejected or not wanted. Often positive and negative feelings about parents went together – 'They can be cruel, but it's for your own good' – and one statement of opinion would be modified or qualified by another.

Home

These sentences were analysed on the same scale as WHAT I LIKE ABOUT SCHOOL . . . As would be expected, the Expressive categories predominate far more than in the school responses, although the Physical and Material needs combined account for the next highest number of mentions (28:37 per cent).

We now look at some of the responses the MRE groups made.

(a) TO A CHILD PARENTS ARE . . .
(b) WHAT I LIKE MOST ABOUT HOME . . .

(a) needed, depended on to survive
(b) I've always got somebody to go to, no matter how much trouble I get into

(a) always saying don't do this, don't do that
(b) it may not be much but it's home

(a) a big worry and a protector
(b) is my own television clothes and food

(a) bossy, trying to own your mind, body and soul, people who expect too much of you. (Earlier, this same girl had written: NOW AND AGAIN I REALIZE . . . that I am very mean to my mother, that she really cares for me, she's just doing what she thinks is best for me.)
(b) home is that I can be alone in my room, thinking and dreaming, so it's like I haven't a care in the world.

(a) cruel
(b) the food

(a) sometimes nuisances and pest, other times they can be loving and caring
(b) is my food and my bedroom, my clothes and my luxury bathroom

Curriculum Innovation

Humble and Ruddack have identified two types of curriculum innovation projects: (a) the grass-roots, teacher-inspired and (b) the officially funded, externally inspired project. The grass-roots, internal projects are those initiated by an individual teacher or small group of teachers, and are not intended to have influence beyond the small unit or the particular school involved. The official curriculum innovation projects are those which have external (research or local education authority) backing or support and are generally intended to influence policy and practice on a scale beyond those schools immediately involved in the project.

Of the four projects reported here, two fall within the (a)

grass-roots category and two within the (b) official category. The two which are seen as internal, grass-roots curriculum innovation projects are the West Indian dialect and the 'Black Images' classes (Groups A and B). The World History and World Religion classes (Groups C and D) are seen as falling into the (b) category of receiving external (to the school) official backing and support.

In terms of aims, the grass-roots projects are seen as being mainly therapeutic, offering to the children the opportunity to give status to their dialect by using it in the formal surroundings of the school and for purposes usually confined to standard English – plays, poems and creative writing. The aims of the more official projects are seen as meeting the need for social justice which is reflected in the belief that schools should compensate children for the inequalities and injustices which exist in society. In this particular case the injustices relate to race, but they may equally relate to class or sex, in another context.

The categories are not as neat as Figure 3.1 suggests: the promotion of therapeutic and social justice aims overlap at several points, as do grass-roots and officially funded projects. It is the degree of emphasis which determines whether a project is seen as aimed at a therapeutic or social justice outcome: single-teacher, single-option, classroom-based projects are by their nature more 'therapeutic' than departmental, integrated projects.

The School-based Projects – Types of Curriculum Innovation

The development of the two 'grass-roots' projects happened as a result of the individual initiative of the two teachers involved: in the West Indian dialect class the teacher had been sent on an exchange visit to Jamaica where she had learnt the local dialect and had become involved in its use as a method of teaching in schools. On her return to England she decided to offer an option on the use of West Indian dialect for creative writing. The other project was the result of a wider study of 'Images' of various kinds run by the Modern Languages Department in the school. The unit on Black Images emerged from the study of racial images and self-image which formed part of the original

Figure 3.1: Styles of Curriculum Innovation

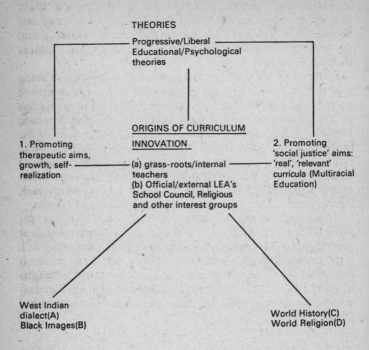

1. Therapeutic aims emphasize growth, self-realization and personal development through the education process: Dewey, A. S. Neil, Susan Isaacs are the educationists who best articulated this view. Currently Rogers as a psychologist and Coopersmith as social scientist stress these aims. The Plowden Report in its statements on the aims of schooling represents the triumph of this approach.

2. Social justice aims are described by Lawton (1977), Barnes, Milner, Schools Council Humanities Project Race Relations Unit (Stenhouse, 1975), Schools Council/NFER, *Education for a Multiracial Society*.

course. The black children became engrossed in this aspect of 'race and self-image' and virtually created the new course, 'Black Images'.

The World History and World Religion courses are not seen as 'grass-roots' in the same way as the two earlier courses. These two projects reflect a much wider base of concern and backing and their objectives are more in line with external agencies, LEA policy, religious bodies, Schools Council and the NFER, which is that education for a multicultural society should reflect something of the history and religions of the various cultural and racial groups which now make up British society. The Inner London Education Authority has stated its commitment to the development of curricula and other resources which are seen as fulfilling this aim; the Afro-Caribbean Educational Resource Project and the World History Syllabus reflect this concern.

Jenkins borrowing the term from Parks, has suggested that the curriculum innovators can be in the position of 'marginal' men, 'looking backward to the grass-roots ideology that produced them . . . and forward through their perceived careers and expectations'. Clearly, where the process of innovation has been institutionalized in an external agency or (having been developed by the teachers) has the support of external agencies, the degree of 'marginality' may be reduced. In the two grass-roots projects this external support was lacking; internal support, though present to begin with, was withdrawn, in one case through change of Head and in another the Head and senior staff were seen as reacting to outside pressure to drop from the curriculum anything that was not clearly 'academic'. The support of the Head is crucial if internal 'grass-roots' innovation is to develop successfully. The effect of the withdrawal of support was a certain end to the projects.

The World History and World Religion classes seen as curriculum innovation had a wider base of support, both internally from the Head and senior staff, and externally from the LEA and other agencies who have an interest in seeing the development of this type of curriculum, for example, the Community for Racial Equality, National Association for Multiracial Education and the National Foundation for Educational Research. Various religious and cultural groups also welcome the multicultural RE programme. In addition, because the projects were backed externally and had adequate resources (Dickinson points to the importance of more than adequate resources for the success of innovatory programmes) they were able to function at an approved 'academic' level, and thus counter any claims to lowering of standards which were the kinds of criticism which the other groups faced.

Aims of the Innovatory Curricula

In Figure 3.1 the West Indian Literature and the 'Black Images' classes have been placed in projects with therapeutic aims, but clearly aims overlap to a considerable degree; it was the degree of emphasis which determined where a particular project would be placed. Whatever the academic or cognitive aims of any one of these projects, overall they also had therapeutic aims, in the sense of wanting to heal the wounds which history and an unequal society had inflicted. In focussing on history and religion the teachers in the 'social justice' group hoped to show all the children in their multiracial classes what different groups had contributed to the history and culture of the world, so that no child could feel that his religion, history or culture was inferior because it was ignored by the school. In the same way the West Indian literature class aimed to show that 'dialect' is an 'acceptable' form of communication, to help each individual child to feel confident and free to use dialect to express himself in the knowledge that he would not be 'corrected' or told to speak 'properly'. Similarly, the 'Images' class explored 'the image' of the individual child's own sense of beauty and personal worth. What makes these two groups more therapeutic is their emphasis on 'the individual', whereas the history and religion groups stressed 'the social' more consciously.

The reasons for the failure of the two grass-roots internal projects appear to be related to:

1. absence of external support;
2. lack of organizational internal support;
3. dependence on one or two staff;
4. lack of resources;
5. isolation of the project – options opened to one year group only and also virtually one racial group;

6. staff changes; depletion of resources.

The success of the other two groups could be attributed to:

1. external support;
2. internal organizational support (especially of the Head);
3. integration of the courses: taught to all the year groups and racial groups. Neither course was an 'option'; both were part of the History and RE courses taught throughout the school;
4. continuity of staff;
5. adequate resources, both inside the school and from external Resource and Teachers' Centres.

In discussing 'Professionality and Innovation', Hoyle suggested that there may be two types of teachers who go in for 'innovation'; these he termed 'restricted and extended' professionals. He described restricted professionalism as being confined mainly to the classroom, child- or subject-centred, deriving satisfaction mainly from relationships with children and depending for assessment of performance on personal observation of pupils' progress. Extended professionalism incorporates all the aspects of restricted professionalism but it operates in a wider theoretical and practical context, including reliance on research literature and collaboration of professional colleagues; this approach tends to favour specified objectives and evaluation of work in terms of these.

Hoyle cautioned against the use of these terms for classifying teachers neatly into categories. But for research purposes these categories are useful, especially in helping to clarify issues involved in the success or failure of small-scale innovatory projects. If we saw the therapeutic classes as reflecting the 'restricted professional' approach to innovation, their failure to become institutionalized becomes clearer; so also does the success of the History and RE projects, in which the teachers adopted an 'extended professional' approach. In this context, the success or failure of the projects can be explained in terms of the strategy of the innovators. However, there are other aspects to this problem. The teachers have agreed that they were unable to widen the internal or external base of support because of indifference on the part of their colleagues and because external agencies had other priorities. We might turn to W. Reid for the final comment on why innovation (of any kind) works in some schools and not in others:

> The innovative school might be the one which has appropriate structures for allowing political accommodation to take place between clients and employees, for developing consensus on goals, for permitting adjustments to outside pressures, and for enabling change to be implemented without undermining the values of those concerned.

This seems to describe the ethos of the school where the successful projects took place.

Comments on Curriculum Innovation as (a) Therapy (b) Social Justice

Marten Shipman suggested that many innovatory programmes were creating a 'Curriculum for Inequality' in the search for 'relevance' in the education of the 'average and below average' child. He wrote that the new curricula 'are often lacking in real academic discipline . . . they could separate the education of the Newsom child from that of the future elite as effectively as when these groups were educated in different school systems'. This problem of 'relevance' is of particular importance in the development of a curriculum which is meant to be 'relevant' to the needs of (1) minority group children and (2) education for a multiracial society. The teachers who develop them and the external agencies who back their introduction hope that curricula of this kind will reduce alienation of minority group children, encourage the development of tolerant attitudes in majority group children and generally lead to the development of a more equal, socially just society which the school has helped to create. In 1975 Lawton argued that the existence of the common school must give rise to the need for a 'common curricula' which gives an equal basis to all forms of knowledge. Lawton believes that the forms of knowledge can be 'manipulated in the service of the common secondary school' towards the achievement of social justice. More recently (1977) he has carried the case for the curriculum as social justice further and argues that a measure of social justice can be achieved through curriculum reform. He sees the curriculum as performing a vital function: focussed not on attainment but on development and giving to children an equal chance for a 'real education'. The trouble is that there is as much difficulty in defining to everyone's satisfaction a 'real education' as a 'relevant education'. A real or relevant education for West Indian children may be seen by some as including the use of dialect with confidence. Others, including most parents and children, may see a 'real education' as having good qualifications thus providing access to 'good jobs'. Yet these aims may not be central to the aims of the curriculum innovators and may even be in conflict with the objectives of the projects. In this sense the questions which Silver raised in connection with the loci of power in decision-making on curriculum innovation, are very apt: 'Who decides what should be "common" in school curricula, and how do profound challenges to the status quo – including a curricular one – gain credence?'

The question of knowledge leads directly to a consideration of Young's critique which holds that the curriculum is socially organized knowledge. When teachers, through the curriculum, extend the knowledge-base of classroom teaching, they do this within a clearly defined framework and acceptance of what constitutes knowledge. Working within this consensus, they adapt the curriculum to include 'knowledge' about other cultures, religions, and lifestyles. This process can be seen as the legitimization of these cultures, religions, dialects etc. which may then be accorded a certain status and acceptability within the school. All innovation is problematic for the teachers, the school organization and the pupils. What I have tried to do is document the background to these four small innovative projects and to clarify some of the issues involved.

Large-scale innovatory programmes react to wide-scale pressure from various interest groups, teachers' unions, Local Authority management and administration, the Department of Education and Science and politicians. Note the controversy over the report of the Schools Council/NFER Working Party on *Education for a Multiracial Society*, and the fate of the Humanities Project Race Relations Unit (Stenhouse, 1975). The debate over the proposal of the Department of Education and

Science (1977), for a 'core curriculum' continues with no apparent hope of resolution. In the matter of small-scale school-based innovation the pressures are of a different kind, the debate is less public, confined mainly to the educational press and professional journals (see *TES*, 24 March 1978).

However the pressures are not simply related to the nature of the school organization, resources, support and so on but also to the wider community in which the school functions – parents, local and national pressure groups and other interest groups. Sieber in analysing the reactions of schools to change, identified four critical features:

1. vulnerability to the social environment;
2. values of personnel;
3. diffusiveness of goals;
4. the need to co-ordinate and control the clients (pupils) and employees (teachers) of the system.

These features apply with particular force to small-scale innovatory projects related to ethnic minority students. Schools in London are becoming more vulnerable to a social environment which incorporates an increase in racial tensions, the growth of Fascism and other extreme political groups, unemployment and general decay in urban areas and increasing bitterness and disenchantment with the school in the West Indian community and scepticism about anything which happens there – including attempts at developing 'relevant' curricula. These developments also affect the values of personnel, who are, as citizens and members of society as well as teachers, part of that overall social structure in both their private and working lives.

In examining the process of adaptation which some schools undergo in coming to terms with numbers of West Indian pupils, we looked briefly at the problems of school-based curriculum innovation projects and at some of the reasons why two of the projects studied in this research failed and have come to an end, whilst two are successful and continue to flourish. Among the factors discussed were teaching styles, the organization of school and whether or not the projects had external support.

Comparison with other groups and further discussion of the results follow in Chapter 5.

4. Poor Self-concept or Poor Schooling?

Introduction

In this section we examine the West Indian community's response to the experiences of their children in British schools. We begin with a look at the development of Supplementary schools, followed by short descriptions of each of the seven community projects, which are included in this research. The research findings for these groups, both officially and voluntarily funded and organized, are supplied and the chapter concludes with a summary and discussion of the results obtained.

Community involvement in education is a contentious issue – the response of the various teachers' unions to the Taylor Report on School Government and Management shows that teachers generally do not welcome such involvement, or are prepared to welcome it only on their own terms. Although it is difficult to make a valid distinction between community participation and parental involvement in schooling many teachers professing to believe in 'parental participation' may not in fact support the idea of community involvement, even though it is clear that parents are part of 'the community'. It is interesting that this widespread suspicion by teachers of community involvement in education is not generally extended to 'immigrant' people living in Britain. Yet the Australian Teachers' Union have banned their teachers from teaching in Saturday schools for immigrant children, the reason given being that this type of 'education' is inferior and that the education authorities should provide proper language facilities. (The Australian Saturday schools provide language tuition for the children of newcomers to Australia.) Teachers' Unions in Britain have made no pronouncement on this issue, so it is not possible to find out what their view is or if they have any views at all. However, all the Official Saturday (Supplementary) schools I visited had some connections with local schools and accepted 'referrals' from these schools. It is not surprising that West Indian community groups have evolved or developed around education issues – education is of great importance to Caribbean people, who view it as a means of social mobility for their children. 'West Indian parents expect the schools to turn out children with great achievements' (Aston Gibson of West Indian Concern). Gibson also argued that West Indian parents do not share the low aspiration and 'realistic goals' for their children of the indigenous working-class. Many West Indian parents give amongst their reasons for immigrating the desire for better education for their children. However, in Britain they are faced with an educational system through which they cannot, as working-class people, fulfil their ambitions for their children. They have to adapt to these conditions, which include a hierarchical schools system which operates to exclude parents generally from decision-making and other processes within. The effects of this structure are felt particularly by working-class parents. The National Children's Bureau study, *Violence, Disruption and Vandalism in Schools* and Finlayson suggest that schools should 'take some blame' in explaining the apparent indifference of many working-class parents, and resulting poor home-school contact. In Liverpool the EPA Project workers 'developed a growing feeling that all parents are interested in their children's welfare and progress but that schools must take positive action to break down the barrier which undoubtedly exists between schools and parents, especially in working-class areas' (Midwinter).

In terms of regarding the Supplementary schools as part of the process of adaptation of the West Indian community to a hierarchical school structure, it is interesting to note the contribution of Austin and Garrison to this discussion. In an article in the *Times Educational Supplement* in 1978 they offered the analysis that the West Indian community is responding to educational failure, high unemployment and both local and central government indifference to the plight of urban black youth. They write:

The community has responded by starting its own sup-plementary schools, to provide the skills it considers lacking in formal educational institutions. These supplementary schools have developed professionalism and expertise. Initially, they were manned by interested parents. Eventually black teachers and other professionals in education took over their running, and related what was being taught to that taught in the conventional schools. They also expanded the basic curricula to include African and Caribbean history, creative writing and black literature.

That same issue of the *Times Educational Supplement* carried a two-page spread on the development of Supplementary schools in the West Indian community and asked the question – how should teachers respond? The report was entitled, 'Can Black Self-help Succeed Where School and Other Social Agencies Have Failed?' An earlier report in the *Guardian* (20 February 1978) entitled 'Old-fashioned Learning by Rote Pays Off' was the first report to draw attention to the development of these Saturday schools by working-class West Indian parents. It provided the first serious acknowledgement of 'the challenge' of the Supplementary schools. In developing these Saturday schools the West Indian community is refusing to accept that significant numbers of their children are intellectually inferior and ineducable. As working-class parents they are engaged in a challenge to the established school system, which says in effect that working-class people cannot play an effective part in their children's schooling.

It is clear from their comments that Austin and Garrison welcome the development of 'professionalism and expertise' which teachers and others involved in education bring to the projects. They should be more cautious; the development of professionalism and 'expertise' is not without its drawbacks which mainly centre on the stifling of the essentially voluntary effort which gave birth to the project in the first place. Professionalism also involves, inevitably, the mystification of knowledge and the exclusion of the 'amateur' in favour of the 'expert' as Illich pointed out. Traditionally, teachers in the state system have come from the lower-middle and upper working class (Tropp). Hargreaves has lamented recent developments in teacher training which have made the main concern of teacher-trainers the achievement of an all-graduate profession with what Hargreaves calls 'an appropriate professional mystique'. He argues that once school teaching is opened only to graduates, it will become an exclusively middle-class profession, and he says that middle-class teachers lack the resources to do anything other than 'cope' with difficult, bored and alienated working-class pupils in schools. He believes that:

> unless we are prepared to de-mystify teacher training and teaching, and allow truly working-class adults into our schools as part-time teachers, we are unlikely to get the kind of debate and reform which is necessary.

The development of Saturday schools within the West Indian community mirrors in many respects the Socialist Sunday school movement of the late-nineteenth and early-twentieth centuries, which offered to working-class children the means to foster a self-image based, not on therapy or charity, but on hard work, disciplined study and the will to succeed (R. Reid). Just as the Socialist Sunday schools were mainly organized and run by working-class people for working-class children, so also in the West Indian Saturday schools we find ordinary working-class people who, as part-time teachers, are 'demystifying' the teaching and learning process as part of the response to a social structure and its institutions which discriminate against them and their children. Similar developments among English parents include the parents' group which runs 'Education Otherwise' with a membership of over 100 parents (*Where*), 25 of them 'actively engaged in teaching their children at home'. Education Otherwise and Saturday schools represent part of the growing dissatisfaction of parents with what is being offered by the school system, a willingness to improve on it and a belief that they themselves have the capacity and the ability to effect this improvement. The implications of official (funded) or self-help (voluntary) status will be discussed later in connection with the organization and management of the various groups. Undoubtedly the legitimization of the Saturday schools through funding and control by central and local government carries with it the possibility that they will lose their parental and grass-roots involvement through becoming more professional and thus more hierarchical in their approach.

Many strategies can be employed in attempts to enhance or

improve self-concept and self-image; to encourage more positive attitudes to school and to increase children's school attainment. In the main, schools have concentrated on 'relationships' and on the 'soft-option' approach. Without exception, people working in the West Indian community groups stress the importance of hard work, high aspirations, willingness to sacrifice and belief in one's ability to succeed as the only possible way forward for most West Indian children in Britain. We turn now to consider the West Indian community's response to the problems which their children face in British schools. Seven Saturday schools are considered. Four are labelled 'Official' and three 'Self-help'. They are all in London.

The Official Projects

Official projects are those which have official backing and support – either being fully funded by local or central government or receiving other forms of help, through the provision of teachers, youth workers, materials and resources, premises etc. There were four projects fitting this description:

Group E: Community Arts and Culture Group (including Supplementary school);

Group F: Youth Project (including Supplementary education and culture);

Group G: Supplementary Education Project;

Group H: Community Development (including Saturday school);

All these projects had one thing in common – they operated in depressed inner city areas of multiple deprivation. Groups E and G followed the community development model of community/social work in their general approach and their Supplementary schools were only a part of this overall strategy. Project F in a sense was part of that same community development strategy, but here the Supplementary school was run as an autonomous unit, entirely separate from all the other activities and was different from all the other projects in having a qualified teacher in charge and being the only project with a woman leader.

Group E: Community Arts and Culture Project

This project was a community development scheme in an inner city area of London. It was financed by an Urban Aid Grant. As well as classes in Drama, Dance, Music and Arts in various centres throughout its area, it also ran an Information and Advice Centre.

Other areas of work included a Senior Citizens Group, Adult Literacy Classes and a Bail Project. There were two full-time community workers in charge of the overall project and other workers and volunteers were employed on a sessional basis.

The Supplementary (Saturday) school was run jointly by the project workers and the local Council for Community Relations. The Annual Report of the Project written in January 1977 stated:

> This school which was started a year ago by Project and CCR staff has been meeting a desperate need in the area, that of helping children in the basic three R's.
>
> The attendance at the Saturday school over a period of 12 weeks has been an average of 24 children. The school is staffed on a rota basis by voluntary teachers who live locally.
>
> Unfortunately we have found that these children have not been achieving a great deal at school and for the future we intend to have continuous dialogue with the schools concerned. In fact, work along these lines has already begun with — School whose Headmaster is very keen and receptive to our ideas.
>
> The school is progressing and methods of work schemes are continually being discussed for later use with the children.

My own observations of the Saturday school confirmed the utilitarian approach of these teachers.

Group F: Youth Project

This was part of a Youth and Community LEA Sponsored Project which ran an Education, Culture and Arts Group. The activities of this group included Dance, Music, Drama, Poetry etc. all with a Caribbean flavour. This was in addition to the Supplementary school run on Saturdays, which many of the children also attended. The day I went to test the children was a particularly bad day; it was cold and raining and many children did not turn up. It was the one group where no teenagers were present.

Group G: Supplementary Education Project

This project was run as a separate supplementary education scheme with evening classes and Saturday school from 10 a.m. – 3 p.m. during the school term. (The timetable provided on p.172 was actually taken from this school when it was under different leadership, but it still follows more or less the same schedule.) It provided facilities for children to do their homework, including assistance from the teacher who was a permanent full-time employee. This was by far the most 'prestigious' supplementary education project I visited (and I have visited, at some time or another most SEPs in the London area). It has its own building, reading room, coffee bar, well-equipped classrooms and the only teacher (female) I came across employed full-time on a supplementary education project. The school was well organized and well attended; there were no voluntary helpers, only trained teachers employed on a sessional basis.

Parents dropped in from time to time to tell the school about something that was happening which might prevent a child coming – the parents of these children seemed particularly anxious that the children should not miss any of the sessions – unlike the other 'Official' projects where regular attendance was a problem for the teachers and helpers. There were times when normal weekend family activities took precedence over attendance at the other Saturday schools. It may be that the environment of this Supplementary school was so businesslike, the building and layout so much like a real school that the parents felt it important that their children should attend each session. Whatever the reason this school had a waiting list of children wanting (or parents eager for children) to come. There were several spin-off cultural activities at the school, concerts for parents, Christmas play, fêtes etc., but as with all the other projects the main emphasis was on learning and teaching basic skills.

As I have said, this was a 'prestigious' project. It was the only one run by a woman teacher – who immediately impressed me as being very capable, efficient and practical in the traditional teacher fashion. She treated the parents in a friendly but distant way, encouraging them to come in and talk at any time but not offering them any role within the school. She listened to their problems and sympathized with them, but it was always on a 'professional level'. There was no nonsense about parental involvement; in her view parents had enough to be getting on with and teachers should not be shirking their responsibility by passing on their problems to parents.

I listened in to an interview between this teacher and a Jamaican parent who had come in to tell her that she was taking her daughter back to Jamaica for six weeks' holiday, so she wouldn't be coming to the Saturday school during that time. The teacher asked her if she had been to see Mr — , the Headmaster at the comprehensive which the girl attended. The mother explained that she did not need to tell Mr — her business as her daughter didn't learn anything at his school anyhow and not being there for six weeks wouldn't make any difference. But she said that she was worried about the girl missing the help she got on Saturdays as that had made all the difference to her. She said that her daughter enjoyed reading now, whereas before she came she hardly ever looked at a book. The teacher promised to give her daughter some work to take away with her.

After this mother had gone I expressed some amazement over what she had said about the Saturday school being more important than the weekday school. The teacher replied: 'A lot of them say that; I get that all the time. They have no faith whatever in the schools around here.' It is interesting to note that in spite of having no faith in schools, West Indian parents do not keep their children away from schools and truancy is not considered a problem amongst West Indian children in ILEA schools.

Group H: Community Development Project

This Supplementary school was part of a much bigger Urban Aid Sponsored project which included an Information Centre, and schemes for Legal Aid and Advice and Adult Literacy. The Saturday school was located on the top floor of the Community Centre with six classrooms and a small library. A woman teacher was responsible for running the school; she was employed by the project and was responsible to its Management Committee. Other helpers were also teachers or trainee teachers. Parents came to bring their children to the school; they did not stay around and did not appear to be involved in running or helping in the school. Again it is possible that these same people used the other facilities on the premises and were part of the project in other respects – but so far as the Saturday school was concerned, they were not involved. This Saturday school had only been going for eighteen months when I made contact so it is possible that they were feeling their way, although from experience one knows that it is difficult to change the style of a project from a professional to a co-operative style of management once it has become established.

The teachers in this group were very outspoken about black consciousness – more so than any group I visited. Virtually all reading material had an African or West Indian theme or background. Project work was connected with 'Black Leaders', 'Blacks in History', 'Great Black Americans/Africans/West Indians' etc. Paintings and drawings also demonstrated this influence – there was no identity confusion in the paintings these children made of themselves of the kind reported by, amongst others, Coard and the North Lewisham Project writers. During one lesson I observed about Africa as the home of all black people, during which the teacher talked about black unity and brother/sisterhood, one little boy asked if he should hate white people? The teacher did not seem perturbed by this question. She answered: 'You don't have to hate anybody – just love yourself and your people.' The boy seemed put out by this. I wondered if he might have received a different answer if a stranger hadn't been present but I think not.

The children in this group were all pre-adolescent; they were all still attending local primary schools in the area.

Self-concept of the Community Official Group

In common with all the other groups tested these children, aged from 11- to 16-years-old, scored in the average range on the self-concept and self-esteem tests. Here are some examples of what the Community Official children wrote about 'self'.

(a) NOW AND AGAIN I REALIZE THAT I . . .
(b) WHAT I LIKE MOST ABOUT MYSELF . . .
(c) SOMETIMES WHEN I THINK ABOUT MYSELF . . .

Boys

Aged 11 (a) I am different
           (b) is liking people
           (c) I think who am I

Aged 15 (a) I am stupid
           (b) that I am good at sport
           (c) I feel free

Girls

Aged 12 (a) I have done something wrong, badness, and I feel sad
           (b) is my complexion, my hair and my clothes
           (c) I feel sad

Aged 14 (a) that I am Black and I have to work extra hard to have the job I want
           (b) is the ability to work hard at school and I am very determined
           (c) I think how lucky I am to be black

Attitudes to School of the Community Official Group

In terms of attitudes to weekday school of the Community Official children, the highest number of responses, 34 (64 per cent) given indicated liking school for its Intellectual function. The Physical category (Sports) came next with 15 responses (29 per cent) giving this as what they liked most about school. Interestingly, 8 respondents (15 per cent) gave Emotional Security-type responses as reasons for liking school. On the negative side, a total of 42 (33 per cent) responses dealt with dislike of teachers' attitudes and the power of teachers. Four (8 per cent) mentioned bad teaching, 11 (21 per cent) mentioned bullying and disruption as things they disliked most about school. Four (8 per cent) mentioned racism and prejudice; 11 (21 per cent) disliked a particular subject and 2 (4 per cent) disliked nothing about school.

(a)   WHAT I LIKE MOST ABOUT SCHOOL . . .
(b)   WHAT I DISLIKE MOST ABOUT SCHOOL . . .

Boys

Aged 10   (a)   I like English
           (b)   I dislike Maths

Aged 14   (a)   is to work and meet different people
           (b)   not being told about Black History and being brainwashed all the time

Aged 13   (a)   the teachers are very kind and treat you well
           (b)   a man named Mr Smith he always picks on the Black boys

Girls

Aged 13   (a)   sports, lesson I like it because it keep me away from home from boring
           (b)   some teachers pick on Black people and they don't give us a chance to explain

Aged 11   (a)   they teach me and help you if there is something wrong with you help you
           (b)   is that if you are working and there is a fight the blame you

Aged 15   (a)   is the companship and the Independance of each other also helping the uncapable
           (b)   is the boredom of some teachers and how they go about their work

Aspirations of the Community Official Group

To get an overall picture of the hopes and aspirations of this group we combine the category dealing with a general wish for Success and Money with that on Self-fulfilment to give a total of 20 responses (or 75 per cent). Some day I would like to . . . be famous, have lots of money, be rich. Or, Some day I want to be free . . . happy . . . do what I like . . . go to bed with my girl/boy friend etc. In terms of career expectations two hoped to be doctors, three teachers and five nurses, which together with five 'other professionals' adds up to a total of 15 (28 per cent) who hope to end up in some kind of professional occupation. Work in entertainment and skilled/semi-skilled occupations came joint second.

SOME DAY I WOULD LIKE TO . . .

Boys

Aged 12   . . . have a lot of money
Aged 11   . . . be a doctor or a mathematician
Aged 13   . . . go to Jamaica for 1 year and visit my gran-dad because I have not seen him before
Aged 13   . . . play cricket for the West Indies and Football for Manchester United
Aged 15   . . . be a motor mechanic

Girls

Aged 13   . . . be a secretary or a teacher
Aged 15   . . . be treated by my mother like an adult not a child to be able to do my own thing
Aged 10   . . . a big young lady and put on some make-up so you look pretty
Aged 14   . . . be a journalist and write Black Literature

Attitudes to Parents and Home of the Community Official Group

The majority of these children saw the role of parents as providing Guardianship (3), Protection (3), Help and Support (8) and Love and Kindness (29). That means that 43 (or 81 per cent) of responses dealt with some positive aspect of parenting. On the negative side, restrictions on freedom got the most mentions with 4 responses (or 8 per cent), 2 children felt bullied or humiliated by their parents and 3 mentioned general negative characteristics – such as parents doing things they had forbidden children to do or wanting to keep them babies or not wanting to admit they were growing up or expecting too much etc. In terms

of home the thing these children liked most was that it provided
a place of safety (16:29 per cent) which gives them the material
comforts they need (15:29 per cent) and identity with the family
(10:19 per cent).

(a) TO A CHILD PARENTS ARE . . .
(b) WHAT I LIKE MOST ABOUT HOME IS . . .

Boys

Aged 12   (a)   kind and without them we would be nothing
            (b)   the warmth and better than going out I could
                 play with my dog

Aged 15   (a)   adult
            (b)   television

Aged 15   (a)   is people who loves there children or should
                 do
            (b)   is when all the family is there

Aged 13   (a)   everything they should be they are fantastic
            (b)   my parents are my home

Girls

Aged 14   (a)   bad tempered
            (b)   doing work, helping cleaning and polishing
                 the stairs and the bedrooms

Aged 11   (a)   loving and kind
            (b)   playing with my dog

Aged 14   (a)   people who should not keep their child from
                 the world
            (b)   is that I can look after my mother

Aged 13   (a)   nice and kind
            (b)   my colour television

The Self-help Projects

Group I

This project impressed me most. It was long established, having
been started over six years ago and still existing in its original

form. This was remarkable as the voluntary Saturday/
Supplementary school movement is littered with the corpses of
projects born and dead within a matter of months. The school
was started by a group of parents all living on an estate in a part
of London which is known as a multi-problem area. The group
of parents came together in the first instance because they felt
that their children were missing out on cultural and recreational
activities, such as outings to museums, visits to the country and
the seaside etc. So in fact the project started out as a social
cultural group. As the group expanded the members found that
most parents were worried about the kind of schooling their
children were getting; they were finding that ten-year-olds
could not read or count properly. The membership decided that
the group's priorities should change from social to educational
and thus the decision was made to start a Saturday school.
Although I have included this group in the self-help category (it
was when I came to know it), at the time when the decision was
taken to start the Saturday school they did in fact apply for a
grant to help get it off the ground and a grant of £50 was given
to them by the local CRC. Since that time it has been completely
self-financing.

Once the decision was made and the small grant obtained, the
group looked for helpers and teachers from amongst its own
membership. It did not have any paid professionals at any time.
Although teachers subsequently joined the group as helpers, the
parents (one parent trained as a teacher), remained in complete
control and the style of co-operation and self-help remained
unchanged. Two members are currently on teacher-training
courses. The professionals came in to an already established
framework into which they had to fit; this was markedly
different from the official groups where the professionals
recruited volunteers or allowed parents in on their own terms to
do clearly specified tasks. Another interesting feature of this
group was the way they got professionals other than teachers to
help the children – thus, for example, an accountant helped with
maths under the general direction of the maths teacher; he sat
with one child every Saturday afternoon for two hours and
helped with a particular problem. Parents heard children read
and helped with general teaching – this meant that each child,
particularly the younger ones, could have (almost) individual

attention. Parents showed a degree of knowledge and confidence in their own ability to help their children which was impressive. Parents also said that they continued to help their children during the week and to plan and work towards the next Saturday session or the next event in which the school was involved. This group and the school were unique; the people had worked together for a long time, lived near each other and they and the children came from one estate.

Group J

This was another long-established (over six years) Saturday school jointly run by two volunteers, one female (a trained teacher) and one male (GPO engineer). This school operated from a local Community Centre – used by a variety of groups representing the many different nationalities who lived in that part of London. The school was run by a management group which was made up of parents and volunteers, but although the parents were involved in the management of the school, they were not as heavily involved in the day-to-day running of the school as were parents in Group I. They were more scattered, coming from a wider area than was usual and this may account for the under-representation of parents. The running of the school was jointly undertaken by a trained teacher-volunteer and a non-teacher under the management of the parent group.

This school ran on a shoe-string. Materials were scarce; parents paid a small sum, 20p per session, to cover drinks and biscuits and what was left went towards the provision of books, pencils, paper etc. The group tried to raise money through jumble sales among the parents and children who came to the school, but this brought in very little money. As the children came from many different weekday schools in the area the Saturday school needed to get single copies of many different maths and reading schemes, which was expensive, especially if the child moved on or changed school. The teacher explained these difficulties with resignation. She tried to keep every child (this of course applies only to primary school children) on the scheme they used at their weekday school. As she said, it was pointless putting the children on to a different scheme for one afternoon per week. Very often children could not identify their reading scheme, especially those who most needed help, and she had to go through all sorts of subterfuges to find out what kind of scheme that particular school used. This teacher had been in on the start of the Saturday school six or seven years ago when she was a student teacher. Since then she had moved away from that area and now lived three or four miles away and taught at a school in the area where she lived, which was part of a different LEA. But every Saturday afternoon she returned to the Saturday school to teach and during the week she often attended meetings in connection with the running of the Saturday school. The co-worker had also been involved from the beginning when his son had been one of the first pupils. His son had grown up and was at college, but he continued to help run the school as before.

Group K

This Saturday school was part of a Methodist Church community scheme to help West Indians in this part of London. The school was started by a West Indian Methodist lay preacher (since upgraded to minister) about three or four years previously, when the Methodist ministry became concerned that it was not doing enough for its West Indian members. The membership of that particular church was about 95 per cent West Indian. Although the church was concerned to do something for the West Indian community, the project was not without its tensions – in particular accusations that the Saturday school was a centre of 'Black Power' and that it encouraged anti-white feelings amongst the children. On one occasion while I was there the local vicar came in to look around; he seemed very uncomfortable and departed after five or ten minutes. It was after that that I heard that he'd been requested to 'keep an eye on' the Saturday school because of the allegations mentioned above.

In fact this group, in common with all other groups, did not pursue any obvious political line, though on the walls were posters of Africa and the Caribbean – MOTHER AFRICA NEED YOU: ENGINEERS, DOCTORS, NURSES, TEACHERS – African hairstyles and costumes, pictures and posters of black Americans etc., creating an environment which said something to the children and to the people working and visiting about what the Saturday school was for. I was at this school the Saturday following the showing of the TV film of the book *Roots*. The teacher stood in the middle of the classroom with a map of Africa, surrounded by a group of children and they talked about Gambia. Where was it? Was there anything recently on TV about that part of the world? Did it have anything to do with you/with us? And so the dialogue went on. It was very moving and completely positive.

The man who was responsible for this school was a trained teacher as well as a preacher, and very 'professional' with it. His lessons were always beautifully prepared, with work cards set out as though he expected an inspector to arrive any minute. He used only trained teachers as helpers and he literally bombarded parents with handouts about the benefits of education, hard work, spelling, sums, anything. But he did this in such a jovial way, with nothing heavy about it, that the parents seemed not to mind; perhaps they never even read the handouts!

Although this group was completely self-financed it was not poor. Affiliated to the Church as it was, fund-raising activities brought in much more money than in other groups. Jumble sales and 'Bring and Buy' sessions were well attended and turned into social occasions for everyone – which made them financially successful for the school. The school was well equipped with books, stationery and other materials and with access to a photocopier which was useful to them in preparing work. All the activities undertaken had some 'educational' value, including visits and outings to places of interest. There was a feeling that everything which happened there was connected with the primary educational goals of the Saturday school – even fun things. Yet the children seemed to enjoy coming. Membership of the school was not tied to Church members or their children, but they were heavily represented amongst the children at the school. The leader told me that he had to turn away children as he did not want 'quantity' but 'quality' and you could not give the children the individual help and attention they needed if the place was 'crowded out'.

Unfortunately the day of the test was one of those bleak autumn days which are all too common and the attendance, which on previous occasions had been well over thirty, was down to around twenty, quite a number of the children being under ten-years-old, and therefore outside the age range for the test. This was very disappointing, especially as the programme for the following weeks meant that it was impossible to fit the testing in before the holidays – so I had to be content with a smaller number in order to get it done at all.

Self-concept of the Community Self-help Group

In common with the findings on self-esteem of the other children in the sample, this group also showed average-high self-esteem.

(a) NOW AND AGAIN I REALIZE THAT I . . .
(b) WHAT I LIKE MOST ABOUT MYSELF . . .
(c) SOMETIMES WHEN I THINK ABOUT MYSELF . . .

Boys

Aged 13
  (a) I must read the newspapers every day instead of twice a week, turn off the television
  (b) is that I am proud of myself and I think I am a special person
  (c) I feel that I am a proud and happy person

Aged 12
  (a) I am alone
  (b) music
  (c) disturbed

Aged 14
  (a) I am doing wrong to my parents feelings and hurt them to
  (b) good looks, figure, good clothes
  (c) I think dirty things about girls and I think of having sex with girls

Girls

Aged 10
  (a) am growing bigger
  (b) I like my clothes most about myself
  (c) I notice that I am sometimes wicked

Aged 11
  (a) would like to be a proud member of a black community who do something for their well being

    (b)   is that I am a person who originated from Africa and that I am black
    (c)   I feel proud of me

Aged 15   (a)   I am a bit bossy and ignorant I do try to check myself though
    (b)   is that people think they can confide in and trust in me and this gives me a feeling of security
    (c)   I feel as if I degrade myself people tell me that I am not as bad as I pretend to be so I must be good

Attitudes to School of the Community Self-help Group

The children in this group said the Intellectual function of school was what they liked most about it – they gave 31 responses (67 per cent) falling into this category. On the negative side, 24 (54 per cent) disliked teachers, teachers' attitudes and the power of teachers. Disruption and bullying was mentioned by 10 (22 per cent) children as things they disliked about school. There were 3 children who disliked nothing about school.

(a) WHAT I LIKE MOST ABOUT SCHOOL . . .
(b) WHAT I DISLIKE MOST ABOUT SCHOOL . . .

Boys
Aged 14   (a)   I like school for my education and for my own sake
    (b)   boys beating you up and pushing you about and the teachers

Aged 11   (a)   Geography History English and Maths because I learn a lot about them
    (b)   I dislike nothing

Girls
Aged 15   (a)   seeing my friends every day, also the teachers and lessons

   (b)   some of the teachers because they think just
         because they have Authority that there are
         always in the Right

Aged 11   (a)   Science, Biology, Chemistry, Physics and
               things like that
         (b)   is that History is misleading and the things
               some History teachers teach us are not right to
               what really happened

Aspirations of the Community Self-help Group

Again, if we combine Success and Money with a general wish
for Self-fulfilment we have a total of 9 responses (20 per cent) in
this category. However the categories of Professional and Other
Professional combined yielded the highest total number of
responses in this overall area of aspirations; 23 (50 per cent) of
these children hoping for a professional career of some kind,
including 7 who hope to be doctors, 6 scientists, 4 teachers and
only 1 nurse. There were no children in this group who saw
themselves in skilled or semi-skilled work, but 3 saw themselves
in manual work.
SOME DAY I WOULD LIKE TO . . .

Boys
Aged 14   . . . do what I like and get married to have 2 or 4
             children with a nice girl
Aged 12   . . . be an electrician
Aged 10   . . . be a doctor
Aged 13   . . . be a farmer in Jamaica
Aged 14   . . . a social worker

Girls
Aged 15   . . . travel around the world and meet a lot of Reggae
             stars
Aged 11   . . . be a singer
Aged 11   . . . be a teacher or teach gymnast
Aged 15   . . . have a very good job with reasonable pay
Aged 10   . . . go to university

Attitudes to Parents and Home of the Community Self-help Group

The attitudes to parents and home life of the children in this group were extremely positive. This was the only group in which mention was made of the home as providing mental stimulation. There were 9 negative and 48 positive responses to parents and home life from this group.

(a) TO A CHILD PARENTS ARE . . .
(b) WHAT I LIKE MOST ABOUT HOME . . .

Boys

Aged 13   (a)   I think parents are very kind to their children
           (b)   I like most about home because I like them. They is no place like home

Aged 14   (a)   everyone are different, they are good and bad persons
           (b)   I could never have a better set of parents than I have

Aged 14   (a)   not all that good except for looking after children
           (b)   I like food, and the house and my baby brother and sister

Girls

Aged 11   (a)   security, love, knowledge, sence of belonging, happiness
           (b)   is that I have parents who love me and do not neglect me for something else. And the thing I like most of all is happiness

Aged 14   (a)   bossy
           (b)   the warmth and security

Aged 12   (a)   I do not no
           (b)   is my bed and how I live

Education, Deprivation and Community Development

> More recently the relevance of traditional education has
> been challenged in a more fundamental way by education-
> ists associated with Education Priority Areas. Dr
> Midwinter argues for a philosophy of 'relevance' . . . .
> although not necessarily with a view to convince but with
> the hope of raising the issue for discussion and appraisal
> . . . This relevance is partly a matter for basing school
> curriculum on a neighbourhood and its culture . . . It is
> also concerned with political awareness embodied in the
> notion of 'constructive discontent' . . . These positions
> share important qualities with strategies of community
> development.
>
> > Kath Jackson and Bob Ashcroft,
> > 'Adult Education, Deprivation and Community
> > Involvement: A Critique'

In presenting the community projects it is necessary to
distinguish between the ideological and philosophical basis of
the Community Official and Self-help projects and their place in
the overall structure of community development and
social/political action strategies currently practised in Britain. In
general, community development is regarded as a means of
organizing people to take part in issues which affect their lives
and to effect change and improvement in their environment.
Redevelopment programmes, housing, planning issues and, of
course, education form a part of the concerns of community
workers. An example which comes readily to mind is the
Liverpool EPA Project run by Eric Midwinter which used
community development strategies to organize the local people
around educational issues. In Britain there has been a tendency
to see community work almost purely in terms of organizing
poor people around issues concerned with poverty and bad
housing and general 'deprivation' mainly because, as Harry
Specht points out, this approach has secured official (financial)
support and backing and also because community workers
themselves are more interested in working with the 'dis-

advantaged' at a local level. Specht, Professor of Social and Community Work at the University of California (Fulbright Scholar at the National Institute of Social Work, London, 1973–4) warned the Association of Community Workers in London that:

> successful programmatic intervention, whether it is with conventional social services or with new experimental innovative programmes, will require the financial and political support of Central Government; therefore community workers and community groups must cultivate their bonds and organizational ties beyond the small local community.

Specht also argued that since the majority of disadvantaged children and people lived amongst the advantaged and did not live in areas defined as 'disadvantaged', community organization must involve organizing people other than those defined as poor. The model of community development I found among the 'officially' sponsored projects was that which Specht had recommended for the future development of community work in having the political support of both central and local government. However in terms of organizational base, the groups tended without exception to be local in the specific sense of organizing among the local West Indian community. Specht had also warned that:

> support for social change must involve a broad cross-section of the body politic and not just the poor. Like it or not, one of the things we can learn from the history of social change movements is that they require the involvement of a wide range of actors including intellectuals, middle-class supporters, people with money, large numbers of people, and so forth.

Only one of the community official projects I visited could call on a support base such as that which Specht believes should form the basis for success in community development projects. Although we may use the general framework of community development to discuss these projects, it is clear that their aims and objectives limit them to organizing not simply among the poor, but amongst a section of the poor – the black poor. However, if as Specht argues, community development programmes must seek a support base in the wider community in order to be successful, these projects must be in a particularly hazardous position. The one project which did have some degree of 'wider' community support in that its Pensioner Club was 'multiracial' and its Advisory Service (having obtained a reputation for being 'good') drew customers from the whole local community, also had workers who seemed convinced that their project did need the support of the local community as a whole.

In discussing the organizational aspects of the projects we have to make a distinction between the projects as a whole and the Supplementary schools which they ran and which were largely independent from the main project – although clearly, in being part of a community project, these Saturday/ Supplementary schools were part of the community development strategy of the project as a whole. It is interesting to note in this connection that there have been and are battles between local authorities and West Indian community groups over the running, staffing and recruiting of children to Saturday schools, focussing on the use of Section XI money. (Section XI of the 1966 Local Authorities Act authorizes local authorities to spend money on the provision of 'extra facilities' in areas of high immigrant population.) It is under this Section that local authorities fund the establishment, staffing and supply resources to Supplementary schools. The West Indian community groups argue that the money is intended for 'immigrant' education and that therefore Saturday schools should have exclusively or mainly West Indian children. The local authorities argue that the money is intended for 'the community' and that Saturday schools should be opened to all comers. The West Indian community groups counter that this would completely change the nature of the schools, which exist solely to supplement the poor schooling which their children get in schools, and to improve their basic skills. They argue that local authorities should set up other projects for other deprived people in the community and not 'adapt' the West Indian Supplementary schools to meet these needs.

In seeking financial and other support from local authorities and central government, the official projects may be ensuring the supply of money, staff, resources and the use of (school) buildings which are clean and heated – none of which can be despised – but by the same token they become caught up in conflicts over the use of these resources and the control of the project which engages them in continual struggles and arguments which must deplete their own (inner) resources. I watched this process over a year as one of the original projects became embroiled in a protracted argument with the local authority over the use of Section XI money. Numerous meetings were held and legal advice was sought but the local authority being in any case better equipped and having more 'staying power' continued simply to put the case that the use of Section XI money was for the 'community'. In the end the West Indian community group withdrew completely from the running of the Saturday school and its control was taken over by the community education officer of the local authority. The Saturday school became a Saturday activity project for all children in the local area. In an interview, the Community Education Officer explained to me that it was a nonsense to have a Saturday school for 'immigrants' which catered solely for West Indians since the nature of population change in the area meant that the largest immigrant group was now Asian – and so the best way round a thorny problem was to exercise no control of membership based on racial grounds but to open the school to those who needed it. What happened once that policy was adopted was that the school reflected the racial distribution in the local community by becoming 70–80 per cent English. This was what the West Indian community group had foreseen. They believed that as all the children in the area were 'deprived' and had nothing much to do on Saturdays anyway, opening the Saturday school up to all comers would mean that West Indian children would soon be in a minority. This would change the nature of the school, and it would become an activity-based rather than a learning or education-based project. It is also true, however, that another Saturday school which I visited in this local authority was multiracial, having about 5 per cent English children and one English teacher, and did in fact function as a Saturday school with the emphasis clearly on giving the children academic rather than social stimulus.

It can be seen from this brief outline that the official projects, although functioning within the main stream of community development ideology and philosophy in having the financial support of local and central government, lack a wider base of community support. Because of this they can become engaged in constant friction with their own sponsors, generally to the detriment of the projects – and sometimes when no effective compromise can be reached the project ceases to function altogether or takes on a different form. The story of how these conflicts developed between community workers and their sponsors because of differences in ideology, philosophy and loyalties has been well documented in the reports of the Community Development Projects Information Unit.

The Idea of Supplementary Education/Schooling

In an article in the *Times Educational Supplement* (9 December 1977) an educational journalist described how the Japanese managed to obtain top scores in a seven nation test of attainment devised by the BBC. The writer commented that Japanese children frequently started the day with private coaching sessions before school and quite often these classes went on after school in the evenings as well. These coaching sessions were supplementary to the regular schooling which the children received. In England supplementary education exists in three main areas.

1. *Private Coaching*. Along the Japanese style mainly for entrance examinations to public schools, but also private lessons for children who are not doing too well at school. This area of activity is solidly middle- and upper-class.

2. *Religious Schools*. Providing instruction in the religion of a particular religious (and/or racial) group. Sunday schools, Jewish Sunday (and evening) schools, Muslim and Hindu schools.

3. *Language Schools*. Offer children of minority (language) groups lessons in their 'mother tongue'. These groups include mainly Europeans (Italians, Poles, Cypriots and Spanish) and Asians (Bengali, Hindi and Urdu speakers).

4. *West Indian Supplementary Schools.* These schools are neither of the first nor the second variety although they more nearly resemble the coaching type of institution than the religious. These schools are present in one way or another in all the urban areas where West Indians have come to settle in this country.

The idea of supplementary education seems then to be a fairly well accepted one. Indeed it is rather interesting to have to regard Sunday schools now as 'Supplementary schools' considering that they predated state schools and for a long time provided the only real schooling which working-class children received.

However, the idea of supplementary education seems to be accepted where the state fails to or cannot provide for some particular educational need for a defined group of children or where (as happens mainly in coaching groups) some people have opted out of the state educational system, and 'buy in' other forms of schooling.

In the West Indies it is quite usual for children to attend classes for 'extra lessons' before and after school and at weekends. The idea of supplementing regular schooling by buying in extra tuition is well established. To illustrate this briefly and anecdotally; I can remember leaving home at 7 am to get to 'lessons' by 7.30. We had one hour of lessons then went off to school at 8.30 am for 9 o'clock. There were several teachers who probably worked as many hours at these lessons as they did at their regular work. Most ambitious parents took it for granted that they had to spend extra money if they wanted their children to succeed educationally. In my childhood and youth there was keen competition for limited places in secondary education and this was reflected in the pressures on children which included many extra hours of schooling. This is still the situation in the former British Caribbean. On a recent visit to Jamaica I found children of three- and four-years-old sitting quite still with pencil and chalk being taught to read and write by 'backyard' teachers (barely literate themselves, I was told) and parents paid by the hour for this privilege. These people lived in extreme poverty and the few pence they spent on these classes represented a good percentage of their income – yet so convinced were they that this was the way for their children to succeed, that they paid up willingly and at some 'backyard' schools there were waiting lists.

Given this type of background, it is therefore not surprising to find that supplementary education for West Indians living in London should take the form of Saturday schools which undertake first, to teach children basic academic skills and secondly, to form cultural or social groups. A typical Supplementary school timetable is given in Table 4.1.

Table 4.1: Timetable of a Supplementary School

	4–6 pm	6–7.30 pm	8–9.30 pm
MONDAY	Homework sessions	English Art	Human Biology Art General English
TUESDAY	Homework sessions	English Sociology General English	Black Literature Creative Writing Sociology
WEDNESDAY	Homework sessions	Maths	French Maths Sociology
THURSDAY	Homework sessions	English Literature	English Literature General English Economics
FRIDAY	Homework sessions	Dance/Drama	Dance/Drama German
SATURDAY	Reading Unit (10.30 am–1.00 pm) General Education (2.00 pm–4.00 pm)		

This school functioned virtually as an alternative to the regular school and the teacher in charge told me that they acted on the basis that children learned nothing in school, so it was their duty to provide some kind of education.

On reading the accounts of Socialist Sunday schools in Britain given by R. Reid one is struck by the similarity between that movement and the Saturday school movement amongst West Indians living in urban areas of Britain today. There is the same belief in 'destiny', in the need to fight oppression – both racial and class – in the value of education as a means of achieving a just and equal society. But whereas the working classes in Britain are a majority of the population, the West Indian population in Britain is minute. After the Second World War, the Socialist Sunday schools died out and Reid reported that in 1965 there were just about one dozen registered in Scotland. Once the Labour movement had succeeded in becoming an established political force in the land and socialist principles became accepted as legitimate, there was no real need for Socialist Sunday schools and when a Labour Government was elected and the Welfare State was introduced, it must have seemed to many that Socialist ideals had totally succeeded and that an equal and just society was round the corner. We know that it was not and that sections of the working class remain poor and educationally and socially disadvantaged, relative to other groups in society.

The process whereby the Socialist Sunday schools ceased to be needed can never of course be reflected in the West Indian Saturday schools. But there will be other processes and these will need to be identified and documented as they develop. At the present time the official response has generally been to treat Saturday schools as a necessary evil. Sums of money are made available under various schemes, Urban Aid and money under Section XI of the 1966 Local Government Act being the most usual forms of subsidy to these community projects. The government has made available funds to provide additional resources for 'language' teaching for children in schools where there are substantial numbers of immigrant children. It is interesting that LEAs have used this money to fund Saturday schools which teach basic skills. They do this applying the widest possible definition to the concept of language:

By 'language' is understood the ability to communicate freely and accurately over a wide range of experience and encounters. Any activity from directly developing specific linguistic/literary skills to increasing self-confidence would be appropriate. Saturday school, with its emphasis on close adult contact and wide experience, is able to make an appreciable contribution to discrete language development and motivation (local authority confidential memo, June 1977).

Saturday schools are tolerated so long as they appear to be fulfilling a specific need, i.e. building language skills, and so long as a form of control can also be exercised over what happens in these schools. Many people, however, are not sympathetic to the schools; they can understand and accept that Jewish and Muslim children need supplementary (religious and language) education but they fail to see why West Indian children should need Saturday schools. This was a question I put to all teachers, community workers, parents and children I met and spoke with in the course of this research. Black teachers, community workers, parents and children were unanimous in their reactions – Saturday schools were necessary because weekday schools were short-changing the kids. I was told of illiterate and innumerate children who were not getting any attention at all in school, and certainly not the individual intensive attention they needed. There is real bitterness in the West Indian community at the way the school system is seen as treating black children. Another illustration often used is the large numbers of black children in schools for the educationally subnormal and the overwhelming concentration of blacks in the remedial and lower streams of comprehensive schools. It is true to say that the West Indian community generally regards the school system as reinforcing and sanctioning the racist views which exist in society at large and which regard people of African descent as basically inferior to people of European descent.

Officially the problems which West Indian children present in terms of attainment are viewed as a reflection of cultural and educational disadvantage. This disadvantage is seen to include the effects of immigration, unstable family relationships and a 'value system' based on immediate gratification. These theories and ideas are reviewed in Chapter 5.

In general, West Indian parents and their adolescent children have very little faith in the British school system as a whole. In looking at the role which formal education has played in relation to working-class people generally in Britain, this would seem to be a sensible and realistic response to the total situation. In an article in the *Economist* in 1977, Leslie Thorow, the American economist, showed how monetary and fiscal policies to counter labour shortages among white adult males in the United States – for whom the unemployment rate is about half the 7 per cent national average – resulted in unemployment rates of 11 per cent for adult blacks, 15 per cent for white youths and nearly 40 per cent for black youths. Commenting on this, Peter Jenkins wrote in the *Guardian*:

> It is the same sort of story in Britain. The young and the old, the black and the brown, the least skilled and the already poor and inadequate suffer the worst scourges of monetarist orthodoxy applied in the vain hope of avoiding bottlenecks of skilled workers or reducing the wage claims of those who are strong or in short supply.

Without wanting to become embroiled in economic arguments or debates which are not central to the main issue, it is important to note that the reasons why 'immigrants' are here in the first place are economic. Black people came at a time of economic expansion in the late fifties and early sixties. They came to do the jobs the natives didn't want. In the eighties we are faced with a different economic situation, where unemployment is being used as an instrument of policy by both Labour and Conservative Governments.

The Saturday School Movement: The Problems of Official or Self-help Status

The issue of statutory or voluntary status in community work is part of an ongoing discussion on the role of social work generally in contemporary British society. Margaret Norris has developed a four-cell model for identifying styles of community work (Table 4.2).

Table 4.2: Styles of Community Work

		Techniques	
		Directive	Non-directive
Theories	Conflict	(a) Community Action Social Action	(b) Community Development (Conflict Style)
	Consensus	(c) Community Organization Traditional Social Welfare	(d) Community Development (Consensus style)

Source: Norris, 1977.

In this context, *Community Organization*, cell (c), is defined as 'working mainly within the existing system of institutions and established organizations and power relations' (Bloomberg). A *Community Action* approach, cell (a), is defined as being 'in opposition to the norms, or at least some of the norms, held by society as a whole' (Norris). Cells (b) and (d) represent the *Community Development* approach but the relative weight given to predominant norms in society will differ according to leadership styles, (d) stressing consensus and (b) adopting an approach which stresses conflict with society's norms. The approach to community work outlined by Biddle and Biddle and Batten would fall into cell (d). This approach avoids conflict and works towards an agreed process of change. Bloomberg offers a definition of community development as 'a challenge to the established system, calling for direct involvement of the organizer with the rank and file citizenry in order to produce new patterns of involvement and power' which fits well with Warren's view that community development is 'an enterprise which sets about deliberately . . . to reorganize power loci and decision making loci . . . not a system-maintaining approach, it is a system-disturbing approach'. In this sense it falls clearly within the conflict model, cell (b).

Official Projects

Within the analysis provided by Norris, the official groups would fall within the Community Development (Consensus style) of cell (d). They operate within the traditional social work, welfare model, are funded by local or central government, have links with schools in their areas, taking referrals and generally operating a support system. Although there is sometimes conflict this is usually contained within the organization and usually means the dismissal/withdrawal of personnel and their replacement by more co-operative staff. Conflict can also be resolved by changing the nature of the project so that its aims are defined in terms less likely to provoke conflict and more likely to secure a wider base of support, thus achieving consensus, as in the example given earlier where the issue of selection of children on racial grounds was resolved by changing the nature of the Saturday school.

Self-help Projects

The Self-help projects would certainly be put within the Conflict style of community development. This is so, not because they set out theoretically or practically to challenge the location of power in relation to the schooling of West Indian children but because they operate outside the established (welfare and school) system. In that sense it is what Warren describes as a 'system-disturbing' approach. The system being disturbed may not necessarily be the school, it may be, as was the case in Group K, the local Methodist Church. The very fact of groups of parents and volunteers running a Saturday school, responsible to no one, supervised by no one, accountable to no one, can be seen as 'disturbing'. Although, the three self-help Saturday schools included in this research have been located in Norris's cell (b) for the purpose of this discussion, in fact groups which truly belonged within this cell for all purposes would not be included in this study because they would refuse to be involved in, or co-operate with, research of any kind. What one is saying is that there is a continuum on the consensus-conflict scale and groups both self-help and official may include elements of the two approaches in varying degrees. Group E represents the extreme (b) approach, highly professional, well organized, working within a consensus view of the effects of deprivation on the attainment of West Indian children in schools. Group G illustrates an official project which veers towards a conflict model in its analysis of the reasons for the poor attainment of West Indian pupils, but by being funded accepts a consensus role in relation to the solution of these problems. Within the self-help groups, Group I could be seen as consensus in terms of its avoidance of a political stance of any kind and its commitment to providing educational, cultural and recreational facilities for its members. This means that Norris's model, although useful, is limited in its application to the styles of community development adopted by these groups.

The organization and leadership within the self-help groups ranged in style from being very like that of the official projects (Group K) to being completely run by parents who recruited professionals to help them (Group I). Group K was unusual for a self-help project in being run completely by a professional (a teacher) who, for the purposes of the Saturday school, became a volunteer. In the self-help projects, the style of leadership was co-operative, the teachers and other professionals came as volunteers and worked along with the parents. A small number of parents and lay volunteers went on to train as professionals. In Group I, for example, there were three people, one of whom had already undergone this process (change from amateur to expert) and two were currently at teacher-training college. It is interesting that their professionalism did not make them reject or question the need for the Saturday schools; they expressed the feeling that as trained teachers they could give more.

In general it could be said that the system of management and leadership within the community official projects was (loosely) hierarchical. They tended to have an appointed leader to whom others were responsible. This structure was loose and adhered to more or less according to the personalities involved and how

Figure 4.1: Styles of Organization and Management in the Two Types of Saturday Schools

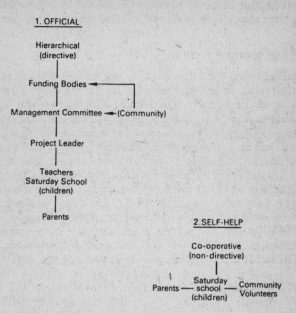

1. OFFICIAL

Hierarchical
(directive)

Funding Bodies

Management Committee — (Community)

Project Leader

Teachers
Saturday School
(children)

Parents

2. SELF-HELP

Co-operative
(non-directive)

Parents — Saturday school (children) — Community Volunteers

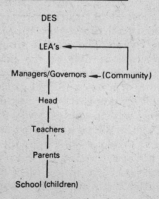

3. THE ESTABLISHED SCHOOL SYSTEM

DES

LEA's

Managers/Governors — (Community)

Head

Teachers

Parents

School (children)

long the projects had been going. The self-help projects were, with one exception, co-operative in style. Again this style was modified to a greater or lesser degree by the personalities involved. But certainly parents ran the self-help projects and they were responsible to themselves and their membership.

Lines of communication:

Organization and management in the official projects closely parallel those of the established school system, with parents near or at the bottom. The recommendations of the Taylor Committee may (if implemented) bring parents in at the level of Managers/Governors in the school system (see (3) Figure 4.1). In the self-help groups the management model and lines of communication followed are horizontal rather than vertical as in (1) and (3). Rowbottom *et al*, whilst acknowledging this co-operative style as a form of 'partnership' for organizational theory purposes, regard it as a 'non-form, without any institutionalized division of functions, duties, or rights'. The self-help groups did all have an 'institutional division' of functions, duties and rights, with treasurers, secretaries, etc.

The status of the group, official or self-help, determined its organizational and management styles. In general, having official status implied a commitment to (or willingness to try) a more formal, hierarchical type of management within a consensus approach to the problems being dealt with. Predictably we associate this approach with more expertise and professional involvement and less lay or amateur participation. This approach is more likely to meet the approval of the funding authorities and therefore attract funds. The self-help groups are truly 'grass-roots'; they function as part of the informal community network of resources which a neighbourhood has developed for itself. The location of power within the group was clearly demonstrated when permission was sought to do the research. In the official projects I was interviewed by the Project Leader: if she/he approved, I was in. With the self-help groups it meant a wait until the next parents' meeting and, after discussion, I might or might not be allowed in. But it was never simply a single person's decision. The major effect of the 'official' formal style of organization and management was that, like the school system, it functioned mainly to exclude parents from active participation in their children's schooling. By insisting on professionalism and expertise, they lost the opportunity of being truly innovative.

It is clear that both groups had problems related to their status as official or self-help – problems of control and management or problems of finance, equipment and the use of volunteers. These problems were felt more by the workers in the projects than by the consumers if the project was run, as most of these projects were, as a service. If the project was actually run by the consumers, i.e. the parents and children, then of course these problems were experienced at all levels. The projects described here do not include any run by parents and children although there was one run by parents and volunteers on a co-operative basis. From my observation of how the Saturday schools actually functioned at the level of the classroom I can only say that I saw no influence there of the status of the group. The Saturday schools seemed concerned to teach basic skills to children – whatever the political and ideological basis of their existence or the views of their leader.

Finance

Having access to funds, premises and other forms of support means that the official projects are more secure and have not got to put a lot of time and energy into fund-raising. The self-help groups may start off in the back or front room of someone's house, them move to a Church Hall or some other premises available for general community use. It is true to say that the resources and premises of the self-help groups compared very unfavourably with those of the community official groups – it was clear that voluntary self-help status also entailed living on a shoe-string. Most groups accepted donations from the children who came, these donations varying from 10 – 25p per session; they were seen as 'donations' rather than charges as they were given on a voluntary basis and were actually meant to cover the cost of orange squash and biscuits. Money left over from 'donations' went to buy books, pencils and other necessities. The two financial statements in Table 4.3 provide a clear illustration of the annual budgets of a community official project and a community self-help project. From these two statements we can see that, although the self-help project obviously spent a lot of time on fund-raising, these raffles, fêtes, discos and dances are clear extensions of the social activities which give the group cohesion. They also extend the support base of the group by involving other members of the public, but most of all they are enjoyable activities.

Thus we can see that the organization, management and finance of community groups which run Saturday schools have implications for the style of work which the group undertakes. The official projects are more formal, having a directive consensus type approach and a (loose) hierarchical structure which tends to exclude parents and other lay people from the decision-making process. The self-help groups adopt a co-operative style of management recruiting professional helpers to work alongside parents on an equal basis. The official projects are better off financially, but the self-help projects, in order to raise money, extend their role into community social activities which have the added benefit of cohesion, extending the base of support and providing enjoyment.

The motives for being self-help rather than official may vary from the clearly political to a simple desire to be independent of official control and to show that ordinary people can do things by themselves. However, the more politically developed argument is that which says that dependence on officials runs contrary to the very idea of self-help and self-reliance. Those who hold this view say that dependence on government and local authorities means control by government and local authorities which restricts autonomy and thus the possibility for change. This basic idea of self-help and self-reliance has a long history in voluntary movements of all kinds and in voluntary welfare movements in Great Britain.

It is within the self-help community groups that one would expect to find more open articulation of the political-activist ideology. However, even where this was true it did not appear to influence what occurred in the actual classroom. That is to say, there were no obvious differences in the way Saturday schools were run in the self-help groups which distinguished them from Saturday schools run by officially-funded projects. However in talking to the workers and volunteers there were clear differences in ideologies between the groups.

Table 4.3: Financial Statement of (a) an Official Project and (b) a Self-help Project

---

(a) Official Project
Receipts and Payments Account for the year ended 31 March 1975

Receipts	£
Community Relations Commission Grant	1188
Donations from Parents	46
	1234

Payments	
Teachers' travelling and disbursements	411
Coach trip to Hastings	53
Books and Materials	152
Christmas Pantomime	50
Christmas Party	25
	691
Surplus carried forward to following year	£543

(b) Self-help Project
Treasurer's Report
Annual Expenditure for year May 1974–April 1975

CR	£	p	DR	£	p
Subscription	106	52	Rent	21	00
Raffle	1	40	Holiday Booking	5	50
Fete	21	75	House Contributions	5	00
Disco	9	27	School Books	141	43
Dance	152	59	Other expenses	60	35
Contribution	3	70			
Odd Money		63			
TOTAL	295	86		233	28

At the end of the financial year 30 April 1975 the Group had a balance of £62 58p.

Saturday Schools and Weekday Schools: Contact

The weekday schools' response to the Saturday schools is interesting and somewhat perplexing. Teachers have fought long and hard to be recognized as 'professionals': it is argued that teaching is based on particular skills and knowledge, the acquisition of which necessitates prolonged formal education and training in specialized institutions (Robbins Report, James Report). The largest teachers' union (NUT) has come out against parents or other 'lay' people being involved in the teaching process, and this policy is generally shared by all the smaller teachers' unions. Yet the writers of the North Lewisham Project Report describe how a list of under-achievers was supplied to them by one of the local primary schools. This type of contact between Saturday schools and schools in the local area was quite common among the Saturday schools I visited – especially in relation to primary schools. Contact with secondary schools tended to be more spasmodic, but this could have been due to the fact that membership of Saturday schools tended to fall off in the over fourteens. The point I am trying to make is that, contrary to expectation and policy with regard to other types of alternative education, teachers and education authorities appear to adopt a rather benign attitude towards the Supplementary schools run by the West Indian communities and local Community Relations Councils and various other grant-aided projects. Indeed many Saturday schools use school buildings and sometimes staff at a local school might also work in the Saturday school. The relationship is not always amicable, however, and I was told of one instance where a Saturday school had been established with help and encouragement from a local primary Head, who later 'turned against' the Saturday school when black children who were attending started criticizing teachers for not telling them about Black History and also started comparing the teachers in the Saturday schools with those in the weekday schools: 'My Saturday school teacher does/doesn't do it like that. S/he says . . . ' etc. The Head called the project leader in and explained to him that he had helped to set the school up in order to make things better for the children, but its effect had been to increase the strain on teachers and this did not ultimately benefit the pupils.

Professional Teachers in Saturday Schools

The teachers in the Saturday schools were mainly West Indian. There was an occasional white teacher involved because of personal contact with one of the members – over a two-year period and visits to some fourteen projects having over eighty staff I met three white teachers – and these were in officially funded projects, two in one LEA which insists that Saturday schools should be multiracial.

The West Indian teachers I met were completely convinced of the need for Saturday schools. They were generally critical of the school system, especially what they saw as its lack of discipline and 'standards' and felt that this meant that West Indian children were at a particular disadvantage. Some said that schools were part of a society that was generally racist, and reflected that racism. Some felt that it was not necessary to see things in those terms. On this question of discipline and whether West Indian children require more formal constraints in order to work successfully in schools, it is generally true that in the Caribbean there are few discipline problems in schools; it is also true that Caribbean schools are more strict, formal and, some say, regimented in their outlook.

In general, these black teachers are still optimistic about what formal education could do for black children. Taking themselves as examples, they felt that black children could succeed by hard work and that once through the educational hurdles 'the world', or at least the Third World, would be their oyster. The view that these teachers took of black talent was quite different from that encountered in the regular school system which was utilitarian in the extreme: 'Africa and the Caribbean need skilled man/womanpower and if these black kids want to make it they can or they can join the dole queues in Britain'. As I mentioned earlier, mobility for West Indians in Britain has a different meaning entirely from that commonly accepted in sociology – it might mean moving around the world, across the Atlantic, anywhere where things are better. There was much bitterness about the indifference and lack of motivation of many black pupils – especially boys. In the Saturday schools it was always the boys who dropped out first, usually when they were about thirteen or fourteen, whereas the girls kept on until sometimes after sixteen. I saw many teenage girls being helped with their 'O' level work at these Saturday schools. The teachers felt that many blacks were reacting against the school system and in the process destroying themselves and any chance they might have of a 'good' life. Teachers made a point of telling the kids over and over that they went to school to learn and that they must ignore 'everything else'. One teacher said to me, 'Once a kid starts reacting to the system, it's suicide', and told me about West Indian children she had known and taught who entered secondary school at eleven bright and eager to learn. By thirteen these same kids were hostile tearaways, who were rejecting everything the school had to offer – including her, a black teacher. She felt bitter and frustrated and said that there was no way to continue except by leaving teaching altogether, which she has since done.

Maintaining Order and Discipline in Saturday Schools

It is well known that in British schools, West Indian children are seen as boisterous, hyperactive children who present teachers with particular problems of classroom management and discipline. Many West Indian teachers and parents regard the schools themselves as being responsible for this state of affairs. They see English schools as being too 'free and easy' and offering children no real discipline. I was therefore interested to see how teachers and others in these Supplementary schools managed the problems of maintaining order and discipline amongst the children who attended them. I should have realized that these problems would hardly exist in a voluntary project which children attended either because they wanted to or to please their parents. It may be that trouble-makers just do not go to Saturday schools, but during all the time I spent observing these projects I did not see any boisterous or hyperactive behaviour; in fact, the children were unnaturally 'good', sitting quietly working alone or in small groups or attached to an adult. Teachers said that they had no problems with discipline;

children knew they came to work and they worked. Of course $2\frac{1}{2}$–3 hours of study is not a long time. Even so, when I think of some of the groups I have been involved in running, the windows that were broken, kids going beserk, smashing chairs and each other (and these were over the same length of time – $2\frac{1}{2}$–3 hours), I know that their brevity is not the full explanation. It must be as the teachers said; the children who came knew what was expected of them and they got on with it.

Teaching Methods

Mostly children worked in small groups or alone on something they had been working on for some time, or were attached to an adult who helped them, over time. There was not a lot of 'talk and chalk' – the small numbers, varying ages and abilities of the children made that impossible. A lot of time was spent by teachers preparing material for the Saturday schools, especially in those projects which placed great stress on using completely or almost completely black teaching material and books.

Aims and Objectives

What was common to all the projects described here, and to others which I visited but which are not included, was the absolute conviction that West Indian children needed supplementary schooling which these Saturday schools had to provide. I expected to find major differences in emphasis between officially sponsored and self-help groups, the officially sponsored being more closely controlled and more accountable to the sponsoring bodies for what they were doing, but this did not appear to be the case. I did not find the self-help groups in particular stressing the cultural background and origins of the kids more; this seemed implicit in all the community groups, but the overriding concern was with teaching the children basic skills. Self-concept did not figure as an issue among the people who were running these groups. It was not something that came up spontaneously in discussion as it had done with the school-based groups; it had to be put to these teachers, whose priorities seemed far more practical. The general feeling I picked up from them was that some black kids believed what the white world told them about themselves and these had to be helped, but the way to help them was to offer them the opportunity to achieve something, to let them see themselves reading well, writing, getting their sums right and then they would have something solid on which to build their self-image. It was felt that positive self-concept could only be maintained through effort and attainment. In listening to this view I was struck by the similarity of these arguments to those that had been going on between social casework and community work where the social worker argues for the achievement of personal autonomy through growth, mainly as the result of therapy, and community workers argue for the achievement of growth and individual autonomy through 'social action' to change the conditions which (in their view) produced the problems in the first place. What we are seeing in the Saturday schools is the development of a strategy based on action, rather than the acceptance of a passive role by parents and the community in the schooling of their children.

Saturday's Children: The Reasons why Children Attend Saturday Schools

The three most common reasons given for attending Saturday school were:

1. *Social* – because a friend/brother or sister is going;
2. *Educational* – to improve school work, usually prompted by parents, but often self-motivated, especially amongst children aged thirteen and over.
3. *Parental* – because their parents sent them.

Parents and children learn about the existence of the Saturday schools through the informal network of communication which operates in all communities. A child will give as his/her reason for coming that he/she came along with 'my friend' or 'my mother sent me because she wants me to learn'. What usually happens is that parents approach an adult in the Saturday school and ask about what goes on there and what kind of help their children will get. Very often the parents may stay all or most of this first session. Sometimes if the parents live outside the area, the project workers may discuss with them the possibility of starting a group in their own area. If they are interested, they will be encouraged to come along to the Saturday school to 'learn the ropes' and it will be suggested that they 'sound out' other parents in their own area. The Saturday schools aim to serve a catchment area within a mile or two of where they meet. When children turn up at the school they are not questioned about their intentions. For the first two or three Saturdays they come and join in. When it seems as if they are going to be regular members, they are given books and attempts are made to find out if they have any particular problems which need immediate help. Otherwise they work with a small group or individually with an adult helper. The system of selection and admission varies and some Saturday schools are more formal in their admission procedure, keeping registers etc., but I never saw any child turned away or told that she/he could only be allowed in if first brought by an adult. This means that many of the children in the Saturday schools come completely voluntarily, and there did not appear to be a lot of pressure from parents to attend. In the case of children under ten-years-old, very often they were brought by parents who were themselves helpers, or by older brothers and sisters.

Although there was no selection procedure, it is clear that some children would get more out of the Saturday school than others. It might be argued that, in the absence of strict parental pressure, or educational welfare officers or social workers to enforce attendance, the children who continued to come would be those who received a considerable degree of success and positive reinforcement and the other children would merely drop out. This argument is difficult to counter in any completely satisfactory way, except to say that there are children in the Saturday school who are classified as ESN or who attend schools for the maladjusted and emotionally disturbed, and these children continue to attend. There are also children with handicaps, including deafness – the schools accept any child who turns up. No Saturday school complained of not having enough children; it was usually the case that demand was too high to be satisfied with scarce resources. The reasons for leaving were usually the family moving away, although one Saturday school felt that the numbers of boys tended to fall after fourteen-years-old. For the over fifteens the Saturday school tends to serve as a study centre where they receive coaching for examinations. Very often they also receive help during the week from one of the project workers or someone attached to the project who has particular knowledge or expertise in their subject area.

If the impression has been created of a 'mental sweat-shop', where children sit working away at sums and reading when they ought to be playing and exploring their environment, this would be a distortion of the Saturday school image. The atmosphere is extremely relaxed, informal and friendly. The children seem happy and since attendance is voluntary one has to assume that they would not come if they did not want to. There are many outings and activities associated with the Saturday schools which make them part of the family's life. There are shows which the children put on, fund-raising activities organized by and for the Saturday schools, day-trips and other outings which take the children and their families and friends exploring the environment together. Where in any case the Saturday schools are run by parents, they are an integral part of all activities and the divisions between Saturday school and home be come somewhat blurred. Where Saturday schools are run by official projects there is less parental involvement, but there is more money to spend and children can enjoy many treats and outings through being at the Saturday schools. So although the main purpose of the Saturday schools is to teach children basic skills, to improve their attainment in weekday schools and to heighten their aspirations, the children who attend them benefit in ways other than those connected with school performance.

The overall impression created by the children in this group is of high motivation and ambition and a belief in their ability to succeed through hard work. On the whole they are very appreciative of what parents are trying to do for them. Even though they can be critical of parents, they tend to modify their criticisms by expressions of understanding. The suggestion that these groups encourage children away from their parents was not borne out by the children in this study.

5. Does Self-concept Make a Difference?

This chapter will draw together all the findings on the groups studied – the MRE group, the Saturday schools, Official and Self-help, and a group of children chosen for purposes of comparison only. This group consisted of eighty-nine West Indian children in primary and secondary schools. In common with all the children involved in this research, these children attended schools in the selected London area. The schools were selected to achieve geographical spread from those schools with above average percentages (40 per cent or more) of West Indian children on roll. The chapter first describes this group and then goes on to compare the self-concept and attitudes of each of the four groups in the sample.

The comparison group consisted of pupils from:

School 1 – girls' comprehensive (3rd year, 14- to 15-year-olds);

School 2 – boys' comprehensive (3rd year, 13- to 15-year-olds;

School 3 – final year primary class (10- to 11-year-olds).

School 1: Girls' Comprehensive

This is an ex-secondary modern school in a very racially mixed area of London, which includes a large West Indian population. The school buildings are old and somewhat dilapidated. There are several wooden prefab buildings, housing additional classrooms. There is a social worker attached to the school, which can usually be regarded as a sign that the school admits to having serious problems. The school has a poor reputation and is not the first choice of school for any of the groups who live in the area, particularly among West Indian parents. It has a falling roll and will probably be closed or amalgamated with another school in the next five to ten years, so its future is by no means secure.

School 2: Boys' Comprehensive

This is a purpose-built boys' comprehensive school which has never reached its full complement of boys – having been built to accommodate 1300 and never exceeding the 800 mark. The Headmaster sees himself as upholding traditional standards of work, dress and behaviour. The school is associated with a Special Education Project, i.e. a centre for children with 'problems'. Many disruptive West Indian children, who make up between 35–40 per cent of the school, are referred to this centre. The English children tend to be referred for truanting. The workers at the centre told me that the centre could easily become 'all black' but they maintain a spread of 'problems' and thus a spread of race by insisting on a variety of referrals. It is interesting to note that the Headmaster was very reluctant to discuss the centre and told me that the links were not 'very strong'. But I later found out that the teachers and workers at the centre had struggled for autonomy and separation from the school against the Headmaster's wishes; he originally wanted the centre as a unit within the school grounds and under his control. Yet when I spoke to him at length on three occasions he insisted that there were no special problems in his school with any of the different groups. In our third interview, when he had still not mentioned the centre, I asked him about its role and its connection with the school. It was then that he explained to me that the links were 'not very strong' and that the centre helped a small number of boys who were experiencing particular personal problems – more or less as an extension of the pastoral care system.

I tried to find out from the Headmaster why the school had never been completely full. He explained this in terms of its single-sex education – which he said was less popular with parents than before. He also said that there was a problem with catchment areas which meant that parents who might prefer a boys' school were unable to send their boys there, as it was outside their area. He thought that a boys' school should cater for a wider geographical area and offer parents more choice.

School 3 : Final Year Primary Class

This school is housed in a nineteenth-century building, very rundown and badly in need of modernization. There are at least 80 per cent West Indian pupils, and a West Indian male senior member of staff. The Headmaster was very reluctant for me to do the research in his school; he felt that there is much too much 'useless' research done and that there was nothing special about his school that warranted it being included in my research project. He did not feel strongly enough to object completely and grudgingly consented, provided I got the required LEA permission and took no more than 45 minutes to complete all the work. Fortunately on the day I went to test the children he was away at a meeting and I found the staff extremely helpful and co-operative.

Although I had been warned to expect difficulties during the test, as many children had reading problems, in fact most of the children finished in the expected time of half an hour and there were no particular difficulties over reading the test. Many of the teachers were extremely curious to know what the children had written and because the two classes were being tested simultaneously for a short while (due to overlap) I could not be present throughout the final minutes of the first session. I found the supervising teacher reading through the test (he had heard me tell the kids that no teachers would see the test) and he expressed great surprise at some of the things the children had written in the sentence completion. Some teachers added further information on to the questionnaires as they were handed in, or made comments about individual children: 'regular truant', 'born liar', 'difficult family background, no father/mother at home'. This was in spite of the fact that I constantly stressed that I did not want any 'school information' on the children. It seemed to me that some teachers were worried that I might get the wrong impression, by believing children who were born liars and those whose family background made them unreliable sources of information. This problem of teachers' curiosity about the test information, although present in some degree in most schools (but no community projects) was especially striking among teachers in this primary school.

Self-concept of the Comparison Group

(a)   NOW AND AGAIN I REALIZE THAT I . . .
(b)   WHAT I LIKE MOST ABOUT MYSELF . . .
(c)   SOMETIMES WHEN I THINK ABOUT MYSELF . . .

Boys

Aged 13   (a)   I am very popular with girls
          (b)   is my way of getting girls
          (c)   I am very nice

Aged 14   (a)   not thinking right
          (b)   is that I got brains
          (c)   superior

Aged 13   (a)   I will not get a job if I don't do my work at
                school
          (b)   everything, the way I make friends easily,
                especially with girls
          (c)   I think how fantastic I am and brilliant and
                great etc.

Girls

Aged 14   (a)   I am getting bad
          (b)   is that I am getting pretty and intellegante
          (c)   I think that I am getting beautiful every day

Aged 10   (a)   might not have the brains to be a teacher
          (b)   is my fingernails
          (c)   I wish I was more brainy than I am

Aged 15   (a)   bully some of my friends
          (b)   is my hair
          (c)   I think I am very lucky

Attitudes to School of the Comparison Group

(a)   WHAT I LIKE MOST ABOUT SCHOOL . . .
(b)   WHAT I DISLIKE MOST ABOUT SCHOOL . . .

Boys

Aged 14   (a)   friends and to learn about things
          (b)   dinner and some teachers

Aged 10   (a) learning about things
            (b) is wakeing up in the morning and short winter
                 holidays

Aged 13   (a) nothing
            (b) everything

Girls
Aged 14   (a) is that I know a lot and I cannot get into
                 trouble for being somewhere else
            (b) is the teachers put you on report for the least
                 little things you do

Aged 10   (a) is when we have games and needlework and
                 when the teachers are kind
            (b) is when the teachers are bothering me

Aged 15   (a) is meeting your friends and going to subjects
                 you like and getting on with the teachers
            (b) is that some pupils are bullies and think they
                 can boss you about

Aspirations of the Comparison Group

SOME DAY I WOULD LIKE TO . . .

Boys
Aged 11   . . . be a good football player
Aged 14   . . . go back to country JAMA (crossed out) very
                   rich
Aged 14   . . . be rich and go anywhere I like and of course help
                   people
Aged 10   . . . work with my father at his work place

Girls
Aged 14   . . . be a secretary or typist
Aged 14   . . . go to the West Indies and become success-
                   ful
Aged 11   . . . be a doctor or a tennis player
Aged 15   . . . have a car, with my mates, share a flat together
                   and enjoy life, go around Europe and most of all
                   have a pleasant job

Attitudes to Parents and Home of the Comparison Group

(a)   TO A CHILD PARENTS ARE . . .
(b)   WHAT I LIKE MOST ABOUT HOME . . .

Boys
Aged 11   (a)   nearly everything one could hope for
            (b)   loving parents and a nice mother

Aged 14   (a)   good
            (b)   it's cool

Aged 13   (a)   sometimes a nuisance and they still think
                   you're babies you can't do this and you can't
                   do that
            (b)   the record player

Girls
Aged 10   (a)   I love my parents very much and I wish to stay
                   home until I get married
            (b)   I like to play about with my parents and have
                   fun

Aged 14   (a)   silly and don't understand you
            (b)   it is cosy

Aged 15   (a)   loving and understanding at times
            (b)   is that I'm at home and I'm with my mother
                   and sisters and parents and I've got most of my
                   freedom

Summary of Findings on the Comparison Group

1. *Self-concept*
The self-concept score was similar to that of the MRE group
falling well within the average range on all three tests.

2. *Attitudes to School*
These were generally negative. Only 35 per cent liked school for
Intellectual reasons, whereas nearly half (48 per cent) liked it for
Friendship and Social reasons and 23 per cent for Physical
(sports, games) reasons. Fifty-five per cent of pupils disliked
teachers, teachers' attitudes and the power of teachers. Children

in the primary school (School 3) were the least critical and
negative towards teachers: 12 replies (34 per cent) included
references to dislike of teachers as compared with 22 (73 per
cent) in the girls' comprehensive (School 1) and 15 (63 per cent)
in the boys' comprehensive (School 2).

3. *Aspirations*
Success, Money/Self-fulfilment account for the largest category
of replies: 44 (49 per cent). Those aspiring to professional-type
occupations account for 25 (28 per cent); 13 (15 per cent) of
these occur in the primary school group, 3 (3 per cent) in the
boys' comprehensive and 9 (10 per cent) in the girls'
comprehensive.

4. *Attitudes to Parents and Family Life*
Seventy-nine (89 per cent) positive and 16 (18 per cent) negative
or critical statements were made about the children's parents.
Similarly, home was seen by the majority in 'expressive' terms:
21 (24 per cent) liked home for its 'emotional security'; 26 (29
per cent) for identity with family; 20 (22 per cent) because of its
safety and 13 (15 per cent) for the opportunity to engage in
physical tasks (including helping with housework and baby-
sitting). Seventeen (19 per cent) mentioned functional/material
reasons – having somewhere to live, features such as type of
decorations, TV, record player, etc.

Does 'Enrichment' Make a Difference to Self-concept?

There were three main hypotheses. These state:

1. On an instrument devised to measure self-concept, West
Indian children will have overall low self-concept scores.

2. Children taking part in cultural enrichment and other
types of compensatory education projects aimed at improving
their self-concept will have higher scores than those who have
not.

3. Children who attend Supplementary schools will have

higher self-concept scores than those who have (a) been 'compensated' or (b) received just ordinary education.

There were two subsidiary hypotheses:

4. West Indian children attending schools where the intake of black children is high (over 50 per cent) will have higher self-concept scores than those where members of their group are in a smaller minority.
5. Overall, girls will have higher self-concept scores than boys.

Table 5.1 shows the sex distribution and the numerical content of the whole sample.

Table 5.1: The Complete Sample

Group Type	Girls	Boys	Age	Total
School-based				
MRE Projects	20	56	13–15	76
Community Official Projects	29	24	10–15	53
Community Self-help Projects	26	20	10–15	46
Comparison Group	44	45	10–15	89
	119	145		264

Table 5.2 Shows the self-concept and self-esteem scores of each group with the scores of girls and boys listed separately.

Table 5.2: Self-concept/Self-esteem Scores of the Complete Sample

Group	No.	Age	Piers-Harris		Girls		Boys	
			M	SD	M	SD	M	SD
School MRE	76	13–15	45.5	9.9	48.4	8.6	44.5	9.7
Comm. Official	53	10–15	48.8	9.6	51.3	7.5	45.8	11.2
Comm. Self-help	46	10–15	49.5	9.2	51.9	7.6	46.5	10.5
School Comparison	89	10–15	47.0	9.8	48.0	9.4	46.2	10.2

Group	No.	Age	Ziller		Girls		Boys	
			M	SD	M	SD	M	SD
School MRE	76	13–15	13.6	2.9	13.6	3.4	13.6	2.8
Comm. Official	53	10–15	12.9	3.0	12.9	2.6	13.0	3.4
Comm. Self-help	46	10–15	13.0	3.8	13.6	3.8	12.0	3.6
School Comparison	89	10–15	12.1	3.0	11.7	2.9	12.6	3.2

Key: M = mean
SD = standard deviation

Piers-Harris

The lowest Piers-Harris group score was 45.5 obtained by the School MRE group. The highest score on the Piers-Harris scale was 51.9 obtained by girls in the Community Self-help group, followed by girls in the Community Official group with 51.3. Girls in the School MRE and Comparison groups had similar scores. The highest boys' score was 46.5 for boys in the Community Self-help group, followed by School MRE with 46.2. The biggest difference, 7.4 points, is between the girls in the Community Self-help group and boys in the School MRE group. In terms of educational intervention, the girls in the school-based MRE group have virtually the same mean score as girls in the Comparison group and boys in the Comparison group actually score slightly higher (1.7) than boys in the School MRE group.

Ziller

On the Ziller item, the School MRE group obtained the highest mean score for any group, boys and girls having the same mean score of 13.6 (total possible score 18). It is difficult to explain the discrepancy between the Piers-Harris and Ziller scores of the School MRE group, except to suggest that the nature of the items themselves elicits a particular type of response. Thus, although some children circled Piers-Harris negative-type responses, when faced with the Ziller circles and a collection of people, including themselves, they may then put themselves 'first' sometimes, inserting facial features and writing 'me' in the circle representing self. The findings for all other groups are fairly consistent between the two measures; it may be that the explanation of the Ziller score for the School-based MRE group is simply, as Carlson has suggested, an indication of male preference for diagrammatic representation. There were 56 boys and 20 girls in the School MRE group.

Examples of Ziller Self-esteem Items

The circles below stand for people. Mark each circle with the letter standing for one of the people on the list. Do this in any way you like but use each person only once and do not omit anyone.

F – someone who is failing
H – the happiest person you know
K – someone you know who is kind

S – yourself
SU – someone who is successful
ST – the strongest person you know

13-year-old girl (high self-esteem, total score of 18)

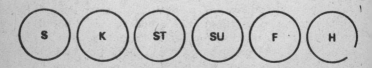

This child placed herself to the extreme left on all three items; she also achieved a raw Piers-Harris score of 63. (Mean Piers-Harris score for girls was 49.7.) Her sentence completion items on 'self' were:

(a) NOW AND AGAIN I REALIZE THAT I . . . sometimes do not do as I should

(b) WHAT I LIKE MOST ABOUT MYSELF . . . I can get on with people and I try to help people when they need it

(c) SOMETIMES WHEN I THINK ABOUT MYSELF . . . I wonder if I will grow up and be able to earn my own living. (She also wants 'to work for enough money and treat my parents to a trip to the West Indies'.)

15-year-old boy (average self-esteem, total score of 12)

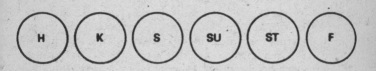

Raw Piers-Harris score 75 (mean Piers-Harris for boys: 45.3). Sentence completion:

(a) NOW AND AGAIN I REALIZE THAT I . . . am handsome

(b) WHAT I LIKE MOST ABOUT MYSELF . . . my hair

(c) SOMETIMES WHEN I THINK ABOUT MYSELF . . . I don't. (He also wants 'to be famous'.)

14-year-old girl (low self-esteem, total score of 4)

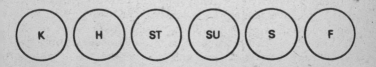

Raw Piers-Harris score of 74 (mean Piers-Harris for girls: 49.7).
Sentence completion:

   (a) NOW AND AGAIN I REALIZE THAT I . . . am growing up
and that now responsibility is held on me
   (b) WHAT I LIKE MOST ABOUT MYSELF . . . is that I am not
dependent and independent. I'm just me
   (c) SOMETIMES WHEN I THINK ABOUT MYSELF . . . I wonder
if what I want to be would come through but it will only come
through if I work at it. (She also wants to 'become an actress, I
would like to sing, too. I like banking'.)

It is difficult to account for the low self-esteem score of this girl,
except to hazard a guess that it probably reflects her uncertainty
about possible success or failure in future life.
   Ziller takes self-esteem to be the value which one places on
the perceived self: 'Self-esteem is the individual's perception of
his worth' (1973). He also postulates that high self-esteem is a
facet of the self-concept 'which enables the person to persevere
during information processing periods involving data relevant
to the self'. Whereas persons with low self-esteem do not possess
this well-developed conceptual buffer for evaluative stimuli, the
person with low self-esteem is field dependent; the individual's
behaviour is directly linked to environmental circumstances. It
is clear that an analysis of black personality and self-concept
which takes into account the African perspective would not
expect to find people of African origin living in the Americas
and Britain being 'field dependent' for self-evaluation, if by 'field
dependency' is meant the objective evaluation of one's own
socio-economic status, or the socio-economic status of the
group of which one is a member.
   It is this assumption which has led to so much mis-
understanding and confusion in theories about black self-
concept. Theorists have assumed that self-concept is related to
objective 'knowledge' about oneself and one's group. But since
one's objective position is dependent on factors largely outside
one's own control, it is difficult to support the logic of this
deduction. We cannot assume that the individual uses objective
knowledge about socio-economic status or the overall position
which has been assigned to his/her group as a basis for his/her

own self-evaluation. Stack, in an anthropological study of lower-class black families, showed the adaptive strategies which these families used to survive and showed how their criteria for self-evaluation differed from that of welfare and other officials with whom they came into contact. Willis (1978b) in his study of 'motorcycle' and 'hippie' cultures, showed how groups develop their own criteria for evaluating self and others; often these are not only different from, but can be in conflict with established 'norms'. Any such 'field dependency' would result in negative self-concept and low self-esteem as it would inevitably be a reflection of the negative value placed on the group by the dominant society.

Hypothesis 1

(a) *Piers-Harris Children's Self-concept Scale*

The mean Piers-Harris self-concept score of the total population of children between the ages of 10 and 15 years was 47.2, SD 9.7 (33 percentile). Piers-Harris state that average scores are those between the 31st and 20th percentile or raw scores of between 46 to 60. Piers-Harris give the mean of their normative sample (based on 1183 public school children, 8- to 13-years-old) as 51.84 with a standard deviation of 13.87. But they add this caution: 'Like many personality instruments these measures of central tendency reflect negative slowness or the tendency of the general population to respond in a generally positive fashion' (Piers-Harris Manual). On the other hand, Wylie (1976) has expressed general concern over rating scales which 'confound' unreliable responding with poor self-regard. She expressed the view that a random response would result in a score of about 40 and quoted Piers' research where 20 per cent of subjects had this score. It was because of the problem of unreliable response on a fixed response 80-item scale that other types of tasks were included. However, if we accept the Piers-Harris self-concept test as a reliable instrument for the purpose of research we have to conclude that Hypothesis 1 was not supported, for this group of West Indian children scored within the average range on this instrument. It must be said that many children objected to the Piers-Harris test because of having to reply yes or no when they

wanted to say 'sometimes', 'now and again' or something fairly
neutral.

(b) *Ziller*

Hypothesis 1 failed to be supported on the Ziller self-esteem
item, the mean score out of a possible raw score of 18 points
being 12.9, SD 3.2 for the total sample, indicating above average
positive self-evaluation for this group.

In completing this item, many children used the word 'first'
for the person put in at the extreme left: 'I will put my
father/mother/myself first' was a comment I overheard on
several occasions. Information gained from discussions with
several groups of children both in the main research study and
also from preliminary testing groups, confirms Ziller's belief in
a general left-right hierarchy. That is to say, there appears to be a
general tendency for people to place themselves or people they
see as important to the left.

In discussing the questionnaire with children, I sometimes
asked, 'Why did you complete it like this? Why did you put
yourself there?' For those who had put themselves to the
extreme left or near, the answer came easily, 'I had to put myself
first.' Very often, mother or father was placed first and the
answer then would be, 'I had to be next to my Mum/Dad.' For
those who had placed themselves to the extreme right, the
replies were not so easy to give: 'I don't know', 'I had to put
myself somewhere' and vague, uneasy replies of that nature were
given.

(c) *Sentence Completion*

The sample as a whole had a total mean score of 3.8, (SD 0.8) out
of a possible total score of 2–6 (2 = high self-esteem, 6 = low
self-esteem). Overall, the 264 West Indian children were found
to have average-high self-concept/self-esteem scores on the
three tests used in this research.

Hypothesis 2

(a) *Piers-Harris*

On the Piers-Harris test, the School MRE group achieved a
mean score of 45.5 (SD 9.6), whereas the School Comparison

group had a mean score of 47.0 (SD 9.8). The score for girls in the School MRE group was 48.4 (SD 8.8) and for boys 44.5 (SD 9.7). There was a disproportionate number of boys in the School MRE group, 56 boys to 20 girls. (This was due to the fact that one of the girls' schools experienced a change of Head and withdrew from the project.) As boys overall had lower Piers-Harris scores, this tended to depress the score of the School MRE group. If the Piers-Harris score for boys in the School MRE group is compared with that of boys in the Comparison group:

School MRE	*P-H Score*		*No.*
	M	SD	
Boys	44.5	9.7	56
Girls	48.4	8.8	20
School Comparison			
Boys	46.2	10.3	45
Girls	48.0	9.4	44

we see that there were no major differences between school groups but that boys in the MRE group had slightly lower scores than boys in the Comparison group, a difference of 1.7. There were differences between boys and girls on the Piers-Harris scale in each group: a difference of 3.9 points in the school MRE group and of 1.8 in the School Comparison group. The Comparison group as a whole had a marginally higher mean score of 47.0 as against the School MRE score of 45.5.

(b) *Ziller*

The Ziller self-esteem item failed to support the hypothesis concerning differences between the School MRE and Comparison groups. The mean scores for both groups were almost exactly the same: 13.6 (SD 2.9) for the School MRE group and 12.9 (SD 3.0) for the School Comparison group, a difference of 0.7.

(c) *Sentence Completion*

The mean score on the sentence completion item was 4.2 (SD 0.8) for the School MRE group and 3.9 (SD 0.8) for the School

Comparison group, a difference of 0.3, indicating that the School MRE group wrote in a slightly more self-critical vein, but again, the differences are minor.

With such slight differences in self-concept and self-esteem scores between groups of children in schools where curriculum innovatory programmes are in progress and schools where there has been no attempt to be innovatory, it is difficult to see any evidence that the innovatory projects have been effective in terms of enhancing the self-concept of the groups of children in this study.

Hypothesis 3

(a) *Piers-Harris*
The Piers-Harris test did lend some support to this hypothesis, the self-concept scores of the Community Self-help group being slightly higher than the scores of the other groups on this item.

	M	SD
Community Self-help	49.5	9.2
Community Official	48.8	9.6
School MRE	45.5	9.6
School Comparison	47.0	9.8

(b) *Ziller*
The scores on this item were similar for all groups.

	M	SD
Community Self-help	13.0	3.8
Community Official	12.9	3.0
School MRE	13.6	2.9
School Comparison	12.1	3.0

The total Ziller score for the Saturday Supplementary school groups is 12.9, which is 0.7 lower than the School MRE group and 0.8 higher then the Comparison group. Again, this is a very slight difference.

(c) *Sentence Completion*

This test is scored from 2–6, the higher the total score the less positive the self-esteem.

	M	SD
Community Self-help	3.3	0.8
Community Official	4.1	0.8
School MRE	4.2	0.8
School Comparison	3.9	0.8

The Community Self-help group scored lowest (3.3), followed by the Comparison group (3.9). The scores of the Community

Figure 5.1: Piers-Harris and Ziller Scores for the Four Groups (Hypothesis 3)

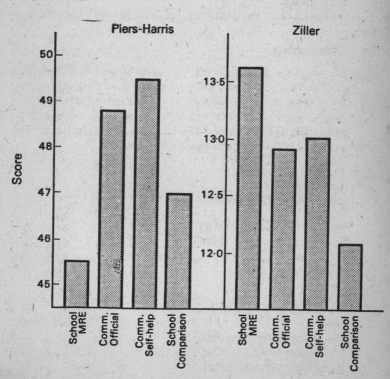

Official and School MRE groups were similar. This means that the joint mean score for children in the Saturday Supplementary schools was 3.7, which is lower than the School MRE group by 0.5 and lower than the Comparison group by 0.2. These differences are very small, but tend to lend weak support to the hypothesis.

Figure 5.1 illustrates the Piers-Harris and Ziller scores for each group. The most striking feature is the difference between the scores of the School MRE group on the two test items – scoring the lowest on the Piers-Harris self-concept scale and the highest on the Ziller social symbols self-esteem task. This will be discussed more fully later in relation to the hypothesis dealing with sex differences, but it is suggested that this distortion is produced by the disproportionate number of boys in the School MRE group.

Overall, this hypothesis received weak support from the data.

Hypothesis 4

This hypothesis dealt with the percentage of West Indian children in a school and its relationship to self-concept scores. There were no major differences on the self-concept and self-esteem scores between children in schools with a high proportion of West Indian children (over 50 per cent), and those where the percentage was less than 50 per cent.

(a) *Piers-Harris*
Schools with high percentage (50 + %) of West Indian Pupils

School	%	No.	P-H M	SD
Boys' Comprehensive (MRE)	65 +	20	44.5	11.3
Boys' Comprehensive (MRE)	65 +	22	45.6	7.5
Girls' Comprehensive (Comparison)	60 +	30	47.6	9.4
Primary (Comparison)	85 +	35	48.6	9.2

Schools with 35-50% West Indian Pupils

School	%	No.	P-H M	SD
Mixed Comprehensive (MRE)	30-40	20	46.1	8.7
Boys' Comprehensive (Comparison)	35-40	24	44.2	11.0
Mixed Comprehensive (MRE)	35	14	45.9	12.0

Schools with over 50 per cent had a mean Piers-Harris score of 46.8; those with 35–50 per cent had a mean Piers-Harris score of 45.4. Thus those schools with high numbers of West Indian pupils had a marginally higher score by 1.4 points.

(b) *Ziller*

The Ziller item confirmed the general trend in terms of similarities rather than differences between the groups.

Hypothesis 5

The fifth and final hypothesis has to do with sex and states that overall the self-concept scores of girls will be higher than the self-concept scores of boys in the sample.

This hypothesis did receive some support from the data. On the Piers-Harris scales used the 119 girls consistently scored higher than the 145 boys.

Test	Girls		Boys	
	M	SD	M	SD
Piers-Harris	49.7	8.6	45.3	10.2
Ziller	12.7	3.2	13.0	3.1

There was a marginal difference of 0.3 in favour of boys on the Ziller item. However, on the Piers-Harris test girls scored 4.4 points more than boys and on the Sentence Completion items the girls scored 3.7 and boys scored 4.1, which means that girls' writing was slightly more positive in content than boys.

Figure 5.2 illustrates the scores for girls and boys on the Piers-Harris and Ziller items. The sex difference is quite marked on the Piers-Harris item – girls consistently score higher than boys. However, on the Ziller self-social symbols tasks, boys actually score higher than girls in the Community Official and School Comparison groups and equal with girls in the School MRE group; only in the Community Self-help group do girls score higher than boys on this item. Carlson has suggested that symbolic spacial ordering of experience, especially represen-tation of self-esteem in terms of height or in terms of degree of left-right location on a page, may be a masculine characteristic. These findings tend to support Carlson's suggestion.

Hypothesis 5 did receive some support from the data, on two of the three items used (the Piers-Harris and Sentence

Figure 5.2: A Comparison between the Piers-Harris and Ziller Scores for Girls and Boys (Hypothesis 5)

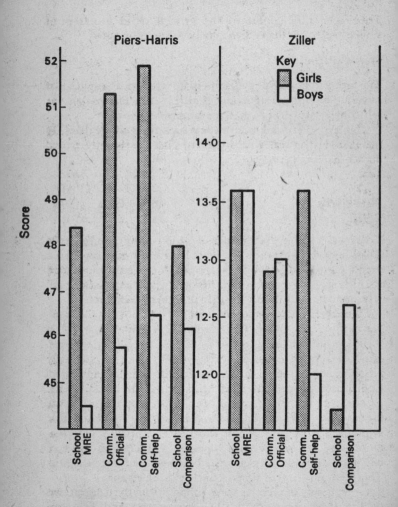

Completion tests). Girls tended to score more highly than boys, although boys scored slightly higher on the Ziller item.

The self-concept/self-esteem scores of children in this study do not indicate a group of children with negative self-concept and low self-esteem. On the whole, the group scores across three measures of self-concept and self-esteem are consistent, being within the average/average-high range.

Bennett *et al.* found that formal and informal teaching styles had little or no effect on the self-concept or self-esteem of the children in their study group. The innovatory projects which we have been studying assume a relationship between self-concept, self-esteem and teaching styles, believing that particular teaching styles and methods will encourage the development of positive self-concept and enhanced self-esteem. Most of the research on self-concept and teaching methods has tended to support the assumption that teachers can influence self-concept. But given the overall status positions of West Indian pupils and English teachers, it is extremely unlikely that these teachers, by whatever means and however well-intentioned, could, within the existing school system, markedly affect the self-concept/self-esteem of black pupils. Even more important is that the teachers' perceptions of the problems may be wrong or misguided in the first place.

Attitudes and Aspirations

(a) Attitudes to School and Teachers

Tables 5.3 and 5.4 show the breakdown of responses from each group to the two sentences dealing with attitudes to school. It can be seen that children in the community Saturday schools demonstrate a highly instrumental attitude to school, 64–7 per cent liking school for the opportunity it gives to acquire intellectual skills. In the MRE group, 54 per cent give this reason and in the Comparison group only 39 per cent. In the total school group (i.e. MRE and Comparison, N = 165) we find 77 (47 per cent) giving Social and Friendship reasons for liking school; in the total Community group (Community Official and Community Self-help, N = 99) we find 23 (23 per

Table 5.3: What I Like Most about School

Statement Category	Comm. Self-help N = 46		Comm. Official N = 33		School MRE N = 76		School Comp. N = 89	
	No.	%	No.	%	No.	%	No.	%
Intellectual	31	67	34	64	41	54	35	39
Physical	9	20	15	28	20	26	23	26
Manual	2	4	2	4	4	5	12	13
Social	6	13	6	11	18	24	23	26
Moral	—	—	—	—	1	1	1	1
Advancement	—	—	4	8	9	12	2	2
Emotional security	4	9	8	15	2	5	9	10
Freedom	2	4	3	6	1	1	—	—
Friendship	7	15	4	8	18	24	18	20
Sense of competence	3	7	3	6	1	1	—	—
Support from adults	3	7	2	4	4	5	4	4
Identity with group	—	—	—	—	—	—	—	—
Sense of purpose	1	2	1	2	—	—	—	—
Place of safety	—	—	—	—	—	—	—	—
Everything	1	2	—	—	—	—	1	1
Functional/material	—	—	—	—	—	—	—	—

Table 5.4: What I Dislike Most about School

Statement Category	Comm. Self-help N = 46		Comm. Official N = 53		Comm. MRE School N = 76		School Comp N = 89	
	No.	%	No.	%	No.	%	No.	%
Absence of challenge	1	2	1	2	1	1	–	–
Bad teaching	1	2	4	8	6	8	6	7
Attitude of teachers/ dislikes teachers	12	26	11	21	30	39	27	30
Power of teachers	9	20	11	21	18	24	22	25
Dislikes everything	–	–	1	2	7	9	4	4
Lack of achievement	1	2	–	–	2	3	–	–
Absence of, or poor, facilities	–	–	–	–	3	4	5	6
Bullying, being picked on	6	13	4	8	4	5	4	4
Disruption	4	9	7	13	5	7	2	2
School dinners/uniforms	2	4	1	2	2	3	4	4
Racism/prejudice	–	–	4	8	–	–	1	1
Dislikes nothing	3	7	2	4	3	4	8	9
A particular subject	6	13	11	21	7	9	12	13

cent) giving Social and Friendship reasons. The strength of feelings against teachers is everywhere evident and must be considered among the important findings of this study, particularly with regard to the concern of teachers to change or improve the self-concept of West Indian children. If we combine Attitudes of Teachers/Dislike of Teachers with Power of Teachers, we find that 140 responses or 53 per cent of the complete sample (N = 264) mention teachers as 'What I dislike most about school'. No other category of dislike can compete with teachers. Dislike of a particular subject comes next with 36 (or 14 per cent), giving specific subjects as what they disliked most about schools.

Davidson and Lang, in their study of 'Children's perception of their teachers' feelings towards them related to self-perception, school achievement and behaviour', suggested that the way children perceive teachers' feelings towards them has a direct effect on their own self-perception achievement and behaviour. Davidson and Lang hypothesize that:

1. there exists a positive correlation between children's perception of their teachers' feelings towards them and children's perception of themselves;
2. there exists a positive relationship between favourable perception of teacher's feelings and good academic achievement;
3. there exists a positive relationship between favourable perception of teachers' feelings and desirable classroom behaviour.

Working with a sample of 89 boys and 114 girls aged from 8 to 10-years-old and using an adjective check list of fifty favourable and unfavourable words, the authors found their hypotheses substantially upheld. The research reported here does not support Davidson's findings. The West Indian children's unfavourable view of their teachers' feelings towards them did not correlate with an unfavourable view of themselves. Although it is not possible to comment on academic achievement, we may use attitudes to school, Intellectual vs. Social/Friendship and Aspirations as an indicator of the influence of children's perception of teachers. We have seen that the children in this study do not show any real differences in self-concept/self-esteem scores either with regard to group membership or type of project. In terms of teachers' feelings towards them, this group of children generally regarded teachers as having negative views of them. However, this did not appear to affect their attitudes towards school.

	School Positive (Instrumental) %	Teacher Negative (Expressive) %
Community Self-help	31 (67)	21 (46)
Community Official	34 (64)	22 (42)
School MRE	41 (54)	48 (63)
School Comparison	35 (39)	49 (55)

We see that children in the Community Self-help group have the highest positive score for school (Intellectual) and also a low negative score (46 per cent) for disliking teachers, teachers' attitudes and the power of teachers. Interestingly, children in the School MRE group have the most negative view of teachers (63 per cent). There were seven children in this group who wrote that they 'liked' nothing about school, as compared with only one child in the Community groups and four in the Comparison group. A possible explanation for this is the high proportion of adolescent boys in this group, but since attitudes to parents should also (presumably) reflect such an influence, but don't, perhaps the explanation may be in another direction: the teaching styles employed, or the group becoming more critical of school teachers as a result of exposure to new curricula.

Other research findings are contrary to those of Davidson and Lang including those reported by Jackson and Lahaderene, who found the correlation between student satisfaction scores and scholastic scores in their sample of 292 sixth-grade pupils to be negligible. In earlier research, Jackson and Getzels found that their adolescent sample of 'satisfied' and 'dissatisfied' students did not differ either in general ability or scholastic achievement. In Britain, Baker-Lunn found that eleven-year-old children's attitudes to school were 'significantly related' to achievement and social class. Westwood also found 'marked differences' in degree of 'satisfaction with school' between high and low achievers. In America, Berk replicated Baker-Lunn's British study and found no relationship between social class and attitudes to school. Wright studied the attitudes to parents and teachers of a sample of fifth-year secondary modern schoolboys and concluded surprisingly that 'it was those attitudes of teachers which make them more human which are rated less favourably' by adolescent boys. Thompson replicated Wright's study with a sample of first- to fourth-year boys and girls which was divided into three groups: (1) adjusted, (2) maladjusted and (3) those who had appeared before a court at any time. This study of a mixed comprehensive school sample reported that these pupils found teachers particularly lacking in 'human qualities'.

> It was found that, overall, teachers were seen as positively as other adults, but also as being somewhat lacking in the more 'human' qualities such as warmth, kindness and happiness. The 'ill-adjusted' pupils had less favourable opinions of schools and teachers.

Finlayson and Loughran looked at pupils' perceptions of school and teachers in high and low delinquency schools including an indication of to what degree pupils perceived teachers to be 'sensitive to the needs of individual pupils'. Boys in the A stream in all schools were found to be more accepting of the work tasks set them by the school and saw their teachers as less authoritarian towards their pupils, than B stream boys. Finlayson and Loughran commented:

> The consistency of the differences between streams . . . indicates that, quite apart from any dispute about whether it is actually so, the B stream boys certainly see themselves to be working in a less supportive and perhaps more anomic atmosphere than the A stream pupils.

They also found that boys in low delinquency schools rated teachers as less hostile than did boys in high delinquency schools: 'pupils perceive their teachers to be defensive and authoritarian in their interaction with their classes'. The authors add the comment that in such a 'cycle of events, the regressive measures which the teachers are perceived to adopt could themselves be an important factor in the contribution which high delinquency schools seem to make to inflating their delinquency problems'.

The research reported here suggests that West Indian pupils in this sample share the views of pupils in the B stream in the high delinquency schools: they perceive teachers as hostile and authoritarian, using their power in an arbitrary way. They generally resent the teachers' attitudes towards them and regard teachers as not liking them. It is interesting to compare these attitudes with Brittan's 1976 findings on teachers' attitudes towards West Indian pupils. Brittan writes that teachers had a self-contradictory array of stereotypes about black (West Indian) pupils who were described as lazy/passive/withdrawn and also boisterous/aggressive/disruptive.

Brittan adds:

> Bearing in mind the varied cultural groups subsumed in the term 'West Indian', the willingness of teachers to make such generalizations and the degree of consensus of opinion leads one to summarize that there is a large-scale stereotyping of West Indian pupils. It is clear that teachers perceive West Indian pupils as of low ability and as creating disciplinary problems. There is therefore an objective problem: whether it should be located in the children or the teachers, or in some interaction of the two, is a critical issue.

What we have seen from Brittan's research is that teachers generally view West Indian pupils in a negative, stereotyped way; from the research reported here we see West Indian pupils viewing teachers in a negative, stereotyped way.

It is interesting that in spite of the suggestion that commnity groups encourage anti-school feelings, it is in fact the MRE group which shows the greatest amount of negative feelings and supplies the largest number of children who can find nothing to like about school. In contrast children in the Community groups have the least negative feelings towards teachers and highest positive feelings towards schools. This suggests that, although children in the innovatory projects may have positive feelings towards the teachers involved in those projects, these feelings are not generalized on to the school or other teachers, whereas the children in the Community groups, encouraged to take a more instrumental, achievement-based approach to school, are able to regard teachers in a more favourable light. Children in the Comparison group see teachers in less favourable terms than children in the Community groups but less unfavourably than children in the School MRE groups.

It is arguable how much teachers' opinions influence children's self-concept at any age although some research appears to suggest that teachers can remould pupils' personality by the use of certain teaching methods (Thomas). It is certainly highly probable that teachers' classroom management, influenced by their perception of pupils, can create situations in the classroom which result in an increase of problems and disruption. What is important is the way the teacher actually behaves towards the pupils. In a recent report, *Children and Young Persons in Custody*, NACRO (The National Association for the Care and Resettlement of Young Offenders) drew attention to the over-representation of West Indian children in Community Home Schools; Cawson (1975) has also studied this problem. The issue of over-representation itself has been well documented by Pearce. In addition there is the continuing problem of the over-representation of West Indian children in ESN schools (Omar; Dhony; *Race Today*, August 1975; Coard; DES, 1973 and 1978). Schools play an important part in the classifying of all children as educationally subnormal and/or delinquent. It is clear that when groups of people as involved with each other as teachers and pupils share negative views of each other, and one group has power and influence, important consequences may follow from this.

This question of attitude to teachers is particularly relevant to the self-concept enhancement concern of some teachers and educationists. It is clear from this research that teachers as a whole would lack the credibility to engage in affective, relationship-based projects with the majority of children in this group. Teachers themselves show equally negative feelings towards black pupils and see their problems as stemming from poor home conditions, 'innate characteristics' and the stress of immigration. It is at least possible that some of the problems may also lie in the schools and in particular in the behaviour (or perceived behaviour) of teachers towards their West Indian pupils.

(b) Attitudes Towards Parents and Home Life

In general all groups showed positive attitudes towards parents
and home life (see Table 5.5).

Table 5.5: Attitude Towards Parents

Group	No.	Parent Positive	%	Parent Negative	%
Comm. Self-help	46	45	98	7	15
Comm. Official	53	50	94	9	17
School MRE	76	50	66	31	41
Comparison Group	89	79	89	16	18
TOTAL	264	224	85	53	20

There were no sex or age differences apparent in the pattern of
responses, except that girls were slightly more critical of
parents, particularly resentful about restrictions and lack of
freedom – but they usually added a rider to the effect that parents
were doing what they thought best. In writing about home and
family life, children constantly expressed feelings of warmth,
belonging, being safe, comfortable, being loved etc. They also
ranked the material benefits – nice bedroom, colour TV, luxury
bathroom – fairly high, but overwhelmingly home was seen in
expressive terms by all the children in all the groups.

> Parental ambitions are high and often unrealistic. There is
> pressure to pass exams but no appreciation of how home
> conditions can help. The negative and repressive child-
> rearing practices designed to produce 'good' children are
> often at variance with teaching methods in schools here
> (National Children's Bureau, 1973).

The sociological view of the black family in America and Britain
is based on the belief that slavery completely destroyed the
African family system and left in its place a fragmented, chaotic
pattern of 'residential units dominated by mothers and

grandmothers, in which the place of father or husband was always insecure' (Higman). This view is represented historically by Greenfield who, after his study of Barbados, concluded that 'the slaves mated, but the plantation system denied them any family life'. Smith (1965) agreed that 'slavery involved the fragmentation of elementary families and encouraged alternative forms of union which were neither obligatory nor stable'. Patterson argued that in Jamaica 'the family was unthinkable to the vast majority of the population . . . the nuclear family could hardly exist within the context of slavery'. Goveia, from her research in the Leeward Isles, concluded that the 'matrifocal' family was the only possible form of 'family life' under slavery.

This background to West Indian or black family life is not simply of historical interest. On the consensus of views among sociologists and psychologists about black family life rest many assumptions related to self-concept, education and school, achievement, aspirations and so on. The Moynihan Report represents the accepted view of the black family in the United States. It stated that the complete destruction of African family patterns left female-dominated, fragmented units which could not prepare children for life in American society; black males were seen to be particularly disadvantaged, having highly marginal status as men or fathers, being indulged as sons. The black family, or absence of such a family, is seen as being responsible for the low status of blacks generally and black males in particular. Patterns of child-rearing which encourage in infants complete oral satisfaction are seen as resulting in the inability to 'delay gratification' which is necessary to the pursuit of long-term goals. The Coleman Report, in deciding that self-concept and parental interest were among the most significant factors in whether or not children achieved in schools, also links up with the unsatisfactory child-rearing patterns of black families which are unable to sustain interest in the performance of children.

In Britain, the view of the West Indian family as represented in the literature essentially mirrors that which is held on the black American family in America. Although studies have been impressionistic, conclusions have been written up authoritatively (e.g. Kitzinger). Studies which have not been impressionistic have usually involved selected samples of children or parents usually receiving psychiatric or some other special care (Feldman; Graham and Meadows; Hood *et al.*; Nicol). One of the effects of this research has been to portray the West Indian family as disorganized and unable to cope. Bagley wrote that immigrant communities in Britain 'especially those from the Caribbean, are faced with a variety of stresses which tend to disorganize family life and depress the possibilities for adequate child-rearing'. Jackson drew pictures of Dickensian squalor in the child-minding conditions in which many under-five West Indian children are left; this was related to Pollack's study which found many West Indian mothers working long hours.

David Hill (1976), in an attempt to explain the differences between West Indian and English attitudes to child-rearing to teachers, has written:

> One could say that the English parents consider they have an obligation to their children, accepting blame for their social inadequacies, whereas West Indian parents believe that the children must please them and should feel guilty if they fail to achieve parental expectations.

Earlier, Hill drew attention to the inconsistencies in West Indian child-rearing: 'Children are treated permissively in such things as feeding and toilet training, but experience considerable repression for rudeness, usually accompanied by unfulfilled threats'. Being 'rude' is defined as the opposite of being 'good'.

However, challenges to the basis of assumptions about slavery and its effects on black life have been made, notably by Gutman (1972, 1978) and Higman. This challenge represents a development in sociology similar to those we have earlier discussed in history with Levine's work and in linguistics with the work of Labov and the socio-linguists. Essentially it argues that, for a number of different reasons (including benefit to the slave-holder) slavery did not completely destroy African family patterns and shows, through the use of historical material, the persistence of forms of family life during and after slavery, which included both nuclear and extended family styles. Again this proves not the 'humanity' of slavery but the force of economics, the ingenuity of people and their persistence in adapting and developing forms of life to give dignity and meaning to existence even under the harshest conditions.

West Indian families in Britain face conditions of extreme stress – both psychological and material. In looking at what these children have written about their parents and home life, we see once again the fact that children and parents are not passive beings reacting to structural forces and introjecting the negative views which the dominant society has of them. They create for themselves patterns of relationships which are meaningful and which serve to insulate and protect against the stressful and dehumanizing environments.

In 1974 John Coleman of London University undertook a study of society and the adolescent self-image. He did so against a background of academic and popular opinion which held that a 'generation gap' existed between parents and children, and that adolescents were unable to communicate with adults and a general polarization existed between the two age groups. What he found when he asked adolescents to write about their parents and themselves was that the majority of adolescents could and did talk to their parents, experienced no feeling of distance or 'generation gap' and generally accepted the values of their parents. In asking West Indian children to write about their parents and home life, we face a similar consensus of views (all the more entrenched for being shared by professional and lay opinion) on West Indian family life, increasing alienation, absence of shared values and so on. Hill (1970) found that West Indian children in his sample generally expressed less regard for parents and home than did their English counterparts; West Indian girls were also more favourably disposed to schools, particularly teachers, than to their parents or home life. The findings reported here run completely contrary to Hill's – this may be a reflection of several factors: (1) changes over eight years in the social, economic and political conditions in the country; (2) regional differences (Hill's sample was located in the Midlands); (3) differences in research methods (Hill used the semantic differential technique), or (4) influence of race of researcher. One is inclined towards thinking that the instrument difference could account for the different findings. Burns called attention to the problems of using the semantic differential which he described as 'a trap for the unwary'. Burns suggested that researchers do not 'bother to investigate whether their chosen scales do in fact represent the evaluative factor with reference to their particular concept'.

Herbert Gutman (1978) has written that the conventional academic wisdom on black families was simple: three centuries of 'injustice' had caused deep-seated structural distortions in the life of the Negro American, a 'tangle of pathology' resulted in which the 'disorganized black family' was at the centre. His own study of the black family showed these assumptions to be false, in the same way that Laurence Levine's study also showed the way African folk culture survived during and after slavery, indicating the ability of human beings to create self-sustaining and self-enhancing conditions even in the most humiliating and oppressive conditions. The assumptions made about black families in Britain are very much the same as those which have been held by white American society about blacks. These families are characterized as 'pathological', the rift between parents and children is assumed to have reached gigantic proportions, emphasized by a 'culture gap' between children born and brought up in Britain and their parents. However we find that given the chance to express a view, West Indian children, including many adolescent boys and girls, regard their parents in a very positive light and value highly their home and family life (see Tables 5.6 and 5.7). The conditions of life for these families are extremely difficult; undoubtedly relationships are affected and some are distorted, but most people manage to make something of their lives and to develop meaningful relationships within their family circle.

(c) Aspirations

The research on self-concept and aspiration has been reviewed in Chapter 2 of this study. The underlying theory states: the more favourable the self-concept the higher the aspiration and is based on Prescott Leckey's 'Theory of Personality' in which he argued that all human motives are instigated by the desire to 'maintain the self and enhance self-esteem'. However, as we have seen in the review of research, findings are contradictory and people with high self-esteem are as likely to be low achievers, and people who are high achievers are as likely to be

Table 5.6: To a Child Parents Are . . .

Statement Category	Comm. Self-help		Comm. Official		School MRE		Comparison Group	
	No.	%	No.	%	No.	%	No.	%
POSITIVE								
Guardians	7	15	3	6	5	7	8	9
Protectors	3	6	3	6	9	12	4	4
Providers	—	—	2	4	4	5	8	9
Help and support	7	15	8	15	12	16	10	11
Love and kindness	14	29	29	55	25	33	46	52
Moral guidance	8	17	4	8	7	9	2	2
Acceptance	3	6	1	2	2	3	—	—
Freedom	3	6	—	—	1	1	1	1
NEGATIVE								
Cruelty	—	—	—	—	5	7	1	1
Unfair punishment	—	—	—	—	1	1	—	—
Bullying, humiliating	1	2	2	4	4	5	1	1
Restrictions	2	4	4	8	12	16	3	3
Rejection	—	—	—	—	4	5	1	1
General Negative	4	8	3	6	5	7	10	11

Table 5.7: What I Like Most about Home . . .

Statement Category	Comm. Self-help No.	%	Comm. Official No.	%	School MRE No.	%	Comparison Group No.	%
Intellectual	2	4	2	4	1	1	—	—
Physical	4	9	2	4	17	22	13	15
Manual	—	—	—	—	1	1	—	—
Social	2	4	1	2	—	—	4	4
Moral	—	—	—	—	—	—	1	1
Advancement	—	—	1	2	—	—	1	1
Emotional security	11	24	7	13	18	24	21	24
Freedom	1	2	1	2	7	9	5	5
Friendship	3	7	—	—	2	3	1	1
Sense of competence	—	—	2	4	—	—	4	4
Support from adults	—	—	2	4	3	4	—	—
Identity with family	11	24	10	19	14	18	26	29
Sense of purpose	1	2	1	2	—	—	—	—
Place of safety	16	35	16	30	29	38	20	22
Everything	—	—	4	8	1	1	6	7
Functional/material	8	17	15	28	11	14	20	22

low in self-esteem. In this present research the self-concept and self-esteem scores were not related to aspiration in any obvious way. Self-concept and self-esteem scores were similar across groups, age and sex, but high aspiration was much more prevalent in the Saturday school groups, and when it occurred in the other school groups was related to age, the primary school children (10–11 years) having higher aspirations than the older comprehensive (13–15 years) pupils.

'Unrealistic' Aspirations

Much has been written and said about the 'unrealistic' expectations of West Indian parents and children. Beetham found Asian and West Indian children had higher job aspirations than did their English counterparts. Nandy queried the definition as 'unrealistic' and stated that with adequate educational provisions this description would not apply to children who had the necessary motivation to fulfil their aspirations.

The aspirations of children in the different groups also show contrasting patterns of hopes and desires (see Table 5.8). Again by combining Success and Money with Self-fulfilment we find that school groups (irrespective of type) have more generalized hopes for a good life, to be rich, famous etc. than the Community Supplementary school groups: 37 per cent (63) of the schools groups see the future in these terms as against 30 per cent (30) of the community based groups. Although not very striking in itself, the difference becomes more significant in the light of future job aspiration: 34 children (34 per cent) in the community groups aspire to a professional career – as a doctor, teacher, nurse, scientist (other professional), air-line pilot etc. which requires an academic background, in contrast to 28 (17 per cent) of children in the school groups (all types) aspiring to professional-type careers. Of the 6 would-be doctors in the school groups, 5 were from the primary school and aged 10- to 11-years-old whereas the would-be professionals amongst the community-based groups showed no such age-related tendency. It is interesting to note that 10 per cent of the School MRE group looked forward to a career in Entertainment – most usually acting and singing. When we remember that the focus of teaching in two of these groups (West Indian Literature and

Table 5.8: Some Day I Should Like to . . . .

Statement Category	Comm. Self-help		Comm. Official		School MRE		Comparison Group	
	No.	%	No.	%	No.	%	No.	%
Success, Money	5	11	9	17	16	21	13	15
General desire to 'get on'	4	9	1	2	1	1	1	1
Travel: General	2	4	3	6	8	11	5	6
. . . West Indies	2	4	6	11	4	5	10	11
. . . . America	—	—	1	2	2	3	4	4
. . . . Africa	—	—	—	—	1	1	3	3
Occupation: Doctor	7	15	2	4	—	—	6	7
. . . Teacher	4	9	3	6	1	1	6	7
. . . Nurse	2	4	5	9	1	1	4	4
. . . Scientist	1	2	—	—	1	1	2	2
. . . Skilled/semi-skilled	6	13	6	11	2	3	9	10
. . . Manual	—	—	—	—	1	1	1	1
. . . Entertainment	3	6	5	10	10	13	6	7
. . . Football	2	4	—	—	4	5	4	4
Marriage and family	2	4	1	2	8	11	4	4
Self-fulfilment	4	8	11	21	14	18	21	24
Other professional	5	11	5	10	6	8	—	8

Images) was drama and the use of photography in communications this is not surprising.

From the sample of 264 West Indian children we find the following choices of occupation.

Occupations	No.	%	
Doctor	15	5.6	Total of 68 (25.7%)
Teacher	14	5.3	aspire towards a
Nurse	12	4.5	professional/semi-
Scientist	4	1.5	professional occupation
Other Professional	23	8.7	
Manual/skilled/			
semi-skilled	25	9.4	25 (9.4%) low status
Entertainment	24	9	jobs; 34 (12.8%) high
Football	10	3.7	status media
			occupations

The 1971 Census statistics analysed by Lomas and Monck showed 54 per cent of West Indian males concentrated in four occupations, all in the skilled/semi-skilled range: Engineering, Woodworking, Labouring and Transport.

Occupations	1966 (%)	1971 (%)
Self-employed	1.4	2.3
Employees: managers and supervisors,	0.7	0.8
Foremen, articled clerks, apprentices	1.0	1.5
Formal trainees	2.4	3.8
Professional	0.9	0.7
Other	93.7	90.8

A comparison of the percentage of West Indians in professional occupations in 1971 (0.7) with the percentage of this sample of children who aspire to such occupations (25.7) shows an enormous gap. In actual fact, the West Indian population in Britain is concentrated in manual, skilled or unskilled work, although the pattern of female employment is more varied and West Indian women are found in clerical and semi-professional work.

Breakdown of Job Aspirations by Group

Of those who hoped for a professional-type career,

　34 (36.3 per cent) were in the Community groups;
　25 (28 per cent) were in the Comparison group;
　9 (7.8 per cent) were in the School MRE group.

The difference between the School MRE group and the two others is quite striking. The School Comparison group had ambitious primary school pupils; 13 (14.6 per cent) of the 25 of the high aspirers occur in this group, and the girls contribute 9 (10 per cent) whereas adolescent boys represent only 4 (3.3 per cent). When we consider the actual employment of West Indian males and that the School MRE group had 42 (55.2 per cent) males we begin to see some possible explanation for the low job aspirations of this group.

Possible Effects of Ability/Attainment on (a) Attitudes to School and Teachers, (b) Aspirations

No direct evidence was collected on the ability or attainment of children in the sample, although it should be noted that all the school-based MRE groups were working to an examination syllabus – CSE or GCE. This would suggest that they were at least of average ability. There is no information on the ability of the Comparison group children; the secondary classes were described by their teachers as typical mixed-ability classes. The primary school warned me to expect reading and comprehension problems, but in fact there were few.

The schools groups therefore were drawn from the 'normal' school population. The community groups were drawn from the 'normal' community population, including children who were attending ESN and other special schools during the week.

If there are to be any assumptions about ability it seems sensible to assume that the school-based MRE groups probably had the largest number of average ability children and that the community groups had the widest spread of ability. If we can assume this we see that (assumed) ability has no influence on (a) attitudes to school and teachers or (b) aspirations. The children in the community groups had the most positive attitudes to school and teachers and the highest aspirations. Conversely, children in the (assumed) average ability MRE groups had the most negative attitudes towards school and teachers and the lowest aspirations of any group.

In educational research it is common to gather statistics on children's attainment and to relate these to other variables in an attempt to correlate them or even to establish a causal relationship between variables. It was decided early on not to include statistics of this kind in this study because it was felt that the factors influencing attitudes were more likely to emerge from observations of the processes involved in the school and community groups, from interviews and discussions than from the collection of even more statistical data.

The qualitative research methods yielded information which suggests that the differences in attitudes and aspirations between the groups could be explained in the following terms.

1. *The School MRE Groups*

a. The methods used in the school-based projects encouraged good relationships with individual teachers but may have resulted in children adopting a more hostile and critical attitude towards other teachers who compared unfavourably with their 'special' teacher.

b. Emphasis on affective-type goals may lead to lower aspirations as participants settle for 'happiness' and self-fulfilment: the responses of the school-based MRE group certainly suggest this.

2. *The Community Groups*

a. The methods used in the community-based groups encouraged children to take an instrumental view of school and to regard teachers as having knowledge which they (the children) would like to share. They are encouraged not to react 'strongly' to difficult situations but 'to get on with their work'.

b. Emphasis on hard work and high expectations may lead to high aspirations as shown by the responses of the Community group children, but – and this is important – children in the Comparison group who had experienced (as far as was known) no MRE were closer to the Community groups in having positive attitudes to school and high aspirations.

Overall the differences in attitudes shown towards school and teachers by children in the School MRE and Community groups appear to be related to the aims and objectives, methods andteaching styles of the teachers, group leaders and parents involved in the projects.

Summary of Findings

1. Self-concept

a. No major differences in self-concept/self-esteem scores were noted in a sample of West Indian children aged from 10- to 15-years-old, comprising three groups: (i) school-based MRE projects, (ii) community-based Supplementary schools and (iii) a Comparison group.

b. There were some sex differences, in that girls tended to score higher than boys on the Piers-Harris children's self-concept scale, and to write more and (slightly) more positively about 'self' on the projective sentence completion item; boys however had a marginally higher score on the Ziller diagrammatic self-esteem item.

c. No age difference emerged.

2. Attitudes to (a) School (b) Teachers

a. Major differences in attitudes to school were noted between groups, the community-based Supplementary school children demonstrating significantly more positive attitudes to school than children in the MRE projects or the Comparison group.

b. Overall, children's attitudes to teachers were negative, but children in the community-based Supplementary schools expressed the least negative views, whereas children in the school-based MRE groups expressed the most negative attitudes towards teachers, the Comparison group falling in between, expressing moderately negative views.

3. Attitudes to Parents and Home Life

Children in all groups showed clearly positive evaluation of parents and associated home life with love, warmth, protection, safety and belonging. Overall, there were no age or sex differences, although teenage girls (14- to 15-years-old) tended to be somewhat more critical of parents for placing restrictions on their freedom and mobility.

4. Aspirations

Differences in aspirations between children in the groups were marked: in line with their most positive attitudes to school and less negative appraisal of teachers, children in the Saturday Supplementary schools also had high aspirations, followed by children in the Comparison group. Those in the MRE group appeared the least ambitious (some would say, most realistic) of any group.

6. Discussion and Conclusions

The Relevance of Self-concept

In a recent work on the nature of 'self', Raziel Abelson quoted Wittgenstein as saying:

> Why should there not be a psychological regularity to which no physiological regularity corresponds? If this upsets our concept of causality, then it is about time it was upset.

Self-concept is seen as relevant by practitioners, theoreticians and researchers because it is held to have a causal relationship to motivation and hence to performance and achievement. When we examined the literature on black self-concept, we saw that before any research was carried out the impression, and the theory based on the impression, was that there was no possible basis for the development of a healthy self-image amongst black people. After the mid-1960s, research began to show blacks having positive self-concept. The fact is, as we have tried to show in our discussion of black culture and consciousness, people derive the means to sustain a sense of self from many sources and do not rely on negative and hostile views as their source of information about self. Through political, social, literary and musical styles, people create alternative sources of selfhood. We should not therefore be surprised to find a normal/average distribution of self-concept scores amongst black children living in Britain. As Abelson has written, it must be possible for us to regard people as 'free agents whose actions and avowables are explainable by . . . reasons, purposes and values . . . in brief, a human being is a person not an automaton'. Taking the view of people as actors, actively engaged in defining their own world, including their sense of self, permits us to see that any human being can create for herself a self-sustaining, self-enhancing environment. Whatever objective values others place on such an environment will be a function of their own status, position and values.

The assumption, however, that actions and behaviour follow from the individual's sense of his own worth, is quite illogical. Thus, from the research presented here, we see no real differences in self-concept scores between groups of children; their ways of thinking about themselves are similar, but their expectations are widely different. Ways of behaving are mediated by factors outside the individual's control; ways of thinking need not be. An individual may feel very worthy, but know that unemployment affects well over half of all black school leavers in parts of London. However worthy he/she may feel about him/herself as an individual, as a worker he/she knows that his/her future (work) behaviour is largely outside his/her own control. The high aspirers in this group are those who go to the community Supplementary schools, i.e. those who have additional information, and those who may be too young to know any better – the primary school children. What I am suggesting therefore is:

1. That it be acknowledged that black children have sources of self-pride and do not simply introject the negative views of the white society. These sources include a history of political, social and religious resistance to stereotyping and racial abuse.

2. Self-concept or self-esteem, which is a psychological function of individual or group values, cannot be regarded as being (overall) in the same category of power or determinism as the social structure prevailing in a given society.

3. Within this analysis, acknowledgement of the subjective reality of the actor leads towards an acceptance of the actor's definition of herself and her world as valid, but also notes the constraints of structures on individuals and groups within a given society.

4. The constraints of structures on individuals and groups lead to strategies for survival and the initiation of processes through which some modifications of the structures are attempted.

5. The (normal) self-concept of black children (and adults) is therefore best understood in terms of the development of a

culture which acts to protect and sustain the individual and the group: 'culture' in this sense is taken to mean the values and world-view of the group as shown in language, dialect, literature, music, religious and political movements which historically reflect the striving for individual and group autonomy.

Curriculum Innovation

The school-based projects reflect the theories and ideas put forward by self-concept theorists and educationists. Although these theories stem basically from an interactionist perspective, they have also been influenced by Freudian theory, social behaviourism and other theories. Overall it is tidy to regard all these theories and ideas as falling within the 'developmental' approach to education which emphasizes the personal growth and development of the individual child as among the primary objectives of formal education.

The examples of curriculum innovation we have been considering indicate a process of adaptation on the part of schools and teachers where there are large numbers of West Indian pupils. The theoretical rationale within which all the teachers operate in MRE projects could roughly be described as liberal and the aims as developmental. However, we have seen that the children in these groups exhibit more negative attitudes towards schools and teachers than any other group, including the Comparison group; these children have aspirations which reflect a general desire to be rich, happy and self-fulfilled. Only 9 (12 per cent) mention the desire for a professional-type career, although 14 (18 per cent) hope for a career in entertainment or football. This is perhaps the one area where the influence of the school projects could be noted, the School MRE group having by far the highest number of aspirants for stage and entertainment careers. One school project dealt with the use of dialect in creative writing including scripts for TV and other plays and another project dealt with the use of photography in creating 'images'.

Of the four projects which were described, the West Indian Literature group has ended and another (Images) is also under threat. The two which have survived (World History and Religion) show a better organized and more 'professional' approach to innovation and in the sense that they have gained the support of the school and the LEA officials and thus ensured their survival, they can be seen as 'successful'. However, in terms of their own objectives: enhanced self-concept, leading to more positive attitudes to school and better motivation, there seems no indication that children in these groups have benefited at all in these terms. That is not to suggest that this type of endeavour should not be undertaken, but rather that objectives should perhaps be more 'realistic' and should be expressed in cognitive, rather than affective, terms.

What is important in establishing objectives in school curriculum-innovatory projects are the assumptions from which the teachers start. These assumptions, shared by all teachers irrespective of teaching style, are based on the belief that black children have poor, negative self-concept and low self-esteem which need compensating and enhancing. While in no way denying the effects of racism and discrimination in society generally and in the school system, I would argue that to see black people and their children as passive beings, simply reacting to structural forces is a limited view which denies the facts of history and is supported neither by commonsense nor by rigorous sociological analysis. Teachers and other practitioners therefore need to question their own assumptions and those which underlie the theories on which their own teaching is based before setting out on curriculum-innovatory projects and particularly in deciding what the objectives of these projects should be.

Community Involvement in Schooling

It has earlier been suggested that West Indian Supplementary schools are part of an historical and sociological process, and that such developments represent a creative and dynamic process whereby people seek to define, influence and change the conditions of their lives. This process may be illustrated by political, religious, literary and other social developments; we have been examining only one aspect of this overall process.

Traditionally, community involvement in schooling is related to the romantic ideal of 'community' which relates back to the Cambridge colleges of the 1930s, the ideas of William Morris (Poster) and to the notion of the 'open school' as a characteristic of 'open education' (Bernstein, 1969). The type of community involvement in schooling which we have been considering is not the attempt by the school system to 'involve' the 'community' (however defined) in some aspect of schooling, in a setting that is already well established and where boundaries are clearly marked out. For example, the contributors to *Teaching in the Urban Community School* (Garner) put forward the argument for more community involvement in urban education and focused on social workers, health visitors, teacher visitors, doctors etc. as the people most likely to encourage this type of 'involvement'. Easthope has argued that such a conception of the community school and community participation suggests a colonial role:

> The school becomes a coloniser of the local area as a source of ideas for an audience comprised of an elite drawn from inside and outside the area . . . far from destroying the hierarchy between school and the local area only serves to strengthen it.

He continues:

> A community school that is not a coloniser is difficult to conceive of in Britain because the concept of the school as an autonomous 'hierarchical community' with a sovereign head precludes any real local control over the process of education.

For the minority group the problems of control over the type of schooling their children receive are even greater than for the rest of the urban community. They are stigmatized (Goffman), regarded as inadequate and incapable of good parenting (Kitzinger). They suffer terrible discrimination in housing and employment (PEP Report). If they are approached at all by schools to take part in the education of their children it will not be as partners. They themselves will be seen as needing help and treatment.

The type of community involvement in schooling which we have been considering here is reminiscent of the kind of activity amongst working-class socialists in the late-nineteenth and early-twentieth centuries.

There is no comparable contemporary English working-class equivalent to the West Indian Saturday schools. Unable to influence the school system, the West Indian community has devised its own response. As we have seen, this response can take different forms and the Saturday school is in any case only one type of response, but it is the one which we are concerned with. We have seen how the Official Community projects ape the hierarchical school system and thus ensure respectability and funding; they also rely more on 'professional' expertise and tend to assign parents a somewhat limited role. However, they can never create for themselves the problems of the established school system, beause they are part of 'the community' in a way which the formal school is not. They are far more accountable and responsive to pressure from the community, being voluntary. Children can vote with their feet; the Saturday schools have no sanctions to apply. In the 'grass-roots' self-help projects we really did see community involvement in schooling, people working together to help youngsters to acquire skills and knowledge which they believe are essential. People volunteer for duties (secretary, treasurer) as they are able and all can join in the teaching of the children. 'Professionals' in the group are not accorded any particular status but help on the same basis as other members.

The research undertaken as part of this study shows that the Community groups are very successful in encouraging children to develop positive (if instrumental) attitudes to school. Children attending them are also very much less critical of teachers than children taking part in innovatory school-based projects and children in a Comparison group. The children in Saturday Supplementary schools have higher aspirations than children in the other groups. They are not more critical of parents or alienated from them, as has been suggested; on the contrary they appear to value their parents and their home life very highly. The children in this group were among the few to associate home life with 'intellectual' skills. This category received four mentions in the Community groups ($N = 99$) as against one in the rest of the sample (N = 165).

For whatever reason, West Indian children continue to under-achieve in British schools, lagging behind white working-class British children in tests of attainment in school subjects (Little, 1978). From the research reported here, we have seen that community-based Supplementary school projects have in them children who exhibit more positive attitudes to school, less negative attitudes to teachers and higher aspirations than children in the other groups with whom we compared them. This is particularly interesting as the population of the community Supplementary schools includes children diagnosed as ESN, children suffering various kinds of physical handicaps and those attending maladjusted and other 'special' schools, whereas the school-based and comparison groups were drawn from the 'normal' school (secondary and primary) population.

In a recent paper on Jewish education in Britain, B. Chazan, of the Hebrew University of Jerusalem suggested that 'the phenomenology of ethnic group education is a promising resource for the understanding of issues related both to ethnicity and education'. Chazan is concerned with a group (Jews) who are an established and accepted part of British society. He writes that British Jewry is a good example of Jewish integration and acceptance in a non-Jewish society, that British society has been receptive to Jews and the Jews of Great Britain have successfully learned how to adjust and be absorbed. In contrast, the West Indian community is barely tolerated in British society and there exists a long history of prejudice and discrimination against people with black skins (Little, 1972; Walvin; Rose *et al.*; PEP Report; Scobie). Thus the development of Jewish schools or educational programmes in the Jewish community and Supplementary schools and educational programmes in the West Indian community may appear similar types of response, but they are in fact reactions to very different objective social conditions. The emphasis in Jewish schools is on a religious and cultural curriculum whereas West Indian schools stress acquisition of skills and knowledge, although this is within a virtually uniracial context where West Indian (and black culture generally) is emphasized and given pride of place.

Chazan's analysis suggests that the development of ethnic education programmes or schools is related to the group's own 'sense of self', to particularistic or assimilationist tendencies in the group and to the values and mores cherished by the group. This is essentially the approach adopted here in relation to the discussion of the West Indian community's involvement in the education and schooling of their children.

The development of Supplementary schools by the West Indian community may be seen negatively as a threat or positively as a challenge. What is certain is that they represent perhaps the only real example of working-class community involvement in schooling at the present time. They therefore represent an area of interest for sociology generally, and for the sociology of education in particular.

Implications, Conclusions and Suggestions

> In reality a mediocre teacher may manage to see to it that his pupils become *informed*, although he will not succeed in making them better educated; he can devote a scrupulous and bureaucratic conscientiousness to the mechanical part of teaching – and the pupil, if he has an active intelligence, will give an order of his own . . . to the 'baggage' he accumulates. With the new curricula . . . there will no longer be any 'baggage' to put in order . . . A date is always a date, whoever the examiner is, and a definition is always a definition. But an aesthetic judgement or a philosophical analysis?
>
> Antonio Gramsci, 'On Education'

Gramsci's argument against the romantic idealism of the Gentile Reform of 1923, which sought to change Italian education from mere 'instruction' to an 'active, creative' process, is very relevant to any discussion on urban schooling in Britain today, and particularly to the schooling of West Indian children within that system. We have seen from our review of the literature on self-concept, self-esteem and schooling that there is almost unanimous agreement amongst researchers and teachers that the development of positive self-concept and high self-esteem are important to attainment in schools. The practical result of these assumptions is that teachers act more and more like social workers and consequently neglect their primary role of 'instruction'. We have seen from the research undertaken as part of this work and the findings presented earlier that there is no basis in fact for the belief that black children have poor self-esteem and negative self-concept. Further, we questioned the belief that high or low self-concept in itself can make a difference to the structural forces in society which largely determine distribution of income which in turn determines class and status positions.

In coming to this final chapter, we examine the implications of the critique and the research for the schooling of West Indian children. We are not here concerned with developing relevant curricula; the details of what Gramsci called 'the baggage' may not be as important as has been recently stressed (Callaghan). What is of overriding importance is that children should acquire the means to put 'the baggage' in order; something they cannot possibly do if they have not mastered the fundamentals and are virtually semi-literate.

The proposals which follow may appear controversial or conservative. The intention is that the debate over the schooling of working-class and black children should be opened up to rigorous academic scrutiny so that discussion of issues such as the place of emotions in the classroom, self-concept and self-esteem should be linked to discussions of the structural factors which regulate social and economic life and so teachers are not further encouraged into teaching methods based on romantic ideas of 'self-realization' and 'self-fulfilment', to the detriment of their pupils' interests.

Neville Bennett, in trying to explain the poorer academic performance of the 'informal' pupils in his sample observed that one explanation may be:

> that the poorer academic progress of informal pupils is an accurate reflection of the aim of informal teachers . . .
> Formal teachers stress academic aims while informal teachers prefer to stress the importance of self-expression, enjoyment of school and the development of creativity.

This seems to lend support to my thesis that teachers who emphasize self-concept, self-esteem and enjoyment, do so at the expense of more concrete objectives. Although it is possible to test whether or not a child can read, write, spell or do sums to most people's satisfaction, there is no agreed method of telling whether a child is 'self-actualized' or not – even if it were important to know. It is for these reasons that the central recommendation of this study is for the use of more formal methods of teaching West Indian children throughout primary and secondary schools. These methods are understood and approved of by West Indian (and other working-class) parents and in the light of the dismal failure of the present approach, formal teaching methods can only offer an improvement on the present situation. The present methods have resulted in low attainment by West Indian pupils and concentration of black children in lower streams of the comprehensive school, remedial classes and special schools for the educationally subnormal.

We turn now to a general discussion of the work as a whole and its implications for (a) policy, (b) theory and research, (c) schools and teachers and (d) parents, children and the West Indian community.

The Aims of Education

With Brian Simon (1965) I would argue that sociological theory must be able to explain and demonstrate plausibly, at a number of levels (of which the empirical is only one), the ways in which anomalies and inconsistencies within schools reflect wider contradictions within the social structure. In looking critically at the ideas underlying self-concept theory and research and in examining the process involved in projects which attempt to apply these theories within schools, one major contradiction has emerged: given the level of dislike of teachers it is virtually impossible for teachers to be 'significant others' in the lives of West Indian children. This factor is compounded by evidence which suggests that teachers are not all that keen on black children either: Brittan showed that teachers in general had negative, stereotyped views of West Indian pupils. Willis (1978b) suggested that the one tension-free area between 'the lad' (who belonged to the school counter-culture) and the teachers was their mutual resentment of the immigrants in their midst. Willis wrote:

Certainly it is quite explicit that many senior staff associate the major immigration of the 60s with the break-up of the 'order and quietness' of the 1950s and of what is now seen more and more retrospectively as their peaceful, successful schools.

My own research suggests that West Indian pupils, at least, have equally negative feelings towards teachers. Individuals or small groups of children develop 'relationships' with a particular teacher or teachers but this does not appear to affect their overall attitudes to most teachers, whom they perceive as having inordinate power over them and generally disliking them. The attitude change which may result from participation in group work projects of the kind described earlier may lead individuals or small groups of children to see certain teachers as being well disposed to them and willing to treat them on a par with English children. These attitudes are not, however, generalized on to *school* – so that, although individual relationships may be good, general attitudes and behaviour may remain unchanged. Since the total school environment is perceived as unhelpful, this is to be expected.

Relationships are not stressed in Saturday schools – work is. If anything, children are encouraged to ignore 'relationships', especially with friends who are not serious about work and might get them into trouble. It may be that in a voluntary situation the need to stress relationships does not exist – children come because they want to learn; teachers and other helpers because they care enough whether children learn to give up free time to teach them. In contrast, teachers in weekday schools who are committed to a 'relationship' based teaching style appear to need to stress relationships continually. One young teacher told me that 'it is impossible to teach these children (there were over 60 per cent West Indian boys in this school) unless you first have a relationship with them'. This is in a school with at least one suspension per week, and where even as he spoke we could hear masters literally screaming at boys and boys shouting back, teaching going on against a continual din and uproar – or so it seemed to me. Yet this teacher, just two years past his probationary year, firmly believed that he could only teach where a relationship already existed. In one day he might take 3/4 classes of 25–30 boys each. Was it possible to have 'a relationship' with each and every one of these boys? I asked. Was it necessary? He felt that not all boys needed a relationship every day or with the same intensity – a death in the family, father gone 'away' etc., could lead to the necessity to help that one boy on a particular day, but the basis for such help had to exist beforehand. Thus he felt that the teacher should aim at developing some kind of a relationship with all the pupils he teaches. His views appeared to be based on the teaching of Carl Rogers and, I suspect, were more in line with what he had learnt in college and what he believed to be ideal, rather than on what actually happened on a day-to-day basis in his school.

The problem is – how is the teacher to develop a relationship with children or groups of children he/she actually dislikes, and who (because likes/dislikes tend to be mutual) also dislike the teacher? Is it really necessary to develop a 'relationship' with a child in order to teach it numeracy and literacy? What if one is a perfectly good mathematics teacher but hopeless at 'relationships'? Should one not be a teacher?

There may be a danger here of relationships assuming importance beyond anything that is useful or meaningful within the context of the provision of schooling for working-class and black children in contemporary British society. Irrespective of the theoretical or other weaknesses of the emotions/ relationships approach to teaching in the classroom, it is clear that, given the negative feelings which both groups (teachers and pupils) generally have of each other, it would be unwise to allow emotions and relationships to assume major importance in urban schools. A black teacher told me that in her view left-wing radical teachers had done more harm to black children in schools than any other group. She said that the perfect teacher for West Indians was a traditional no-nonsense teacher who knew her subject and knew how to teach. 'Politics don't matter – unless the teacher is really right-wing, of course – NF or something like that – otherwise it's a non-issue.' Many community workers and youth workers also blame left-wing teachers for over-indulging black kids, letting them 'get away with anything so long as they had a good relationship with the child'. In my experience, this analysis transcends political boundaries and is as common among liberal as among so-called radical black teachers.

What should be the aim of schooling for West Indian children? Historically, traditional liberal education theory has as its distinguishing characteristics belief in:

1. *The Integrative Function of Education.* The process whereby the young are integrated into the roles expected and required of them in adult society (Durkheim).

2. *The Egalitarian Function of Education.* Whereby society is serviced, governed and controlled by a meritocracy of intelligentsia drawn equally from all social classes and all groups, the only criteria being intelligence (Dewey).

3. *The Developmental Function of Education.* Whereby the process of education promotes in the individual autonomy, self-realization, self-actualization and self-understanding – the 'rational man'/person created as a result of exposure to liberal ideas and education.

Examined against these criteria the school system as a whole would seem to fail West Indian children on all counts.

Integrative schools are not 'integrative'. Increasingly West Indian youngsters are rejecting 'the roles expected and required of them by adult society' (Donna and Marcia). They are refusing to do the menial jobs which their parents were glad to do; they call this 'shit work'.

Within the West Indian working class there has developed a distinct grouping of unemployed men and women, which increases at the end of every school year. It is not a reserve army of labour – that is to say, held in reserve to be called upon at the will of London Transport, Fords, night cleaning agencies, hospitals and all other employers of black immigrant labour. Call as they might, the youths have uncompromisingly refused to budge. It is an overwhelming refusal of shitwork (Race Today Collective, 1975).

The counter-culture developing amongst young blacks in Britain, including membership of the Rastafarian religion and alternative lifestyles around it, clearly indicates an unwillingness on the part of young West Indians to accept the position offered to them in British society. Even though, to many observers, the alternatives they create for themselves appear equally unattractive and lead to equally bad results.

It follows from what has already been said that the egalitarian function of schooling too is a dream. As far as most West Indian parents and children are concerned, the schools do not even begin to offer anything like equal opportunity; they suffer all the disadvantages of the urban working-class and the additional ones of prejudice and racism. It was interesting to be told that all the most successful West Indians in this country were educated in the Caribbean, at least for most of their school life. Whether this is true or not I have no idea, but it is widely believed in the West Indian community. I was told by one West Indian Deputy Head that Britain is a long way from producing its first 'home-grown' black university lecturer! Whatever the reason, black children do not do well in schools and since the basis of the meritocracy is intelligence demonstrated by a suitable number of certificates and degrees, the school system clearly fails on that count as well.

What of the final criterion, the developmental function of education? This, of course, is the area with which the book has been mainly concerned – and the data presented earlier relate to this question. From the data presented we saw that West Indian children in the total sample had average self-concept scores and average-to-high self-esteem and thus the need for self-concept enhancement for all West Indian children must be questioned.

Gramsci in his *Notes from Prison*, argued against relationship-based teaching. He insisted on the value of hard work and discipline and for the need of the potential working-class intellectuals to acquire mastery over the knowledge and skills of the elite if they were to effect any change in their own class position and in society. However, Gramsci did not see social change simply in economic terms, indeed he believed in 'critical self-consciousness' as the means towards personal awareness resulting in cultural and intellectual change. He required education to 'produce people who could both master the skills of intellectual production and use them in engaging the forces of history in active critical self-consciousness'. But the self-awareness he stressed was not the reflexive self-indulgence of the highly individualistic, idealized, romantic liberals but part of a historical process whereby the individual knows herself as 'part of the historical process which has deposited in one an infinity of traces'. Gramsci argued against the developmental role of education because he knew that such emphasis would result in an almost totally ignorant and illiterate working class. He knew that for the working class to succeed they had to produce intellectuals capable of mastering elite culture and turning it to their own use – the working-class intellectual would have to develop and sustain, through the rigour of disciplined study, a coherent world-view.

> What is required then is that children be instructed in the often tedious rote learning of a whole intellectual tradition . . . it is through such a process that each child will be enabled to analyse and think on a par with those intellectual traditions he/she must overcome in order to take up his proper place in civil and political society.

In Gramsci's terms, such aims required that the traditional curricula provide both the historical forms of the various worlds as well as the intellectual rigour through which such worlds may be viewed. Professor Brian Simon (1976) has warned Marxists about the dangers of 'relativism' in these words:

> The 'radical' nature of this relativist ideological position, and the danger of taking it seriously, is shown in the practice of those young teachers who, accepting this view of knowledge, and in their sentimental generosity, identifying with their working-class pupils, begin to see their role as shielding them from the demands of formal schooling and acting more in the role of the social worker . . . rather than as teacher, with the specific function of inducting pupils into the knowledge, skills and abilities that derive from the objectives of an education appropriate to the mid-late 20th century. The dangers are evident: it provides means . . . of denying to the working class access to knowledge, culture and science.

Another leading Marxist intellectual, Maurice Levitas, has also dissociated himself from the relativist position with regard to knowledge and has argued that the working class must first subject themselves to knowledge before they can master it.

We have seen that both in terms of the traditional liberal objectives based on the developmental role of education, and in terms of the supposedly radical phenomenological Marxist approach, the efforts made meet with small returns. More fundament-ally they appear to work against the interest of the working class as a whole.

Implications
Policy

Policy decisions should encourage teachers in urban schools to have as their primary objective the teaching of skills and knowledge and the development of associated abilities in children. Teacher training should emphasize that teachers' professional interest lies in 'the inducting of children into knowledge, skills and abilities' rather than in the provision of social work or therapy to children. Training courses could encourage teachers to consider the use of more formal methods of teaching which appear to have more overall parental support and which may be more effective for certain children.

Another observation concerns the disproportionate stress which has been placed on knowledge of the cultural and home background of 'immigrants' in teacher training. Since most British research and writing on West Indian family life is ethnocentric and portrays the West Indian family as a pathological variant of the European middle-class family (Lowensthal; Fitzherbert; Hill, 1976) it is very likely that the effect of much of it is counter-productive in terms of the schooling of West Indian children. It may reinforce already held stereotypes and not enable the teacher to regard black children as potential intellectuals, worthy of their best teaching effort, instead of potential clients for therapy.

If there is significant demand for Black or Ethnic Studies from the West Indian community, this would need to be examined sympathetically by the LEAs and the DES – but it should not be assumed that the introduction of Black Studies programmes in schools will in itself have a notable effect on (a) the performance of West Indian children as a whole, or (b) reduce the tendency towards alienation, and the development of what has been termed (Willis, 1978b) 'school counter-culture' amongst West Indian adolescents. The issues are far too complex, and are tied in with other economic, social and political factors which schools in themselves can do little about.

Saturday Schools

The DES, the ILEA and LEAs with numbers of West Indian children may be interested to find out more about the numbers of Saturday schools in their areas, the teaching methods they use and the success they have in increasing the attainment of West Indian children in schools. Since all official Saturday schools are known to the authorities, it should be possible to acquire this information using existing channels of communication and thus obviate the need for further academic research. Thus, project leaders could be asked to supply information on children attending their projects based on the use of attainment tests at six- or twelve-monthly intervals. Formal examination passes of children attending these schools could also be monitored over time. The information yielded would be far from perfect, but it could provide a useful beginning. By encouraging the Saturday schools to be self-monitoring, this could increase efficiency and help ongoing evaluation which could provide valuable feedback on performance etc., which more academic research might lack.

Any policy decision on the education and schooling of West Indian children might consider the giving of funds and other types of support to community-based cultural and educational projects. This would be in preference to extending the influence of the schools (via Black Studies, the use of Creole, steel bands etc.) into difficult and sensitive areas which are fraught with problems.

Theory and Research

The findings have important implications for self-concept research and theory in relation to schooling. In particular the need to develop a substantive theory based on the use of both empirical and phenomenological research methods. Willis (1978b) has drawn attention to the development of a particular kind of school counter-culture amongst young West Indians in the schools he studied. He has indicated that research in this area is urgently required and recommends that it should employ the methods of research he used with his sample of working-class boys, the Observer Participant method, which lays stress (almost exclusively) on the subjective reality of the actor and the actor's interpretation of his own world as the basis of social science research. Such research, if it were possible, would be helpful in clarifying issues of self-concept, impact of school-culture on West Indian children and their response to it. On a more practical level, research is needed to identify the process whereby the school system labels West Indian children as (a) maladjusted, (b) educationally subnormal and (c) emotionally disturbed, and thus consigns them in increasing numbers to special schools and treatment groups of one kind or another. It is clear that what Willis has labelled the school counter-culture, as well as being a response to a prospective wageless condition, is also a reaction by West Indian pupils to the violence which is done to them virtually from the moment they enter the formal school system. If research has a role to play it must be in helping the school system and educational authorities to be less racist and discriminatory in their practice. As far as self-concept research itself is concerned, it has yet to prove its relevance or usefulness in relation to the schooling of the black child in Britain. It may also be useful for social scientists, as well as identifying what they take to be the pathology of the black family and lifestyle to devote some time to investigating the capacity for survival and cohesion amongst minority group families in the face of the oppressive and destructive forces which characterize British and American societies in their dealings with people of African descent (Scobie; Walvin; Little, 1972).

Schools and Teachers

Most self-concept theory and research appears to offer to teachers the opportunity of creating 'new selves' for children out of the raw material they were offered by parents. The research reported here and the general theoretical stance adopted throughout is that schools should be places for acquiring skills and knowledge and developing abilities associated with these skills and knowledge. The teacher's job should be to teach children these skills and knowledge and encourage the development of general abilities.

Many (particularly young) teachers are put under enormous stress by the requirement to develop relationships as the basis of their teaching methods. This can lead to feelings of inadequacy and loss of enthusiasm for the job which they still have to continue to perform. If teachers felt sure that their primary aim is to teach one feels sure that this would lead to an easing of stress and consequent improvement in overall 'relationships'.

Schools and teachers must accept that West Indian parents care enormously about their children's education, and they must take some responsibility (at least) if parents hesitate to come to their schools or are hostile and unco-operative when they do. Schools and teachers should attempt to build on the obvious enthusiasm which West Indian parents have for education and resist the temptation to label as 'over-ambitious' or 'unrealistic' expectations which they would take for granted in white middle-class parents.

Although I have stressed the need for teachers to teach basic skills, this should not be taken as a desire for rigid traditional curricula – the curricula can only ultimately express the basic power relationships of society as a whole.

As Bourdieu (1977) has written, 'relationships of communication are always, and inescapably, power relations which depend for their form and content on the material or symbolic power accumulated by the agents (or institutions) engaged in these relations'. Although curricula can be mediated and modified by the teaching process itself and by the pupils to whom they are directed, they remain an expression of power and it seems that only by mastering the traditional curricula will more West Indian children have that basis of choice which many middle-class people take for granted.

We may gain some insight into the realities of the problem of 'choice' for working-class and 'immigrant' black children by reading what Kelvyn Richards wrote in an article on multiracial schools about the 'ambivalence' of the school in helping youngsters decide about future careers and prospects:

> The ambivalent position of the school is more clearly illustrated if we consider careers guidance and placement. Many young Asians and West Indians aspire to jobs in the Civil Service, local government, or the professions. They are concerned to stay on at school, or to go to a college of further education, and gain as many qualifications as possible.
>
> On the other hand, careers teachers strongly advise these people to get a job, and to obtain training on the factory floor or an office and criticize them for having aspirations beyond their abilities. Perhaps teachers must recognize that it is in the factory and the office that 'colour bar' and racialist sentiments are most openly expressed. We must counsel more carefully.

Richards also advises 'the multiracial communities' that their demand for 'the best of British education' will have the inevitable consequence of the 'westernization' of their young people. This argument suggests that mastery of traditional curricula involves complete absorption into the dominant value system, resulting in higher levels of alienation due to raised expectations, better education etc. He writes:

> What are we really doing? Schools profess their aim to be equality of opportunity for all, and yet guide these non-white pupils into factory and office, where they are not really wanted. The factory owners say they welcome all, and yet employ – predominantly white workers.
>
> The multiracial communities demand the best of British education, and yet refuse to recognize that an inevitable consequence of this will be the 'westernization' of their young people.

But a feature of post-industrial society is the mobility of labour on an international scale, and it is possible that the mastery of traditional curricula may extend the choice of these young people in a way that would have been considered impossible a decade or two ago. They should at least have the choice.

Parents, Children and the West Indian Community

Parents, children and community leaders should press for a return to achievable goals by teachers; by the same token, the West Indian community itself must assume responsibility for keeping alive what elements of their own language and culture they think worth preserving. In that they will be in company with the Jews, Irish, Turks, Poles, Muslims and Hindus, who also constitute minority groups in this country, all of whom have established Saturday/Sunday schools and other supplementary education projects with the aim of preserving culture and language.

As well as this, the West Indian community must, for the forseeable future, continue to supplement the regular schooling which children receive in the weekday schools, but they must continue to press for better State education for their children, in the meantime making good, as far as possible, the deficit in basic skills of literacy and numeracy.

This study has very little direct information to offer on the issues which concern West Indian parents most – except perhaps to indicate some of the reasons why (some) schools fail (some) children – and the ways in which certain theories, ideas and research findings may have influenced the development of teaching styles and methods which are particularly unhelpful to West Indian children.

Conclusions

The conclusions of this study based on the total perspective presented here, are that self-concept research and theory and teaching styles based on these ideas have little to contribute towards an understanding of how West Indian children in Britain should be educated, and may have contributed towards the low attainment of such children – because they stress affective goals of self-expression, self-fulfilment, happiness and so on as the basis of their teaching methods. It has been suggested that teaching methods associated with mastery of skills and knowledge and the development of abilities should be substituted for affective-type goals which are vague, and give teachers access to aspects of pupil personality which should be private, extending teacher control of areas of pupil personality which are unnecessary for instructional purposes. Whilst not decrying all attempts at curriculum innovation and creativity, the need for schools to retain a commitment to the mastery of basic intellectual skills and competencies by all children has been expressed.

APPENDIX: Notes on the Self-concept Test Used

The test instrument consisted of three items:
1. Piers-Harris children's self-concept scales;
2. Ziller self-social symbols tasks;
3. Sentence Completion item.

1. Piers-Harris

The Piers-Harris children's self-concept scale is a self-report 80-item test designed for children over a wide age range. The instrument was designed primarily for research on children's self-attitudes and correlates of these attitudes. It was developed from Jersild's collection of children's statements about what they liked and disliked about themselves: (a) physical characteristics and appearance, (b) clothing and grooming, (c) health and physical soundness, (d) home and family, (e) enjoyment of recreation, (f) ability in sports, play, (i) special talents (music, art), (j) just me, myself, (k) personality, character, inner resources.

There were two minor alterations to the Piers-Harris instrument.

Item 5.: from I am smart to I am clever.

Item 55: from I have lots of pep to I am a lively person.

Scoring is by a pre-set formula provided with the manual. Average scores are raw scores of between 46–60. Piers gave a figure of 51.84, 13.87 as the mean for her normative sample.

2. Self-social Tasks

This measure was devised by Ziller (1976) and developed from a social psychological theory of personality involving ten

components of self-other orientation:
1. self-esteem;
2. social interest;
3. self-centrality;
4. identification;
5. majority identification;
6. complexity;
7. power;
8. openness;
9. inclusion;
10. marginality.

Self-other orientations are maps of the subject's perceived relationships with significant others – people such as friends, relatives, work groups, teachers and groups of people. The method of impressing these perceived relationships involves arrangements of symbols representing the self and significant others.

Although several of the Ziller items were included in the test only those dealing with self-esteem were actually analysed.

Self-esteem

The stem of this item presents a horizontal array of six circles and a list of significant other people, such as a friend, a selfish person, mother, father and teacher, doctor and yourself. The task requires the subject to assign each person to a circle. The score is the weighed position of the self. In accordance with 'the cultural norm', Ziller has shown (1969, 1973) that people place persons horizontally in descending order of importance; positions to the left are associated with high self-esteem. Three self-esteem items are used with different sets of 'others'; to score the circles are numbered 1 to 6 starting at the right.

The sum of the scores on all three items represents the self-esteem score.

Sentence Completion

The final section was a sentence completion item with eight stems:

The stems: WHAT I LIKE MOST ABOUT SCHOOL . . . and WHAT I DISLIKE MOST ABOUT SCHOOL . . . are meant to yield more detailed information regarding children's attitudes to schools both in terms of negative and positive responses.

The stems: WHAT I LIKE MOST ABOUT HOME . . . and TO A CHILD PARENTS ARE . . . provide an opportunity for children to express views on the role of parents, and to say what home means to them. These four sets of sentences have been analysed in terms of functional and expressive categories of needs or wants (Musgrove) and full details of the analysis and the results appear in Chapter 5.

The stem: SOME DAY I WOULD LIKE TO . . . has been analysed in terms of aspirations, hopes and desires, job expectations, family life, marriage, travel etc. Details of analysis and results for each group appear in Chapter 5.

The stems: NOW AND AGAIN I REALIZE . . . and SOMETIMES WHEN I THINK ABOUT MYSELF . . . have been coded on a score of 1–3: 1 = positive, 2 = negative and 3 = neutral.

The self-items and method of scoring them are based on the London Sentence Completion Test developed by John Coleman (1976) at the Institute of Psychiatry, London. In scoring a response as positive we take: 'any positive self-evaluation, realization of individual potential, or wish for something better.'

Positive Examples
I could work harder
I pity everyone else because they're not me
Must not think about myself but must help others

Negative Examples
Any negative self-evaluation, realization of failure or statement of insignificance.

am no use to anybody
I hate myself
I feel sick
am ugly

Neutral Examples
Any statement of role, or position in the family, any statement
concerning natural processes such as getting older, or curiosity
about identity or others' view of self.
am growing up
one day must die
can't understand myself

The stem WHAT I LIKE MOST ABOUT MYSELF . . . was meant to
provide further descriptive information on self-feeling.

Analysis of Attitudes to School and Home

Two main classifications were used for analysing these
statements; these are based on T. Parson's distinctions between
Instrumental and Expressive categories of needs and wants.
Parsons wrote: 'Action may be oriented to the achievement of a
goal which is an anticipated future state of affairs, the attainment
of which is felt to promise gratification'. These he termed
'Instrumental' attitudes. Further: 'there is a corresponding type
on the adjustive side which may be called *expressive* orientation'.
Here the primary orientation is not to a goal anticipated in the
future, but the organization of a 'flow' of gratifications.

Musgrove adapted Parsons' classification for use with his
sample of 250 members of 6 mixed youth clubs in a northern
conurbation. His study was concerned with satisfaction with
home, club, work and school; his sub-divisions proved useful
for analysing the responses of this sample in relation to their
feelings about school, teachers, parents and home. Musgrove
developed thirteen sub-divisions, six Instrumental and seven
Expressive:

Instrumental:
  1. Intellectual = understanding, enlightenment
  2. Physical = competence at games and sport
  3. Manual = woodwork, needlework, domestic skills

4. Social = poise, self-assurance in relationships with others

5. Moral development = including references to 'forming a good character', becoming 'a good citizen', 'learning to be self-reliant and stand on your own feet'

6. Personal advancement = passing examinations, getting on in life

Expressive:

1. Ease, emotional security = feeling at ease, wanted, loved, welcome

2. Freedom/self-direction = including the freedom to express your views, have your say, 'be yourself'

3. Friendship

4. Sense of competence = 'having a chance to prove yourself'

5. Support from adults = knowing you can take your problems to parents/teachers

6. Sense of identity with group = feeling one of the crowd/a member of the family/as if you belong

7. Sense of purposeful activity

In scrutinizing the statements, three additional categories emerged:

8. Place of safety = 'where you can be safe, protected'

9. Everything

10. Material = 'nice colour TV, luxury bathroom/bedroom'

Statements could be allocated to more than one category, expressing both Instrumental and Expressive attitudes. Thus: 'the friends, games and when we do interesting subjects' would be allocated to three categories: Friends, Physical and Intellectual. However, no statement would be allocated to the same category more than once.

The category Intellectual was taken to include any mention of school/home as a place for learning. Thus mention of books, equipment, tasks, skills, knowledge, would be classified under this heading.

Analysis of Attitudes to Teachers

Analysis of the stem WHAT I DISLIKE MOST ABOUT SCHOOL . . .
yielded most information on attitudes to teachers. This stem was
included in the final test instrument on the instigation of
children in the preliminary test group. Many children,
particularly boys, in that group (11- to 12-year-olds, first-year
comprehensive) found it difficult to complete the stem WHAT I
LIKE MOST ABOUT SCHOOL . . . because, in their words, they
liked 'nuthink' about school. After completion of the test, many
children said 'that to be fair' it should include something
on 'what we dislike about school'. The point was taken and
the final test included the stem WHAT I DISLIKE MOST ABOUT
SCHOOL . . .

All the statements were scrutinized and thirteen categories
emerged after complete scrutiny of each individual statement.
Categories were now defined and statements allocated to them.
One statement could be allocated to more than one category, but
no statement would appear under a single category more than
once.

Analysis of Aspirations

For an analysis of SOME DAY I WOULD LIKE TO . . . all statements
were scrutinized and five main categories emerged:
  1. general desire for success, money, wish 'to get on';
  2. desire for happiness and self-fulfilment;
  3. wish for marriage, children and family life;
  4. travel – generally or to specific destinations;
  5. specific occupations/professions.
The categories were further subdivided in order to provide
more detailed information; thirteen categories were used in the
final breakdown. These were: Success; Money; General desire
'to get on'; Travel – general, West Indies, America, Africa;
Occupation – doctor, teacher, nurse, scientist; Skilled; Semi-
skilled; Manual; Entertainment; Football; wish for Marriage
and Family; Self-fulfilment; Other Professional.

Thus it can be seen that the measuring instrument provided
children with:

1. a force choice response format;
2. a diagrammatic sociometric format, and
3. a projective, sentence completion item to be used as the child pleased.

In using the Piers-Harris and Ziller instruments I assumed their validity as Wylie, in reviewing over 200 instruments designed to measure self-concept, recommended these two as being amongst the best for research work with children. I also tried to use a test which was suitable in carrying no threat to the child.

Checking

During the preliminary testing, an independent check was made on the method of scoring the sentence completion items. A psychologist who specializes in the self-concept and self-esteem of children and adolescents scored the self-concept items for children in the preliminary test group. Comparison with my own scoring showed near perfect agreement of 95 per cent between the two scores.

Selection of Descriptive Material

Descriptive material was selected to give a representative sample of responses in terms of sex, age and type of response.

Bibliography

Abelson, N. R. (1977), *Persons: A Study in Philosophical Psychology* (Macmillan)

Austin, S. and Garrison, L. (1978), *TES* (24 February)

Bagley, C. (1975), 'Sequels of Alienation: A Social-psychological View of Adaptation of West Indian Migrants in Britain', University of Surrey (unpublished)

Bagley, C. and Coard, B. (1975), 'Cultural Knowledge and Rejection of Ethnic Identity in West Indian Children in London', in Verma, G. and Bagley, C. (eds.), *Race and Education Across Cultures* (Heinemann)

Bagley, C., Mallick, K. and Verma, G. (1975), 'Pupil Self-esteem: A Study of Black and White Teenagers', in Bagley, C. and Verma, G. (eds.), *Race, Education and Identity* (Macmillan)

Bagley, C. and Young, L. (1979), 'Identity, Self-esteem and the Evaluation of Colour and Ethnicity in Young Children in London and Jamaica', *New Community*, 7, 154–69

Baker-Lunn, J. C. (1969), 'The Development of Scales to Measure Junior School Children's Attitudes', *Br. Jrnl. of Edcnl. Psych.*, 34, 1, 64

Baratz, S. and Shuy, W. (eds.) (1969), *Teaching Black Children to Read* (Center for Applied Linguistics, Washington DC)

Barnes, J. (1975), *Educational Priority: Curriculum Innovation in London EPAs* (HMSO)

Barrett, L. E. (1968), 'The Rastafarians: A Study of Messianic Cultism in Jamaica', Monograph, University of Puerto Rico

—— (1977), *The Rastafarians: The Dreadlocks of Jamaica* (Heinemann)

Bastide, R. (1971), *African Civilisation in the New World*, trans. Green (Hurst & Co.)

Batten, T. R. (1967), *The Non-directive Approach* (Oxford University Press)

Beetham, D. (1967), *Immigrant School Leavers and the Youth Service in Birmingham* (Institute of Race Relations)

Bell, D. (1973), *The Coming of Post-industrial Society* (Basic Books)

Bellaby, P. (1977), *The Sociology of Comprehensive Schooling* (Methuen)

Bennett, N. *et al.* (1976), *Teaching Styles and Pupil Progress* (Open Books)

Berk, L. E. *et al.* (1970), 'Attitudes of English and American Children towards their School Experience', *Jrnl. Educ. Psych.*, 61, 1, 33–40

Bernstein, B. (1964), 'Elaborated and Restricted Codes', quoted in Gumperz, J. J. and Hymes, D., 'The Ethnography of Communication', *Am. Anthro.* (6 February 1966)

——(1969), 'Open Schools, Open Society?', *New Society* (14 September)

—— (1970), 'A Critique of the Concept of Compensatory Education', in Rubinstein, D. and Stoneman, C. (eds.), *Education for Democracy* (Penguin)

Biddle, W. and Biddle, L. (1965), *The Community Development Process* (Holt, Rinehart and Winston)

Billingsley, A. (1968), *Black Families in White America* (Prentice-Hall)

Bloomberg, W. (1966), 'Community Organisation', in Becker, H. S. (ed.), *Social Problems: A Modern Approach* (Wiley)

Blyden, E. (1893), 'The African Personality', *Sierra Leone Times* (27 May)

Blyton, E. (1973 edn), *The Three Golliwogs* (Pan Books)

Boudon, R. (1973), *Education, Opportunity and Social Inequality* (Wiley)

Bourdieu, P. (1971), 'Systems of Education and Systems of Thought', in Young, M. F. (ed.), *Knowledge and Control* (Collier Macmillan)

—— (1973), 'Cultural Reproduction and Social Reproduction', in Brown, R. (ed.), *Knowledge, Education and Social Change* (Tavistock)

—— (1977), 'Symbolic Power', in Gleeson, D. (ed.), *Identity and Structure* (Nafferton Books)

Bowles, S. and Gintis, H. (1976), 'Schooling in Capitalist America', in *Educational Reform and the Contradictions of Economic Life* (Routledge and Kegan Paul)

Box, S. (1977), 'Hyperactivity: A Scandalous Silence', *New Society* (1 December)

Brittan, E. M. (1976), 'Multiracial Education III', *Educnl. Res.*, 18, 3

Brook, J. R. (1977), 'Secondary Education for All: Reconsidered', *Durham Edcnl. Rev.* 38, 1–8

Bruckman, R. and Sheni, F. (1966), 'Personality Characteristics of Ineffective, Effective and Efficient Readers', *Personnel and Guid. Jrnl.*, 44, 837–44

Bullock Report (1975), *A Language for Life* (HMSO)

Burns, R. (1976), 'The Concept-scale and Interaction Problems: A Trap for the Unwary on the Semantic Differential', *Edcnl. Studies*, 9, 2, 121–7

Burt, C. (1961) 'Intelligence and Social Mobility', *Br. Jrnl. of Stat. Psychol.*, 14, 11

Callaghan, J. (1976), Speech at Ruskin College, Oxford

Carlson, R. (1970), 'On the Structure of Self-esteem: Comments on Ziller's Formulation', *Jrnl. of Cons. and Clin. Psych.*, 2, 264–8

Carmichael, S. and Hamilton, C. (1967), *Black Power: The Politics of Liberation* (Vintage Books)

Carrington, L. D. *et al.* (1974), 'Linguistic Exposure of Trinidadian Children', *Caribbean Jrnl. of Edcn.*, 1, 2

Cassidy, F. G. and Le Page, R. B. (1967), *Dictionary of Jamaican English* (Oxford University Press)

Cawson, P. (1975), *Survey of Immigrants in Approved Schools* (DHSS), unpublished

CDP (1972–8), *Community Development Projects* (CDP Information Unit, London)

Cesairé, A. (1945), 'Cahier d'un Retour au Pays Natal', *Présence Africaine*, 50 (Paris)

—— (1956), 'Talks on Colonialism', *Présence Africaine*, 75 (Paris)

Chazan, B. (1978), 'Models of Ethnic Education: The Case of Jewish Education in Great Britain', *Br. Jrnl. of Edcnl. Studies*, XXIV–V, 1, 55–72

Cicourel, A. V. and Kitsue, J. (1963), *The Educational Decision Makers* (Bobbs-Merrill)

Clark, R. and Clark, M. (1947), 'Racial Identification and Preference in Negro Children', in Newcomb, M. and Hartley, L. (eds.), *Readings in Social Psychology* (Holt)

Clark, B. R. (1961), 'The "Cooling out" Function of Higher Education', *Am. Jrnl. of Soc.*, 65, 6, 569

Clarke Sir F. (1923), *The Politics of Education* (University of London Press)

Clegg, A. and Mogson, B. (1968), *Children in Distress* (Penguin)

Coard, B. (1971), *How the West Indian Child is Made Educationally Subnormal in the British School System* (New Beacon Books)

Coleman, James (1966), *Equality of Educational Opportunity (The Coleman Report)*, (US Government, Dept. of Health, Education and Welfare)

Coleman, John (1974), *Relationships in Adolescence* (Routledge and Kegan Paul)

—— (1976), *London Sentence Completion Test-scoring Manual*, Institute of Psychiatry, University of London (unpublished)

Commonplace Workshop, *Stepping Out*, Ealing Community Magazine (Summer 1977)

Coopersmith, S. (1975), 'Self-concept, Race and Class', in Verma, G. and Bagley, C., *Race and Education Across Cultures* (Heinemann)

Craig, D. R. (1968), 'Education and Creole English in the West Indies – Some Sociolinguistic Factors', in Hymes, D. (ed.), *Pidginisation and Creolisation of Languages* (Cambridge University Press)

Cronon, E. D. (1955), *Black Moses: The Story of Marcus Garvey* (University of Wisconsin Press)

Cross, D., Baker, G. and Stiles, L. (1977), *Teaching in a Multicultural Society: Perspectives and Professional Strategies* (Collier Macmillan)

Damas, L. (1965), 'The Birth of Negritude', *NMSAC Newsletter*, New York, 7, 5

Davidson, H. and Lang, G. (1960), 'Children's Perception of their Teachers' Feelings Towards Them', *Jrnl. of Exp. Educn.*, 29, 109–18

Davis, K. (1938), 'Mental Hygiene and the Class Structure', *Psychiatry*, 1, 55

DES (1973) *Statistics of Education, 1972. Vol. 1: Distribution of Immigrant Pupils by Type of Authority* (HMSO)

—— (1973), 'Educational Arrangements for Imigrant Children who Need Special Education', letter to Chief Education Officers

—— (1977), *Education in Schools: A Consultative Document* (HMSO)

—— (1978), *The West Indian Community: Observations on the Report of the Select Committee on Race Relations and Immigration* (HMSO)

DES/Welsh Office (1977), *A Study of School Buildings* (HMSO)

Deutsch, M. (1960), 'Minority Group and Class Status as Related to Social and Personality Factors in Scholastic Achievement', Society for Applied Anthropology, Monograph 2

Dewey, J. (1915), *Democracy and Education* (Dent)

Dhony, F. (1974), 'The Black Explosion in Schools', *Race Today* (February)

Dickinson, N. (1975), 'The Head Teacher as Innovator: A Study of an English School District', in Reid, W. and Walker, D., *Studies in Curriculum Change* (Routledge and Kegan Paul)

Dixon, B. (1977), *Catching them Young – Sex, Race and Class in Children's Fiction* (Pluto Press)

Donna and Marcia (1978), *Uptown Top Rankin'* (Decca Records, London)

Dove, L. (1974), 'Racial Awareness among Adolescents in London Comprehensive Schools', *New Community*, 3, 3

Douglas, W. E. B. *et al.* (1968), *The Home and the School* (Peter Davies)

Dubois, W. (1908), *The Souls of Black Folk* (McChung)

Durkheim, E. (1956), *Education and Sociology* (Free Press)

Easthope, G. (1975), *Community, Hierarchy and Open Education* (Routledge and Kegan Paul)

Edwards, V. K. (1976), 'Effects of Dialect on the Comprehension of West Indian Children', *Edcnl. Res.*, 18, 2, 83

Eisher, E. W. (1969), 'Instructional and Expressive Objectives', in Popham, W. T. *et al* (eds.), *Instructional Objectives* (Rand McNally)

Erikson, E. (1963), *Identity, Youth and Crisis* (Norton)

Eynsenck, H. (1971), *Race, Intelligence and Education* (Temple Smith)

—— (1973), *The Inequality of Man* (Temple Smith)

—— (1975), 'Equality and Education: Fact and Fiction', *Oxford Review of Education*

Fanon, F. (1967), *Black Faces, White Masks* (Penguin)

Feldman, H. (1969), 'Diagnostic Patterns and Child/Parent Separation in Children Attending the Jamaican Child Guidance Clinic', *Race Today* (September)

Field, F. (ed.) (1977), *Education and the Urban Crisis* (Routledge and Kegan Paul)

Finlayson, D. S. (1971), 'Parental Aspirations and the Educational Achievement of Children', *Edcnl. Res.*, 14, 1, 104

Finlayson, D. S. and Loughran, R. (1976), 'Pupils' Perception in High and Low Delinquency Schools', *Edcnl. Res.*, 18, 2, 138

Fitzherbert, K. (1968), *West Indian Children in London* (Bell)

Ford, J. (1969), *Social Class and the Comprehensive School* (Routledge and Kegan Paul)

Frazier, F. (1939), *The Negro Family in the United States* (University of Chicago Press)

Freud, S. (1953–4), *Collected Works* (Hogarth)

Garner, N. (1973), *Teaching in the Urban Community School* (Ward Lock)

Garrison, L. (1976), 'The Rastafarians: Journey out of Exile' (unpublished)

—— (1977), 'Self-image of West Indian Black Youth in Britain' (unpublished)

Gibson, A. (1977), quoted in Mack, J., 'West Indians in Schools', *New Society* (8 December)

Giddens, A. (1976), *New Rules of Sociological Methods* (Hutchinson)

Giles, R. (1975), *Black Studies Programs in Public Schools* (Praeger)

—— (1977), *The West Indian Experience in British Schools* (Methuen)

Goffman, I. (1959), *The Presentation of Self in Everyday Life* (Double-day)

Gorbutt, D. (1972), 'The New Sociology of Education', *Education for Teaching*, 89, 3

Gordon, C. and Gergen, K. J. (eds.) (1968), *The Self in Social Interaction* (Wiley)

Goveia, E. (1965), *Slave Society in the British Leeward Islands at the Turn of the Eighteenth Century* (New Haven)

Grace, G. (1978), *Teachers, Ideology and Control: A Study in Urban Education* (Routledge and Kegan Paul)

Graham, P. G. and Meadows, C. E. (1967), 'Psychological Disorders in the Children of Immigrants', *Jrnl. of Psych. and Psychiatry*, 8

Gramsci, A. (1971), *Selections from the Prison Notebooks* (Lawrence and Wishart)

Grassroots, West Indian community paper, London

Greenfield, S. (1966), *English Rustics in Black Skins: A Study of Modern Family Forms in Pre-industrial Society* (College and University Press)

Greenwall, H. and Oppenheim, D. (1968), 'Reported Magnitude of Self-misidentification among Negro Children – Artifact?', *Jrnl. of Pers. and Soc. Psych.*, 8, 49

Guardian (1977), 'Teaching the European Jet Set' (23 November)

Gursslin, D., Hunt, R. and Roach, J. (1959/60), 'Social Class and the Mental Health Movement', *Social Problems*, 7, 2, 10

Gutman, H. (1972), 'Persistent Myths', *Jrnl. of Soc. History*, 6, 41

—— (1978), *The Black Family in Slavery and Freedom, 1750–1925* (Basil Blackwell)

Halsey, A. H. *et al.* (1980), *Origins and Destinations: Family, Class and Education in Modern Britain* (Oxford University Press)

Hare, B. (1977), 'Black and White Child Self-esteem in Social Science: An Overview', *Jrnl of Negro Education*, 46, 141–56

Hargreaves, D. (1978), 'What Happens to Teachers', *New Society* (9 March)

Hartman, P. and Husband, C. (1974), *Racism and the Mass Media* (Davis-Poynter)

Hebdige, R. (1975), 'Reggae, Rastas and Rudies', in Hall, S. and Jefferson, T. (eds.), *Resistance through Rituals* (Hutchinson)

—— (1979), *Sub-culture: The Meaning of Style* (Methuen)

Herrnstein, J. (1973), *IQ in the Meritocracy* (Atlantic Press)

Herskovits, M. (1965), 'The Ancestry of the American Negro', reprinted in *The New World Negro* (annual, University of Indiana Press, 1966)

Higman, B. (1975), 'The Slave Family and Household in the British West Indies, 1800–1834', *Jrnl. of Interdisciplinary History*, 2, 261

Hill, D. (1970), 'The Attitudes of West Indian and English Adolescents in Britain', *Race*, 11, 313

—— (1975), 'Personality Factors amongst Minority Ethnic Groups', *Edcnl. Studies*, 1, 1, 43

—— (1976), *Teaching in Multi-Racial Schools: A Guidebook* (Methuen)

Hollingworth, B. (1977), 'Dialect in Schools – A Historical Note', *Durham and Newcastle Res. Rev.*, VIII, 39, 11

Home Office (1975), *Protection Against Vandalism* (HMSO)

Hood, C. *et al.* (1970), *Children of West Indian Parents* (IRR)

Hopper, E. (1971), 'A Typology for the Classification of Educational Systems', in Hopper, E. (ed.), *Readings in the Theory of Educational Systems* (Hutchinson)

Hoyle, E. and Bell, R. (1972), *Problems of Curriculum Innovation* (Open University), E283

Hughes, L. (1966), 'The Twenties Harlem and its Negritude', *Africa Forum*, 1, 4, 19 (New York)

Humble, S. and Ruddack, J. (1972), 'Local Education Authorities and Curriculum Innovation', in Hoyle, E. and Bell, R. (eds.), *Problems of Curriculum Innovation* (Open University), E283

Illich, I. (1973), *Deschooling Society* (Calder and Boyars)

Isaacs, S. (1946), *The Children We Teach* (University of London Press)

Jackson, B. (1973), 'The Child Minders', *New Society* (29 November)

Jackson, B. and Marsden, D. (1966), *Education and the Working Class* (Penguin)

Jackson, K. and Ashcroft, B. (1972), 'Adult Education, Deprivation and Community Development: A Critique', University of Liverpool (unpublished)

Jackson, P. W. and Getzels, J. W. (1959), 'Psychological Health and Classroom Functioning: A Study of Dissatisfaction With School Among Adolescents', *Jrnl. of Educnl. Psych.*, 50, 295

Jackson, P. W. and Lahaderene, R. (1967), 'Scholastic Success and Attitudes to School in a Population of Sixth Graders', *Br. Jrnl. of Edcnl. Psych.*, 39, 1, 15

James Report (1972), *Report of the Committee of Inquiry into Teacher Education and Training* (HMSO)

Jenkins, D. (1972), 'Curriculum Development and Reference Group Theory: Notes Towards Understanding the Plight of the Curriculm Innovator', in Hoyle, E. and Bell, R., *Problems of Curriculum Innovation* (Open University), E283

Jenkins, P. (1978), in the *Guardian* (22 December)

Jensen, S. (1969), 'How Much Can We Boost IQ and Scholastic Achievement?', *Harvard Edcnl. Rev.*, 62, 546

—— (1972), *Educability and Group Differences* (Methuen)

Jones, P. (1977), 'An Evaluation of the Effect of Sport on the Integration of West Indian School Children', PhD thesis, University of Surrey (unpublished)

Kahl, J. (1953), 'Educational Aspirations of "Common-man" Boys', *Harvard Edcnl. Rev.*, 23, 186

Kamin, L. (1977), *The Science and Politics of IQ* (Penguin)

Kardiner, A. and Oversey, K. (1951), *The Mark of Oppression* (World Books)

Kelly, G. A. (1955), *The Psychology of Personal Constructs, Vols. I and II* (Norton)

King, M. L. (1966), *Conscience for Change* (CBC Publications, Toronto)

Kitzinger, S. (1972), 'West Indian Children with Problems', *Therapeutic Education* (Spring)

Labour Party Advisory Committee on Education (1921), Memorandum 43, p.1 (18 January)

Labov, W. (1969), 'The Logic of Non-standard English', in Giglioli, P. (ed.), *Language and Social Context* (Penguin, 1972)

—— (1972), *Language in the Inner City: Studies in Black English Vernacular* (University of Philadelphia Press)

—— (1978), *Sociolinguistic Patterns* (Basil Blackwell)

Lassett, R. (1977), 'Disruptive and Violent Pupils: The Facts and the Fallacies', *Edcnl. Rev.*, 29, 3

Lawrence, D. (1971), 'The Effects of Counselling on Retarded Readers', *Edcnl. Res.*, 13, 2, 119

—— (1972), 'Counselling of Retarded Readers by Non-professionals', *Edcnl. Res.*, 15, 1, 48

Lawton, D. (1968), *Social Class, Language and Education* (Routledge and Kegan Paul)

—— (1975), *Class, Culture and Curriculum* (Routledge and Kegan Paul)

—— (1977), *Education and Social Justice* (Sage)

Leckey, P. (1945), *Self-Consistency: A Theory of Personality* (Island Press)

Le Page, R. B. (1968), 'Problems to be Faced in the Use of English as the Medium of Education in the West Indies', in Fisherman *et al.* (eds.), *Language Problems in Developing Nations* (Wiley)

—— (1973), *Linguistic Problems of West Indian Children in English Schools* (Community Relations Commission)

Levine, L. (1977), *Black Culture and Consciousness* (Oxford University Press)

Levitas, M. (1976), 'A Culture of Deprivation', *Marxism Today* (April)

Little, A. (1975), 'The Background of Under-achievement in Immigrant Children in London', in Verma, G. and Bagley, C. (eds.), *Race and Education Across Cultures* (Heinemann)

—— (1978), Inaugural Lecture, Goldsmith College, University of London

Little, K. (1972), *Negroes in Britain* (Routledge and Kegan Paul)

Lomas, G. and Monck, E. (1977), *The Coloured Population of Great Britain* (Runnymede Trust)

Lomax, P. (1977), 'The Self-concept of Girls in the Context of a Disadvantaged Environment', *Edcnl. Rev.*, 29, 107–19

Louden, D. (1977), 'A Comparative Study of Self-esteem and Locus of Control in Minority Group Adolescents', PhD thesis, University of Bristol (unpublished)

Lowensthal, D. (1972), *West Indian Societies* (Oxford University Press)

Maran, R. (1912), *Batonala*, trans. Beck and Mbonkon (Black Orpheus Press, Washington DC, 1972)

Maslow, A. H. (1973), *Dominance, Self-esteem and Self-actualisation* (Brooks-Cole)

Merson, M. and Campbell, R. (1974), 'Community Education: Instruction for Inequality', *Education for Teaching* (Spring)

Midwinter, E. (1973), *Priority Education* (Penguin)

Milhum, T. (1977), 'The Study of Images', *Screen*, 23

Milner, D. (1975), *Children and Race* (Penguin)

Morris, J. (1975), 'Babylon', *West Indian World* (18–25 July)

Morris, M. (1977), in the *Guardian* (22 November)

Morris, S. (1973), 'A Treatise on Black Studies' (London Committee on Black Studies, unpublished)

Moynihan, D. (1965), *The Negro Family: The Case for National Action* (*The Moynihan Report*) (US Government, Dept. of Health, Education and Social Welfare)

Mphahlele, E. (1974), *The African Image* (Faber)

Musgrove, F. (1976), *The Family, Education and Society* (Routledge and Kegan Paul)

Myrdal, G. (1946), *An American Dilemma* (McGraw Hill)

NACRO (1977), *Children and Young Persons in Custody* (National Association for the Care and Resettlement of Young Offenders, London)

Nandy, D. (1969), 'Unrealistic Aspirations', *Race Today* (October)

NAS (1975), *Discipline in Schools* (National Association of Schoolmasters)

—— (1976), *The Retreat from Authority* (National Association of (Schoolmasters)

NAS/NUWT (1977), *Effects of Stress on Teachers* (National Association of Schoolmasters and National Union of Women Teachers)

National Children's Bureau (1973), 'Problems of the Children of West Indian Immigrants', *Highlight* (Spring)

—— (1977), 'Violence, Disruption and Vandalism in Schools',
Highlight (Autumn)

Neil, A. S. (1966), *Summerhill: A Radical Approach to Child Rearing*
(Gollancz)

Newson, J. and Newson, E. (1976), *Seven Years Old in the Home
Environment* (Allen and Unwin)

Newsom Report (1963), *Half Our Future*, Report of the Minister of
Education's Central Advisory Council (HMSO)

Nicol, A. (1971), 'Psychiatric Disorders in West Indian Schoolchildren
Race Today (January)

Nobles, W. (1973), 'Psychological Research and the Black Self-
concept: A Critical Review', *Jrnl. of Soc. Issues*, 22, 1

Norris, M. (1977), 'A Formula for Identifying Styles of Community
Work', *Comm. Dev. Jrnl.*, 12, 1

North Lewisham Project (1977), *Report of the North Lewisham Project*,
unpublished

Omar, B. (1971), 'ESN Children – Labelled for Life', *Race Today*
(January)

Ousmane, S. (1962), *The Proceedings of the First International Congress of
Africanists, Accra* (North Western University Press, 1964)

Osgood, L. E. *et al.* (1957), *The Measurement of Meaning* (University of
Illinois Press)

Pack, D. C. (1977), *Report on Truancy and Discipline in Scottish Schools*
(HMSO)

Parks, R. (1928), 'Human Migration of the Marginal Man', *Am. Jrnl. of
Soc.* (May)

Parsons, T. (1964), *Social Structure and Personality* (Collier Macmillan)

Patterson, O. (1967), *The Sociology of Slavery* (Oxford University Press)

Peach. C. G. (1968), *West Indian Migration to Britain* (Oxford University
Press)

Pearce, K. S. (1976), 'West Indian Boys in Community Homes', PhD
thesis, University of Leicester (unpublished)

Pearson, A. (1974), 'West Indians in Easton: A Study of their Social
Organisation', PhD thesis, University of Leicester (unpublished)

PEP Report (1967), *Racial Discrimination in Britain* (Population and
Economic Planning, London)

Pettigrew, T. (1964), *A Profile of the Negro in America* (Van Nostrand)

Pines, J. (1977), 'The Study of Racial Images: A Structural Approach',
Screen, 23

Piers, E. *et al.* (1964), 'Age and Other Correlates of Self-concept in
Children', *Jrnl. of Edcnl. Psych.*, 55, 91

Plowden Report (1967), *Children and their Primary Schools* (HMSO)

Piers-Harris (1976), *Manual for Children's Self-concept Scale*, counsellors' recordings and tests (unpublished)

Pollack, M. (1971), *Today's Three Year Olds in London* (Heinemann)

Poster, C. D. (1971), *The School and the Community* (Macmillan)

Power, M. *et al.* (1974), 'Delinquency and the Family', *Br. Jrnl. of Soc. Work*, 4, 13

Race Today Collective (1975), *The Police and the Black Wageless* (Race Today pamphlet)

Radkhe M. *et al.* (1953), 'The Role of the Parents in the Development of Children's Racial Attitudes', *Child Development*, 21, 13

Radkhe, M. and Trager, H. (1950), 'Children's Perceptions of the Social Roles of Negroes and Whites', *Jrnl. of Psych.*, 29, 93

Rainwater, L. (1966), 'Crucible of Identity: The Lower Class Family', *Daedalus*, 95, 172, 216

Reid, R. (1965), 'Socialist Sunday Schools: 1892–1939', *Int. Rev. of Soc. History* (1966)

Reid, W. (1975), 'The Changing Curriculum: Theory and Practice', in Reid, W. and Walker, D. (eds.), *Case Studies in Curriculum Change* (Routledge and Kegan Paul)

Rex, J. *et al.* (1967), *Race, Community and Conflict* (Oxford University Press)

Reynolds, D. (1975), 'The Delinquent School', in Hammersley, M. and Woods, P. (eds.), *The Process of Schooling* (Routledge and Kegan Paul/Open University)

Richards, K. (1977), *TES* (9 December)

Richmond, K. (1975), *Education and Schooling* (Methuen)

Robbins Report (1963), Report of the Committee on Higher Education (HMSO)

Rodney, W. (1975), *The Groundings With My Brothers* (Bougle L'Overture, London)

Rogers, C. R. (1948), 'Some Observations on the Organisation of Personality', *Am. Psych.*, 2, 358

—— (1951), *Client Centred Therapy: Its Current Practice, Implications and Theory* (Houghton Mifflin)

—— (1958), 'The Characteristics of a Helping Relationship', *Personnel & Guid. Jrnl.*, 37, 6

—— (1959), *Counselling and Psychotherapy: Theory and Practice* (Harper and Row)

—— (1962), 'Towards Becoming a Fully Functioning Person', in Combs, A. W. (ed.), *Perceiving, Behaving, Becoming* (Harper and Row)

—— (1965), 'Theapeutic Relationship: Recent Theory and Practice', in

Baldadelis, G. and Adams, S., *The Shaping of Personality* (Prentice-Hall)

—— (1969), *Freedom to Learn* (Bobbs-Merrill)

—— (1967), 'Interpersonal Relationships in the Facilitating of Learning', in Leeper, R. (ed.), *The Person in the Process* (Prentice-Hall)

—— (1974), *Marriage and its Alternatives: Becoming Partners* (Houghton Mifflin)

Rogers, M. and McNeal, J. (1971), *The Multi-Racial School: Suggested Approaches* (Penguin)

Rose, E. *et al.* (1969), *Colour and Citizenship* (Oxford University Press for IRR)

Rosen, B. C. (1956), 'The Achievement Syndrome: Psychocultural Dimensions of Social Stratification', *Am. Soc. Rev.*, 21, 203

Rosenberg, M. (1965), *Society and the Adolescent Self-image* (Princeton University Press)

Rosenberg, M. and Simmons, R. (1974), 'Black and White Self-Esteem: The Urban School Child', American Sociology Association Monograph

Rowbottom, R. *et al.* (1974), *Social Services Departments* (Heinemann)

Ruston, J. and Turner, J. (eds.) (1975), *Education and Deprivation* (Manchester University Press)

Rutter, M. and Madge, C. (1976), *Cycles of Deprivation* (Heinemann)

Schneiderman, L. (1965), 'Social Class Diagnosis and Treatment', *Am. Jrnl. of Orthopsychiatry*, 35, 99

Schools Council (1974), *Education for a Multiracial Society –Need and Innovation*, Working Paper 50 (Evan Methuen)

Schutz, R. (1962), *Commonsense and Scientific Interpretations in Human Action* (Martinius Nijhoff)

Scobie, E. (1972), *Black Britannia – A History of Blacks in Britain* (Johnson)

Screen (1977), Screen Education, 23 (Summer). Society for Education in Films and Television

Select Committee on Race Relations and Immigration (1974), *The West Indian Community in Britain, Vols. I and II* (HMSO)

Senghor, L. (1956), 'Ethiopiques', in *The Complete Poems of Leopold Senghor* (Editions de Seuil, 1964)

—— (1962), *A History of Neo-African Literature* (Faber)

—— (1967), 'The Foundations of "Africanite" or "Negritude" and Arabite', *Presence Africaine* (Paris 1971)

Sewell, W. *et al.* (1957), 'Social Status and Educational and Occupational Aspirations', *Am. Soc. Rev.*, 4, 326

Sharp, R. and Green, A. (1975), *Education and Social Control* (Routledge and Kegan Paul)

Shipman, M. (1971), 'Curriculum for Inequality?', in Hooper, R. (ed.), *The Curriculum : Context, Design and Development* (Oliver and Boyd)

Sieber, S. D. (1968), 'Organisational Influences on Innovative Roles in Educational Organisations', *Soc. of Edcn.*, 45, 363

Silver, H. (1976), *Education Research*, 18, 1

Simon, B. (1965), *Studies in the History of Education, Vols. I – III* (Lawrence and Wishart)

—— (1976), 'Contemporary Problems in Educational Theory', *Marxism Today* (June)

Smith, M. G. *et al.* (1960), *Report on the Rastafarian Movement in Jamaica* (University of the West Indies Press)

Smith, M. G. (1965), *The Plural Society in the British West Indies* (University of California Press)

Specht, H. (1974), *Community Development in the United Kingdom: An Assessment and Recommendations for Change* (Sage)

Stacey, B. (1965), 'Some Psychological Aspects of Inter-generation Occupational Mobility', *Br. Jrnl. Soc. and Clin. Psych.*, 4, 275

Stack, C. (1974), *All Our Kin: Strategies for Survival in the Black Community* (Harper and Row)

Steinberg, J. (1978), 'The Confusion of Tongues – Dialect in Europe', BBC Radio 3 (12 April)

Stenhouse, L. (1970), *Humanities Project – An Introduction* (Heinemann)

—— (1975), 'Problems of Research in Teaching about Race Relations', in Verma, G. and Bagley, C. (eds.), *Race and Education Across Cultures* (Heinemann)

Stone, M. (1976), 'From Approved Schools to Community Homes: Changes Since the '69 Act', University of Surrey (unpublished)

Swift, D. F. (1967), 'Social Class, Mobility, Ideology and Eleven Plus Success', *Br. Jrnl. of Soc.*, 18, 165

—— (1978), 'Black Culture, Self-concept and Schooling', PhD thesis, University of Surrey (unpublished)

Tawney, R. H. (1922), *Secondary Education for All* (Allen and Unwin)

Taylor Committee (1977), *Report on the Government and Management of Schools* (HMSO)

—— (1977), reported in the *Guardian* (21 October)

Thiong'o, Ngugi Wa (1978), 'On National Languages', *Weekly Review*, (13 January) Nairobi

Thomas, J. B. (1977), 'School Organisation and Self-concept', *Durham Edcnl. Rev.*, 38

Thompson, B. (1976), 'Secondary School Pupils' Attitudes to School and Teachers', *Edcnl. Res.*, 18, 62

Thorow, L. (1977), in the *Economist* (24 December)

Tomtide, West Indian monthly magazine

Tropp, A. (1957), *The School Teachers* (Heinemann)

Troyna, B. (1977), 'The Reggae War', *New Society* (10 March)

Turner, B. (ed.) (1974), *Truancy* (Ward Lock)

Turner, R. H. (1966), 'Acceptance of Irregular Mobility in Britain and the United States', *Sociometry*, 29, 334

Tyler, W. (1977), *The Sociology of Educational Inequality* (Methuen)

Verma, G. and Bagley, C. (eds.) (1975), *Race and Education Across Cultures* (Heinemann)

Walvin, J. (1973), *Black and White* (Heinemann)

Wardle, D. (1973), *The Rise of the Schooled Society* (Routledge and Kegan Paul

Warren, R. (1964), *The Community in Action* (Rand McNally)

Watson, D. (1975), 'Sociological Theories and the Analysis of Strategies of Educational Redress', *Int. Rev. of Edc.*, 22

Weinreich, P. (1979), 'Cross-ethnic Identification and Self Rejection in Black Adolescents', in Verma, G. and Bagley, C., *Race and Education Across Cultures* (Heinemann)

West, D. J. and Farrington, D. (1973), *Who Becomes Delinquent?* (Heinemann)

West Indian World, West Indian weekly newspaper

Westwood, L. J. (1971), *Constructive Education Report* (NFER)

Where (1978), 136 (March), Advisory Centre for Education, London

Wight, J. (1971), 'Dialect in School', *Edcnl. Rev.*, 24, 1

Willis, P. (1978a), *Learning to Labour* (Saxon House)

—— (1978b), *Profane Culture* (Routledge and Kegan Paul)

Wright, D. S. (1962), 'A Comparative Study of the Adolescent's Concepts of his Parents and Teachers', *Edcnl. Rev.*, 14, 3

Wylie, R. (1961), *The Self-Concept* (University of Nebraska Press)

—— (1976), *The Self-Concept, Vol. I* (revised) (University of Nebraska Press

Young, M. F. (ed.) (1971), *Knowledge and Control – New Directions for the Sociology of Education* (Collier Macmillan)

Ziller, R. (1969), 'The Alienation Syndrome: A Triadic Pattern of Self-other Orientation', *Sociometry*, 32, 3, 287

—— (1973), *The Social Self* (Pergamon)

—— (1976), *Manual for the Social-self Symbols Tasks*, University of Florida

Zirkel, P. (1973), 'Self-concept and the "Disadvantage" of Ethnic Group Membership', *Rev. of Edcnl. Res.*, 41, 3, 211–25

Index

Index